Domestic Perspectives on Contemporary Democracy

DEMOCRACY, FREE ENTERPRISE, AND THE RULE OF LAW

This series is sponsored by the Cline Center for Democracy, which is devoted to the study of democracy throughout the world, of institutions that sustain and extend it, and of forces that perpetually challenge and endanger it.

Series Editor
Peter F. Nardulli, University of Illinois

A list of books in the series appears at the end of this book.

Domestic Perspectives on Contemporary Democracy

Edited by

PETER F. NARDULLI

UNIVERSITY OF ILLINOIS PRESS
Urbana and Chicago

Manufactured in the United States of America
1 2 3 4 5 C P 5 4 3 2 1
This book is printed on acid-free paper.

Library of Congress Cataloging-in-Publication Data
Domestic perspectives on contemporary democracy /
edited by Peter F. Nardulli.
p. cm. — (Democracy, free enterprise, and the rule of law)
Includes bibliographical references and index.
ISBN-13 978-0-252-03319-3 (cloth : alk. paper)
ISBN-10 0-252-03319-1 (cloth : alk. paper)
ISBN-13 978-0-252-07521-6 (pbk. : alk. paper)
ISBN-10 0-252-07521-8 (pbk. : alk. paper)
1. Democracy
2. Pluralism (Social sciences)
3. Political sociology.
4. Information society—Political aspects.
I. Nardulli, Peter F.
JC423.D668 2008
321.8—dc22 2007030881

To Richard G. and Carole J. Cline,
whose vision and generosity made
this undertaking possible

Contents

Preface

As a form of government, democracy enjoyed unparalleled prestige as the twenty-first century began. The most prosperous nations in the world were democracies. Moreover, democracy's "third wave" had generated an unprecedented number of new republics in southern and eastern Europe as well as Latin America. Reflecting on these developments, some see the "end of history." They argue that democracy has vanquished its competitors, and that it is the only legitimate form of government in the modern era. Others are more cautious; mindful of the challenges to democracy in the new century, as well as its ebb and flow throughout history, they envision a more problematic future.

Several salient challenges confront democracy's durability and portability: the increasing racial, ethnic, and religious diversity of many contemporary societies; the rapid diffusion of innovations in information and communication technologies; and the emergence of global forces and institutions. While these developments present new possibilities for democratic governance, they also have the potential to disrupt its formulation and implementation. Moreover, in conjunction with the demise of the cold war era in the 1990s, these developments give rise to barriers that could affect the diffusion of democracy beyond its current frontiers. In the twenty-first century, the joint effects of these developments could

- affect the ability of individuals to discharge the responsibilities of democratic citizenship;
- undermine the commitment and identification of citizens to their domicile;

- affect the structure, the operation, and legitimacy of institutional mechanisms for linking elite behavior to mass preferences;
- place extraordinary burdens on democratic political and civic leaders;
- limit the legitimacy of traditional conceptions of democratic institutions in non-Western settings; and
- constrain and curtail the actions of democratically elected governments in historically unprecedented ways.

The confluence of two milestone events on the Urbana-Champaign campus of the University of Illinois made it possible to organize a set of activities around these important concerns. One was the centennial of the university's Department of Political Science; the second was the inauguration of a newly endowed center within the College of Liberal Arts and Sciences, the Cline Center for Democracy. To mark these events the college, the department, and the center hosted a week-long conference.

In preparation for this conference, the editor initiated a wide-ranging consultative process to clarify the implications of increasing social heterogeneity, Information Age innovations, and globalization for the health and practice of democracy in the twenty-first century. Once these topics were clarified he used them in conversations with leading political scientists to identify a wide range of accomplished scholars (comparativists, theorists, political economists, communication scholars, law and society students, etc.) who were equipped to make original and important contributions to the topics. Discussions with these scholars led to new insights and further refinements in the topics to be adessed.

These scholars were then commissioned to prepare original essays that focused on assigned, clearly developed themes for a general academic audience, refraining from excessive jargon and focusing on the "big picture." These essays were initially presented in October 2004 at our centennial conference in a leisurely collegial setting, and exchanges among the participants were lively and enlightening. The reflective atmosphere was due in large part to the fact that the conference brought together scholars from a variety of subdisciplines, scholars who seldom interact with one another.

A set of discussants was also commissioned to prepare detailed reviews of the papers, which were supplemented by a review written by the editor. The essayists then revised their papers in light of insights gained from the conference. The result is a collection of wide-ranging essays that make original and important contributions to issues facing democracy at the beginning of the twenty-first century. This volume examines two issues that affect mass-elite linkages within democratic societies: social heterogeneity and Information Age challenges. The companion volume, *International Perspectives on Contemporary Democracy,* deals with two cross-national phenomena: the prospects for a fourth wave of democratization and the challenges that globalization poses for democratic governance.

1

Democracy Challenged

Demography, Technology, and Democratic Possibilities

BRIAN J. GAINES AND
PETER F. NARDULLI

By its very nature, democracy is messy and chaotic, akin to making sausage. It is hardly surprising, then, that the process of establishing, maintaining, and improving democracy has been challenging and untidy since its reappearance in the eighteenth century. Just because "everyone is a democrat" now does not mean that making democracy work will be any easier in the twenty-first century. Indeed, not too long ago "everyone was a Keynesian." Thus, democracy's enviable, and historically unprecedented, global status means little in terms of implementing its laudable values, principles, and goals in the world's diverse and ever-changing societies. The theoretically minded can point to a huge literature on social choice theory, rife with "impossibility" theorems and paradoxes that demonstrate that aggregating the preferences of a large group of people is, inescapably, a profoundly difficult problem. The empirically minded can underscore the implications of a half-century of survey research that casts doubt upon the capacity of individuals to discharge their democratic responsibilities. Or they can simply catalogue contemporary problems with elections and governance in the world's putative exemplars of democratic rule. These include the embarrassing spectacle of the "tied" 2000 presidential election in the United States, plummeting turnout in European Parliament elections, and the corruption scandals that recently brought to an end more than a decade of Liberal rule in Canada. As this list could be multiplied many times over, it suggests that democratic deficiencies continue to plague the world's most mature regimes and are likely to continue to do so for the foreseeable future.

Despite the record of recurring problems in supposedly exemplary regimes, it would be myopic to be nonchalant or complacent about the maladies of established democracies, dismissing them as endemic. A dominant theme in this book's companion volume, *International Perspectives on Contemporary Democracy,* is that the performance of established democracies has profound implications for democratization. Thus, those committed to democratic values and principles would do well to think about both the types of difficulties that established democracies have had in the past and the challenges they will face in the twenty-first century. This volume is concerned with the latter. While its companion volume addresses issues presented by globalization, this work is concerned with those posed by the specter of ever-increasing social heterogeneity and technological advances in communication and information processing.

The issues posed by social heterogeneity affect both the establishment of new democratic regimes and the operation of existing ones. Any time a new government is created, important structural issues have to be addressed. Resolving these issues is always difficult, especially in multiethnic societies. Strategic choices must be made by political elites with different motives and different bases of political support. Those committed to democratic consolidation face difficult questions. Should they embed existing cleavages within governmental structures? Or should they create institutional structures that force competing groups to work together? How do they create these structures when dealing with skeptical, acrimonious masses and competing elites working at counter purposes? How these issues are resolved could have profound, long-term implications for the operation of government and the incidence of ethnic conflict, which many believe to be undesirable. But is ethnic strife always undesirable or inevitably counterproductive? Are there episodes of ethnically based political conflict that can actually enhance the quality of democratic life? In situations where ethnic conflict is counterproductive, what role can political leaders play in mollifying their supporters? What role can electoral engineering play in alleviating political stresses in ethnically divided democracies?

Various technological advances in communication and information processing pose different challenges and opportunities. Citizens play a vital role in any model of democracy, and mass-elite dynamics are at the core of electoral accountability and democratic responsiveness. Recognizing the importance of individuals, drafters of liberal democracies have been careful to give "space" to citizens by providing them with core freedoms, liberties, and protections. Without these protections and liberties it would be difficult to maintain the proper relationship between citizens and leaders in democratic societies. But some modern technological advances, using information freely provided by individuals, provide private entities with unprecedented capacities to assemble massive data banks. Technology also provides these private entities with the capacity to distribute that personal information, unbeknownst to the provider and without explicit consent, to third parties, including governments. These unprecedented capacities create the potential for heretofore unforeseen intrusions into the private lives of individuals. While these intrusions are likely to permit invasions into the space needed by individuals to perform their roles as democratic citizens, they fall outside the reach of existing legal doctrines on privacy. Can liberal societies deal with the privacy implications of these technologies? If not, what will their impact be on the new age of democracy? These same technological advances also have the potential dramatically to affect mass-elite linkages in unprecedented ways. But what will be the import of those effects? Will these technologies be used to empower ordinary citizens? Or will elites use them to manipulate mass attitudes and behavior? Finally, advances such as the Internet have the potential to fragment political communities in the future, perhaps to such an extent that this fragmentation will undermine the capacity for common understandings and meaningful dialogues. How realistic are these concerns about fragmentation? What are the chances that fragmentation will undercut the basis for reaching consensual policy decisions in the future?

SOCIAL HETEROGENEITY AND DEMOCRATIC GOVERNANCE

Jack Snyder (chapter 2) underscores the difficulty and tenuousness of democratic transitions, which are particularly challenging in multiethnic societies. In these societies, the generic challenges of creating a new regime are often compounded by conflicting nationalist sentiments and elites working at cross-purposes. Some elites want to integrate diverse groups within the new state to aid its consolidation; others place a higher priority on advancing self- and group interests. Snyder is concerned with how these competing motives affect democratic transitions. He discusses the trajectories that democratic transitions can take in ethnically diverse societies, as well as the factors that affect those trajectories.

In reviewing the institutional and constitutional strategies for handling ethnic divisions, he highlights the surprisingly poor record of most of the popular approaches. Federalism easily slides into separatism, assimilation is generally infeasible, defenders of "power sharing" have, over time, watched one after another of their success stories go sour, and so on. In the end, Snyder eschews the search for an optimal constitutional scheme. Instead, he emphasizes the value of "civic solutions," the establishment of a multitude of diverse, cross-ethnic institutions. He also argues that reformers must pay close attention to sequence and context; simply relying on clever institutional designs to control deep ethnic schisms will not be sufficient to create a stable democratic state.

Mark Q. Sawyer (chapter 3) makes the case that struggles among racial and ethnic groups are both endemic in democracy and a means of gauging how successful a polity is at channeling self-expression by diverse groups into responsible government. His most original contribution is his discussion of the advantages that social diversity can bring to democratic governance. He argues that what he terms "contentious pluralism" provides vitality to democratic processes. If the legitimate grievances of racial and ethnic minorities are properly channeled, the issues and challenges they raise can lead to the extension and realization of democratic ideals and values. His discussion underscores the point that, while no government has ever completely met the lofty ideals embedded in democratic theory, a complacent conformism does little to eliminate the gap between democratic practices and ideals. His chapter amply demonstrates the need for more careful attention to the effects of social diversity on the realization of democratic ideals.

Paul M. Sniderman (chapter 4) is concerned with the role that democratic leaders can play in dealing with ethnically based conflict rooted in deeply ingrained prejudices. To generate insight into this problem he uses an innovative technique he helped pioneer, embedding experiments within opinion surveys. What he finds is a twist, worthy of O. Henry, on one of the oldest and most fundamental problems of democracy in heterogeneous societies. Those members of society who are most susceptible to appeals of prejudice, by virtue of their abnormally strong desire to conform, are likewise most susceptible to interpersonal pressure to *suppress* discriminatory views, pressure that party leaders are well-positioned to apply. Sniderman's findings documenting this paradoxical syndrome throw new light on the importance of political leadership. He concludes that democracies can make use of "top down" situational pressure from elites that lead followers away from the more dangerous implications of group rivalries. Sniderman elucidates these conclusions with a tour of recent history and opinion data from the Netherlands, but the dynamic he uncovers is a general one that is likely to be useful in a wide range of societies.

The quiddity of democracy is popular elections, and scholars have long believed that electoral arrangements could be valuable aids in weaving multiethnic societies into functioning democratic polities. The essay by Bernard Grofman and Jon Fraenkel (chapter 5) delivers a two-step tour of electoral engineering designed to achieve this goal. They first review the expansive literature on effects of electoral formulae, theoretical and empirical. They then provide a brief tour of the South Pacific, where experimentation with a wide array of rules has generated extremely useful, mostly overlooked data. Like Snyder, Grofman and Fraenkel are too well acquainted with the theoretical arguments and real-world data to fall prey to a magic-bullet, one-size-fits-all proposition on how elections ought to be set up when societies are crosscut by deep ethnic schisms.

They report that, while most states in the Pacific inherited electoral laws from past colonial masters, they later revised these laws in an effort to accommodate unique local features. But engineering is tricky and there are few simple success stories where social problems were tamed by revising voting laws. Indeed, their clearest conclusion from the experiences of these small states is that close attention must be paid to the exact details of the electoral rules. Reformed laws nearly always produce systematic effects in behavior that, even if they seem sensible after the fact, were unanticipated. Their work suggests that the notion of cultural determinism is almost surely mistaken. But the truism that "institutions matter" understates the importance of seemingly small details in affecting how mass preferences are translated into electoral outcomes.

Technological Innovations and Democracy in the Modern Era

Wayne V. McIntosh and Stephen Simon (chapter 6) begin part 2 with an intriguing survey of technological advances that have great import for the enjoyment and jurisprudence of privacy. Information and communication technologies, while expanding choice and convenience, are simultaneously making ever more data on the personal lives of individuals more readily accessible to others. When it is the government employing these technologies while seeking to combat terrorism and crime, there obviously is a sharp tension between individuals' rights to spheres of private activity and the public's interest in security and safety. But the enhanced capacity of private entities to capture, store, and share traces of individual action is equally problematic, even though it is not often covered by legal protections. Compounding efforts to deal with these problems through existing legal doctrines is the fact that much of the increased monitoring and documentation of private lives by private entities takes place through voluntary actions by individuals. Often it does not matter, within existing legal doctrine, that individuals voluntarily releasing information are unaware of the extent to which technological advances make their personal behavior transparent and traceable.

Present law hangs, in part, on whether or not individuals have a *legitimate* expectation that transactions are private, and expectations are clearly subject to revision as new technologies emerge. McIntosh and Simon's examination of the existing "privacy paradigm" in legal thinking demonstrates a cause for real concern. Existing understandings of privacy are rapidly becoming anachronistic, and personal spheres of privacy are shrinking in ways that few in the general public appreciate. Classical liberal thinkers had no doubt that privacy is a core liberal value, one that is essential to the proper functioning of democratic government. Thus, the authors call for urgent adaptation of privacy rights theories and jurisprudence to take into account the blitzkrieg of technological change in collecting, storing, and sharing information about individuals.

W. Lance Bennett (chapter 7) shifts the focus on technology away from the issue of privacy to that of mass-elite linkages. He approaches this issue by providing a sweeping historical review of elite efforts to use communication technologies in shaping public opinion. He sees three distinct eras of "managed" communication over the past century. Until the 1960s, parties and interest groups communicated with citizens via social groups. As group memberships declined, an alternative route developed in the shape of the mass media, and particularly television network news. By the 1980s, however, a proliferation of media sources undercut this second era, and we arrived at the age of the "isolated citizen." Now, competing political elites, with consultants at their side, direct a multitude of messages narrowly tailored to specific segments of the population. By Bennett's telling, then, American democracy has, for decades, labored under a stifling "engineered consent," wherein successful governance depended on elite domination of the masses.

But current technological advances, which are still unfolding, provide the possibility of either still more sophisticated management of public opinion or a revolutionary shift away from "managed communication." New "stealth technologies," wherein information is collected, stored, and used without explicit consent (and outside of public view), permit construction of large databases of personal information that facilitate ever more specialized targeting of appeals. By contrast, "transparent technologies," such as the Internet, have made communication so easy that coordination of all kinds is inevitably decentralized, making bottom-up or two-way communication more prevalent. Looking ahead, Bennett sees the vitality of democracy bound up in an unfolding race between transparent and stealth technologies, one whose outcome is uncertain at this point.

Bruce Bimber's essay focuses on one component of what Bennett terms transparent technologies, the Internet. Like Wendy Rahn (whose essay, "Globalization, the Decline of Civic Commitments, and the Future of Democracy" is in *International Perspectives on Contemporary Democracy*) and Bennett, he is interested in the Internet's potential for creating political fragmentation; that is, for dividing polities into ever smaller and narrower subsets. Fragmentation is a concern of considerable import for democracies in the Information Age, insofar as technologies that contribute to fragmentation can weaken social bonds, create political polarization, erode the distinction between news and "noise," and so on. Bimber conducts a probing reassessment of contemporary concerns over political fragmentation and puts these concerns in historical perspective by reviewing earlier eras of fragmentation in the American experience.

His review suggests that the current concerns with fragmentation are rooted in an overly simplistic understanding of contemporary modes of political communication. He proposes, instead, a two-dimensional model, underscoring the point that the multiplication and differentiation of communication structures have multiple consequences. These changes lead to increasingly heterogeneous structures for political engagement, some centralized, some decentralized; some involving cross-group communication, some involving within-group communication. The result, he argues, is not fragmentation but complexity. He concludes that forecasting the future of political communication has become harder than ever before, and predictions that democracy is bound either to flourish or flounder in this new era ought to be regarded as dubious.

The essays included in this volume address some of the most pressing issues democracies face in the twenty-first century. Hence it is quite remarkable that the overriding theme herein is that, rather than being insurmountable, these challenges are capable of being addressed using conventional democratic practices and without abandoning fundamental democratic principles. This is especially true with respect to the matter of social heterogeneity. It is reassuring, for example, that stable democratic regimes can conceivably be formed in ethnically divided societies by creating institutions and processes that require ongoing engagement across groups. Pluralistic dialogues, with which democracies have a great deal of experience, can play a role in even the most divisive conflicts. No less significant is the point that seemingly ubiquitous ethnic conflicts, when properly channeled, can enhance the quality of democratic governance. Just as reassuring is the notion that political leadership and electoral engineering, two tools that are well within the control of democratic societies, can be of use in ameliorating ethnic and racial conflicts.

The challenges emanating from the rapid advancement of information and communication technologies are no less daunting than those generated by the existence of socially diverse polities. What is most unnerving about technological advances is that their political effects are incremental and far less visible than those generated by ethnic and racial conflicts. These "stealth-like" qualities, joined with the collateral benefits they produce for modern societies and the ambiguity of their political effects, make them difficult to address. But there is nothing inherent in the challenges they pose that makes them impervious to being addressed by open political debate. Innovative jurisprudential doctrines have routinely, if not easily, emerged throughout the history of common law nations. These innovations have accommodated changed circumstances and the inadequacy of existing doctrines; when judicial bodies have failed to act, legislatures frequently stepped in. Moreover, technological advances have often produced solutions to the problems that they have created. What is perhaps most important is that the issues these technological advances pose be the subject of ongoing research, dialogue, and debate.

PART I

Social Heterogeneity and Democracy

Challenges and Opportunities

2

Problems of Democratic Transition in Divided Societies

JACK SNYDER

Moments of transition toward democracy are fraught with the danger of violence in ethnically divided societies. Democratization is typically intertwined with the rise of nationalism, a doctrine that demands self-rule for the nation. At such heady moments, nationalist movements in multiethnic societies often forge competing national aspirations. Since the fall of the Berlin Wall, wars or large-scale civil violence broke out following experiments with mass electoral democracy in Armenia, Azerbaijan, Burundi, Ethiopia, Indonesia, Lebanon, Pakistan, the Palestinian territories, Russia, and the former Yugoslavia (Mansfield and Snyder 2005). Elections did not cause the fighting in Iraq, but their polarizing effect did nothing to dampen it. Multiethnic societies that undertake a transition to democracy are, moreover, more likely to revert to authoritarianism than are homogeneous societies (Przeworski 2000).

In this context, ethnicity is an especially potent axis of cleavage because ethnic groups typically combine the characteristics of size, territoriality, dense social networks, and historic myths that make national self-determination a plausible goal for the group (Hechter 2000; Smith 1986). Nonetheless, ethnicity is not the only cleavage that endangers democratic transitions. Since the French Revolution, the transition to mass politics, including electoral politics, has often energized divisions over class, religion, ideology, region, tradition versus modernity, and urban versus rural interests. These cleavages, including ethnicity, are no longer crippling once a society navigates the turbulent transition. In mature, stable democracies, such cleavages are often politicized, but parties and interest groups that define themselves in these terms play by democratic rules.

The turbulent dawn of the era of mass politics forces political elites to make momentous strategic choices. Those who want to consolidate democracy need to decide whether to work within the constraints of existing cleavages or to create disincentives to politicize those cleavages. Those who want to wreck the democratic project that threatens them need to decide whether to suppress mass participation or promote a populist ideology to hijack it for their own purposes. And those who want to advance the narrow goals of their group need to decide whether democracy or authoritarianism serves their interests best.

Sometimes these choices can lead to unintended consequences. Seemingly expedient strategies to speed the democratic transition in the short run, such as ethnofederalism or power-sharing arrangements, may lock in cleavages that bedevil efforts to consolidate democracy later. Moreover, institutional solutions that work well in mature democracies, where institutions are strong, may be counterproductive or simply irrelevant in transitional democracies, where participatory institutions are ineffectual and easily exploited for antidemocratic ends.

This chapter examines the strategic choices that elites do make—or could make—in transitions. It stresses the need to take into account sequencing and context to avoid unintended consequences. The first section discusses the reasons why democratization causes violence and the factors that make transitions go smoothly or not. Subsequent sections discuss the archaeology of social cleavages that come into play during democratic transitions. A final section assesses commonly advanced policy prescriptions for dealing with cleavage problems in turbulent transitions.

Trajectories of Democratization

Although the process of democratization tends to increase the risk of war, many countries go through the process peacefully. During the 1980s and 1990s, numerous states consolidated their democratic transitions fairly successfully with little if any external or internal violence. These fortunate cases included many in the southern cone of South America, in northeastern Europe, and in East Asia. South Africa, too, despite some internal violence, experienced a reasonably smooth transition.

These countries had a number of important advantages. They tended to enjoy relatively high per capita income and literacy; thus, their citizens had the resources and skills to build the institutions and civil society organizations that democracy needs. Before the transition began, many of these success cases had well-developed state institutions and, in particular, administrative bureaucracies that functioned in a reasonably efficient way to advance state objectives with minimal corruption. Some of these successful states enjoyed the benefit of some past experience with independent legal and journalistic institutions that could be adapted for use by the democratizing state. In most of these states, powerful elites did not feel threatened by a successful transition to democracy, in part because trusted state institutions made guarantees that they would have a soft landing credible, so they were less likely to put up resistance to change. Where, under such conditions, strong democratic institutions emerged quickly, democracy was fairly easily consolidated, and the transition was largely peaceful, as in Brazil, Chile, Hungary, and Poland. Where institutional groundwork was in place, transitions were peaceful even in geopolitically challenging cases where unresolved national partitions raised the risk of war, as in South Korea and Taiwan. In contrast, where the institutions needed by democracy were weak and democratization remained incomplete, war was more likely, as in Ethiopia, Pakistan, and Peru.

This finding bears out arguments advanced by the seminal scholar of democracy and democratization, Robert Dahl. He argued that the peacefulness of the transition to democracy depended on getting the sequence of the transition right. Where rules, habits, and institutions of competitive politics were well established before the holding of unfettered mass elections, as in Great Britain after the Second and Third Reform Bills of 1867 and 1884, the transition to democracy went relatively smoothly. In contrast, where mass electoral politics developed before the institutions to regulate political competition were in place, transitions were prone to conflict. In countries that tried to take shortcuts to democracy, Dahl argued, elites tended to feel threatened by political change, and leaders often deployed nationalism as a justification for intolerance and repression (Dahl 1971, 36–38, 44). Exactly these causal mechanisms are at work in many wars of democratization.

It is possible to imagine several reasons why democratization might be associated with an increased likelihood of war and ethnic conflict. Some scholars speculate, for example, that perhaps all kinds of regime change, not just regime change toward democracy, lead to instability and war. Or one might guess that the new democracies are vulnerable and hence targets of attack but are not aggressors themselves. Edward Mansfield and I have explored such alternative explanations and show that none of these is convincing (Mansfield and Snyder 2005). Instead, we found that war is most likely in incomplete democratization that has stalled during the transition from an authoritarian regime to a mixed regime, when the state suffers from serious institutional deficits. Weak institutions per se do not increase the chance of war; they do so only during the early phase of an incomplete democratic transition. It is often a strategic mistake for an institutionally weak state that is handing over power to its people to initiate war, and yet such states often do exactly this. Why?

Such states face a gap between rising demands for broad participation in politics and inadequate institutions to manage those popular demands. Where the institutions of autocratic authority are crumbling, yet new institutions of democratic accountability have not yet been constructed to take their place, routine institutional authority is lacking, and political leaders frequently turn instead to ideological or charismatic appeals to bolster their rule.

Rallying popular support by invoking threats from rival nations is a common expedient for hard-pressed leaders who seek to shore up their legitimacy. During the unraveling of the Yugoslav communist regime, for example, Slobodan Milosevic employed demagogic rhetoric about the alleged danger of Albanian nationalism in Kosovo to gain a popular following in Serbia's first elections (Gagnon 1994–95). The institutional weaknesses of early democratization create both the motive to use this strategy of rule and the opportunity to dodge accountability for its high costs and biased rhetoric.

The contest over national self-determination takes place as the fortunes of both elites and mass groups are shifting. Elites left over from the old regime are desperately seeking strategies that will prevent their fall, while rising elites are trying to muscle in, and both are scrambling for allies among the newly aroused masses.

Elites often seek to solve these political dilemmas by invoking nationalism, the doctrine that a distinctive people deserve to rule themselves in a state that protects and advances their distinctive cultural or political interests.[1] Nationalism helps elites to rally the support of the masses on the basis of sentiment, rather than seeking their loyalty by providing responsive institutions that protect their interests. Nationalism also helps to define the people who are exercising self-determination. It thus clarifies the lines between "the people" and their foes, who become scapegoats in a self-fulfilling strategy that rallies support in protection against external threats.

Nationalism is attractive to rising groups, who use it as a populist club that can be wielded against elites who are insufficiently zealous in promoting the interest of "the nation," that is, "the people." At the same time, nationalism can be co-opted as a counter-tactic by elites, old and new, who want to evade new democratic constraints on their rule. Claiming to rule for "the people," but not submitting to direct accountability to them, these elites can tar their opponents as "enemies of the nation" who are in league with external foes, and thus justify curtailing their opponents' political and civil rights. This nationalist club may be particularly attractive to military elites, economic protectionists, or ethnic entrepreneurs. The nearly universal emergence of nationalist ideology in the early stages of democratization suggests that its usefulness at this formative political juncture is generic and can be adapted for use by almost any would-be ruling group (Hroch 2000).

In the absence of strong state institutions to knit together the nation, leaders must struggle for legitimacy in an ill-defined, contested political arena. Nationalism is both an easy and an effective way to rally popular support without actually offering accountability for results to a newly mobilized mass public. Democracy requires national self-determination, but people in weak states who are just emerging into political consciousness often lack clear, agreed-upon answers to the questions, Who are we? What is our nation? Although nationalists often believe that the identity of their own nation was fixed by immutable nature or culture, on the contrary, it is generally a people's shared experience and shared fate in a strong state that solidifies and demarcates their sense of nationality. Even in a country with a long and venerable history such as France, for example, it was only the shared experiences in the late nineteenth century—common military service, national railways, standardized education, and mass democracy—that completed the process of forging a culturally diverse peasantry into self-conscious Frenchmen (Weber 1976).

War and ethnic conflict may sometimes result from this potent political brew, as a direct result of explicitly nationalist political objectives, such as competing claims of groups for the same territory. War may also result indirectly from the complex politics of transitional states. It may come as an unintended by-product of belligerent and untrustworthy diplomacy that provokes neighbors' fears. Nationalists' mobilizing rhetoric may make war more likely by distorting the nation's view of the chances of success in a fight, or of the feasibility of reaching a compromise with the enemy. Political leaders may become entrapped in their own swaggering rhetoric, their reputations mortgaged to the nationalist commitments they have made. Heterogeneous political coalitions may become stuck with their own reckless policies when uncompromising nationalism becomes the indispensable common denominator that keeps them together. In short, it would be misleading to say that nationalistic publics in incomplete democracies simply "want war." Instead, violence is often an indirect by-product of the nationalist politics of the transitional regime.

Political Cleavages in Transitions to Democracy

What are the origins of the political cleavages that are the basis of contention in democratizing states, and to what extent are they subject to manipulation, for good or ill?

Such cleavages are often explained through an archaeology of the layered formative processes that prevailed at different stages of a country's social history (Lipset and Rokkan 1967). Ethnic, dynastic, or colonial processes laid down loose parameters of demography and boundaries in which later processes played out. At the very dawn of the era of mass politics, politicized religious movements in the early modern period formed enduring cleavages that often continued to affect political alignments in the later democratic era. Even in Britain, commonly invoked as the paradigmatic case of territorially inclusive national identity, conflicts over religion in the seventeenth century led to a ban on office holding by Catholics that shaped nationalism during the formative period of democratization (Marx 2003).

This religious stratum is typically overlaid with a subsequent ethnically based linguistic or cultural stratum, which is in turn overlaid by economic sectoral cleavages (urban/rural, labor/capital, export/national) in the course of capitalist and industrial development. Some of these cleavages appear before democratization, whereas others develop during the course of democratization as the broad mass of the population becomes more politically aware. Sometimes earlier cleavages lose their salience as they are buried under newer divisions. Sometimes they remain intact, either crosscutting or reinforcing later cleavages. Sometimes the line of cleavage remains, but it takes on new content in the modernized society (Gellner 1983; Smith 1986).

Several processes may lock in cleavages. Cultural myths about Golden Ages, ancient homelands, and longstanding enemies can be powerful reinforcers of the practical divisions that result from ethnic differentiation, such as language barriers and cultural rules against fraternization. The moment of mass literacy is often a decisive phase in the locking in of ethnic identity. Reading in a common vernacular creates a community of discourse and sometimes a vehicle for homogenizing propaganda (Anderson 1983). Assimilation of ethnic minorities to a majority national identity is vastly easier before mass literacy than after (Cederman 1997; Byman 2002). Nonetheless, literacy alone does not guarantee that ethnicity will be politicized around a goal of national self-determination. This happens only as the result of a campaign by nationalist political entrepreneurs, which includes state officials trying to drum up enthusiasm for paying taxes and serving in the army as well as proselytizers for state-seeking movements in a multiethnic state or empire (Hroch 2000; Posen 1993). Once such a campaign gains mass adherents, it is very hard to obliterate nationalist consciousness.

Not only ideas but also institutions can lock in cleavages. This may include the institutions of authoritarian states, such as the ethnofederal structure of the Soviet Union or the millet system of the Ottoman Empire, which gave administrative salience to ethnic distinctions, creating ethnically defined elites with the capacity to act together politically (Brubaker 1996; Hechter 2000). In more democratic regimes, institutions may likewise lock in cleavages, for example, by creating reserved seats or separate electorates for religious or ethnic groups, as was done in Lebanon's power-sharing system, or in local elections in the British Raj in India.

Conversely, institutions can also have integrative effects. The state can devise institutions to try to unify a people, for example, imposing a common language of administration, common school curricula, and universal military service. In this way, says a classic study by Eugene Weber, the French state gradually turned polyglot, localistic "peasants into Frenchmen" in the latter half of the nineteenth century. The state can also devise electoral rules that split ethnic minorities into different voting districts and create incentives for politicians to appeal to multiple groups to get a majority (Horowitz 1991a).

Sometimes policies aiming at national integration can have unintended effects. The history of national identity building is littered with casualties from would-be homogenizing policies that provoked a backlash on the part of the groups targeted for assimilation. Conversely, federalist strategies of gaining the loyalty of minorities by indulging their desires for limited self-rule sometimes facilitate separatism by helping state-seeking nationalists to organize administratively.

Another problem is that institutional engineering may have very minor effects in states where political institutions, especially institutions of democratic participation, are only weakly established. This is often the case in states that are just beginning to embark on democratization. If true power depends on the struggle of gangs, militias, or guerrillas, then even the best-designed electoral system will have no impact. Sri Lanka discovered this when it instituted a second-preference voting scheme in 1978 that was designed to create incentives for cross-ethnic electoral appeals just as the real contest was migrating to the streets (Horowitz 1991b). The same problem plagues Afghanistan and Iraq today.

Policies to Manage Ethnically Divided Democratizing Societies

Democratization in weakly institutionalized political systems tends to heighten cleavages between ethnic groups and often becomes an occasion for violence. How can this problem be managed during democratic transitions?

One solution is to delay mass democracy until stronger institutions of rule of law, public debate, and impersonal administration can be established. However, waiting is often not an option in contemporary circumstances. For better or worse, peoples who want self-determination may demand majority-rule elections, as have the religious leaders of the Shi'a majority in Iraq. Likewise, the international community often desires early elections as a shibboleth of legitimacy that provides an excuse for an early exit from vexing circumstances. How can ethnic divisions be managed in light of these pressures?

Several would-be solutions are prominent in academic writing, among international public affairs experts, and/or in the practices of political leaders on the ground. These solutions can be arrayed on a chart that is defined by two intersecting axes, depending on whether the solution would separate or integrate the divided groups, and whether it would appease or repress their demands (see fig. 2.1). Thus, the extreme points in the four quadrants define four distinct strategies. Separation with appeasement, for example, characterizes the strategy of ethnofederal autonomy. Repressive integration, conversely, characterizes the strategy of coercive assimilation. Repressive separation is expulsion. Finally, appeasement with integration is a strategy of co-optation of individuals. Other strategies, each with a distinctive theoretical and political logic, occupy intermediate locations on the chart. These intermediate strategies include the prominent option of group rights and formal power sharing among ethnic groups.

The adoption of some of these strategies, even as a temporary expedient, may have implications for the ease of moving to a more preferred solution at a later stage of democratic development. Short-term solutions, such as formal power sharing, can create political constituencies and habits of alignment that constrain later choices in unintended ways. Each of the main alternatives has its advantages and disadvantages, which may come in different proportions depending on the situation.

EXPULSION OF THE MINORITY

The strategy of the so-called ethnic cleansers is to expel unwanted groups from the state's territory. A devil's advocate might argue that this paves the wave for stable democracy by eliminating the cultural divisions that un-

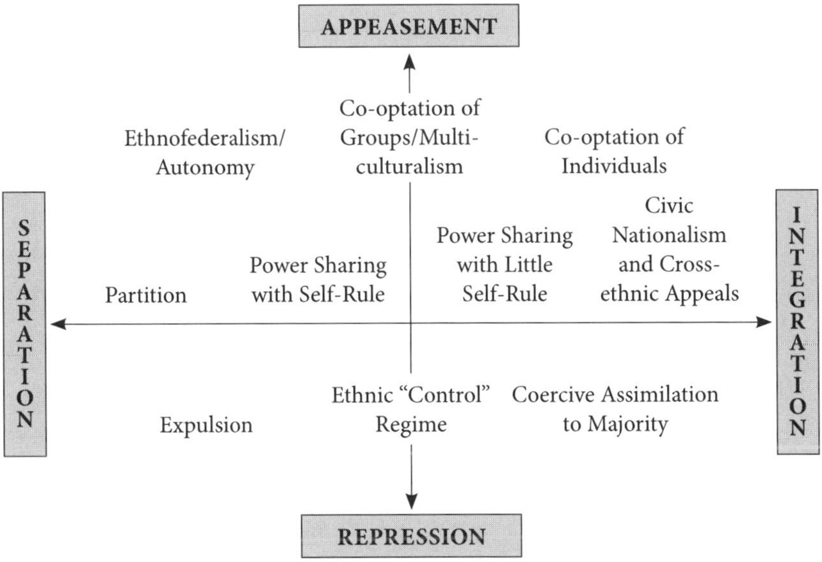

Figure 2.1. Policies to manage ethnically divided societies

dermine it. Stretching, one might make such a case for Israel in 1948 and perhaps for Croatia in 1995. However, other evidence fails to support this view. Incompletely democratizing states in the early 1990s, such as Serbia, Armenia, and Azerbaijan, expelled their minorities and then became more authoritarian. Ethnonationalist violence was employed as a strategy to justify taking away the political rights of all parties, not just the minority's (Gagnon 2004). Expulsion may be a symptom of the problems of democratization, but it is not a solution to them.

HEGEMONIC CONTROL BY THE MAJORITY

One strategy that often gets left off the list of "solutions" to ethnic conflict, due to its unpalatability to a liberal audience, is hegemony. In many multiethnic societies, one ethnic group monopolizes the power of the state and uses it to dominate other groups. In some cases, this is accomplished by outright repression; in other cases, by stratagems that divide minorities in order to conquer them. Repression can sometimes be effective in preventing ethnic conflict, if the power of the dominant group is so overwhelming as to preclude rational resistance. This worked for decades in the Soviet empire, for example. On balance, however, political repression and economic exploitation tend to be associated with a greater risk of ethnic conflict (Gurr 1993, chaps. 2–5).

The classic article on this type of ethnic "control" regime (Lustick 1979, 330) lists as examples South Africa under apartheid, the American South before World War II, Israel, Iraq vis-à-vis the Kurds, Burundi vis-à-vis the Hutu, Ethiopia, and the Soviet Union—all of which have met their demise and/or erupted in severe violence since the article appeared. Repression per se is not very reliable as a strategy of ethnic conflict management.

Domination works more reliably when those who are deprived of power tolerate their situation because they calculate that being second-class citizens is better than being first-class rebels. Ethnic minorities may be co-opted if they are granted benefits smaller than those of the dominant group, yet greater than their next-best alternative. For example, Russians in Estonia and Latvia compared their situation to that of Russians in Russia, and decided to favor independence from Moscow, despite the prospect of unequal citizenship rights in their new states.

Such hegemonies work best when tangible side benefits are reinforced by ideological justifications of ethnic subordination. Sometimes this is accomplished by the fiction that status inequalities are based on neutral legal criteria, not on ethnic ascription. For example, measures excluding most Russians from Estonian citizenship are based not on ethnicity per se but on one's ancestors' citizenship in the interwar Estonian state (before most Russians arrived), and on knowledge of the official language of the state, which happens to be Estonian. Insofar as this seemingly civic justification for ethnic exclusion has helped to create an opening for more inclusionary outcomes, many Russian-speaking Estonians have found the ideology to be one they can work with (Raun 1994; Laitin 1996). The selective inclusion of Russians in Estonian political life has served to co-opt a stratum of Russian-speaking loyalists to the ethnonational Estonian state.

Though majority hegemonies or "ethnic control regimes" may be quite effective in moderating ethnic conflict, they nonetheless have some major drawbacks if they are implemented in too harsh a manner (Lustick 1979; McRae 1991). The systematic deprivation of equal civic rights to ethnic minorities creates an ideological climate in which the democratic rights of the majority are also held to be less than absolute. If the collectivity is held to count for more than the individual, this insidious principle can be, and often is, used to undermine the rights of individuals of the majority ethnic group as well. In places like contemporary Armenia and Croatia, for example, it has been a short step from the expulsion of ethnic minorities to the abrogation of democracy and journalistic freedom for ethnic majorities as well. Ethnic hegemonies would be less objectionable as temporary expedients than as permanent vehicles for civic inequality. Insofar as Estonia continues to gradually infuse real content into its nominally civic principles, for example, its long-run prognosis as a liberal democracy will be good. Unfortunately, few dominant ethnic groups are far-seeing enough to soften their own hegemonic position voluntarily through gradual civic reforms.

One lesson from the Baltic experience is to place moderate, but relentless, pressure from the international community upon quasi-democratic ethnic control regimes, thus gradually breathing life into the nominally civic provisions of their constitutions. The Council of Europe pressed Estonia to loosen its initially draconian law on resident aliens. This influence was successful because it was exercised discreetly, and because it was backed by the perceived incentives of economic integration into the West and a future security guarantee against Russia. As a counterpart to such pressure, tolerance should be shown for ethnic hegemonies if their reforms are heading in the right direction, even if slowly. At the same time, the international community should be supporting the development of the institutional infrastructure that will be needed when the disadvantaged minority is finally allowed to play a full role in the civic life of the state. This means, for example, training ethnic minority journalists to take over responsible positions in mainstream media serving an ethnically mixed audience. It does not, however, mean jump-starting the creation of ethnic opposition media to give voice to the demands of excluded minorities. That only exacerbates the segmentation of the marketplace of ideas, making it easier for ethnonationalists to sow myths unchallenged.

ETHNIC PARTITION

Another unattractive but important strategy is ethnic partition. One does not have to hold primordialist theories of ancient hatreds to believe that, once popular identities are mobilized to fight along lines defined by cultural differences, it will be difficult to erase fears and hatreds rooted in the memory of those conflicts. Once intermingled cultural groups have fought, it is likely that their subsequent cohabitation in the same state will be wary, and consequently that they will fight again in the future. Any of a number of triggers—retreat of the imperial order-keepers, democratization, economic changes, shifts in the demographic balance of power—may ignite conflict. For that reason, a number of scholars have been making the case for ethnic partition as the best solution for certain cases of very highly mobilized nationalist enmities (Kaufmann 1996).

Among the objections to this strategy, the most obvious is that the creation of ethnically homogeneous states in places like the former Yugoslavia,

Rwanda, Burundi, and the Transcaucasus would require the resettlement of huge numbers of unwilling people. Yet the history of many ethnic conflicts shows that homogenization happens anyway, but through the vilest kind of warfare rather than through internationally supervised, preventive operations in peacetime. One reason for ethnic peace in much of Eastern Europe today is that the two world wars occasioned a vast "unmixing of peoples" through what today's Serbs would term ethnic cleansing (Brubaker 1996). Even such civilized folk as the Czechs expelled over a million Germans at the end of the war in 1945. In the present period, expulsions have accompanied many ethnic conflicts. During the breakup of the Soviet Union, hundreds of thousands of Armenians and Azerbaijanis were hounded from each others' countries through pogroms and other forcible measures (Anderson and Silver 1996). Fighting and intimidation in the former Yugoslavia has likewise made many areas more homogeneous and thus made partition more plausible. The de facto partition of Bosnia into Serbian and Muslim-Croat parts coexists awkwardly with the international community's insistence on maintaining the Dayton Accord's de jure fiction of political integration. In future cases of this type, the UN High Commissioner for Refugees might be wise to make a preventive offer of low-interest mortgages to fearful individuals stranded in minority enclaves who wish to purchase housing in their ethnic home republic. Israel has included such offers to induce Jewish settlers to leave Gaza voluntarily, though it has simultaneously created incentives for settlers to move to the West Bank.

Opponents of this strategy argue, however, that partition rarely resolves conflicts, in part because populations often remain somewhat intermingled. In part for that reason, endemic conflict persists despite partition in Ireland, Palestine, Kashmir, and other cases. Most important, partition—and the anticipation of partition—may itself be a cause of conflict. Many more died in communal violence in the aftermath of partitioning India and Pakistan, as a result of the turmoil and insecurities of migration, than before it. Indeed, plans to divide the former British Raj may have acted as a self-fulfilling prophecy, creating needless fears and uncertainties about the status of religious minorities who were to be abandoned in the wrong state (Kumar 1997). For these reasons, while preventive partition should not be viewed as unthinkable, it should not be seen as a preferred strategy applicable to a wide range of cases.

FEDERALISM

A related strategy is federalism. Instead of partitioning ethnic communities into separate sovereign states, this strategy would divide them into partially autonomous territorial sub-units within the state, whose boundaries are designed to coincide with ethnolinguistic concentrations. This method has a poor track record, especially in the formerly communist states, yet it remains popular with liberal problem-solvers, in part because it seems to allow national self-determination without the nasty fuss and bother of full-fledged partition. In fact, ethnofederalism is frequently a recipe for subsequent partition, often needlessly so.

In the wake of communism's collapse, the only states to break up were the three ethnofederal systems—Yugoslavia, the Soviet Union, and Czechoslovakia—the former two with violent consequences. Arguably, in each of these states ethnofederalism was a strategy of rule actively chosen by its communist founders, not a necessity forced upon them by the irresistible demands of ethnic groups. As numerous studies have demonstrated, ethnofederalism tends to heighten and politicize ethnic consciousness, creating a self-conscious intelligentsia and the organizational structures of an ethnic state-in-waiting (Brubaker 1996). When mass political participation expands, these ethnofederal structures channel it along an ethnic path. This process has played itself out even in Quebec. In the 1990s, it was the fear of a slippery slope to ethnofederalism—and beyond—that made central governments in Eastern Europe wary of any proposals for group rights or local autonomy for ethnic minorities. For these reasons, ethnofederalism is at best a last resort, which risks fueling rather than appeasing the politicization of ethnicity.

One of ethnofederalism's very few success cases is India, which reluctantly acceded to demands to reorganize some of its provincial boundaries after 1956 to coincide more closely with linguistic divides. Nehru and the Congress Party, at this point still at the height of their authority, were adamant secularists. Thus, the central government kept a tight rein on the process of ethnofederal reorganization. Rules of thumb guiding this process were that no concessions would be made to secessionist groups, that demands for redrawing boundaries along religious lines would be rejected out of hand, that large-scale popular support for the change had to be demonstrated, and that reorganization had to be requested by all the affected linguistic groups (Brass 1990, 169, 172–73). Most observers credit these controlled boundary adjustments with redressing a reasonable grievance without compromising the basic principles of the centralized, secular, communal-blind state. Subsequent problems leading to heightened communal mobilization in Indian politics were caused by the breakdown of the Congress system at the center, not by ethnofederalism per se.

ASSIMILATION

The opposite strategy is the assimilation of ethnic minorities to the cultural identity of the ethnic majority. This is possible for groups that are culturally similar, like Russians and Ukrainians, for groups that share a common religion, like the Iranians and the Bakhtiaris or the Moroccans and the Berbers (Byman 2002), or for minority cultures that are assimilated before they achieve a literary consciousness or political organization beyond the kinship level (Deutsch 1966, chap. 6; Cederman 1997, 157–61). But for most groups who are already in sustained ethnic conflicts, the window for cultural assimilation to the foe's ethnic identity has already closed. In such circumstances, attempts at coercive assimilation almost always backfire, heightening the political salience of ethnicity.

POWER SHARING VERSUS CROSS-ETHNIC APPEALS AND CIVIC NATIONALISM

This leads us to the two opposite strategies of ethnic conflict prevention that have stimulated the most academic debate: *power sharing* between ethnic groups, and institutional engineering to foster *integrative, cross-ethnic political alliances* (Sisk 1996, chap. 3; Roeder and Rothchild 2005). The power-sharing approach developed by Arend Lijphart takes the politicization of ethnic groups as a given in deeply divided societies and offers guidelines for elite-led pacts between the groups that will allow them to live in peace and mutual security (Lijphart 1977, 1991). In contrast, the integrative approach of Donald Horowitz tries to depoliticize ethnic identity by means of institutional arrangements that create incentives to align on the basis of crosscutting cleavages (Horowitz 1991a, 1991b). The link between democratization and ethnic conflict underscores the problems with elite-managed ethnic power sharing. More promising are integrative approaches like Horowitz's, though these must be embedded in a broader context of supportive institutions than the constitutional and electoral schemes that Horowitz himself emphasizes.

Lijphart lists the central characteristics of power sharing as joint control of executive power of the state, substantial autonomy of ethnic groups to regulate their own internal affairs, a minority veto on important issues, and proportionality of parliamentary representation, bureaucratic appointments, and state financial benefits (Lijphart 1991, 494–95; Nordlinger 1972, 21–33). Underpinning these arrangements is a system of bargaining between leaders of the participating ethnic groups and deference to those leaders on the part of each group's ethnic rank and file. Lijphart lists nine factors as conducive to power sharing: the absence of a single majority group, no economic disparity among the groups, a balance of power among the groups, a small number of groups, a country with a small total population, the existence of an external threat common to all groups, overarching loyalties that reduce the exclusiveness of ethnic attachments, prior traditions of compromise, and geographic concentrations of ethnic residence. However, he adds that power sharing is always the best approach in deeply divided societies, even when those factors are absent (Lijphart 1991, 497–98).[2]

Though there are numerous criticisms of the power-sharing approach, I will focus only on the points that are most relevant to the context of democratizing societies. Power sharing, as Lijphart conceives it, depends on mass groups deferring to the judgments of moderate elites who represent their ethnic segments. However, deference can hardly be taken for granted in democratizing societies. Mass groups clamoring for a greater say in politics will use any available argument, especially the argument that traditional elites are selling out the nation's interests by being too accommodative toward an out-group. In this context, elites jockeying for power within the ethnic group often have an incentive to be immoderate. Institutionalized power sharing exacerbates this by defining all politics as ethnic politics. As mass groups enter the political process, anyone who wants to participate must go through ethnic channels. Mobilizing support by definition means making sectarian appeals. Cross-ethnic politicking is reserved to elites, who may be too pressured from below to be accommodating toward elites of the opposing community.

The empirical record is not very favorable to power sharing. Lijphart points to Belgium and Malaysia as textbook cases of successful power sharing in ethnically divided societies. Setting aside the example of Belgium, a rich country in the heart of a peacefully democratic continent, Malaysia hardly counts in Lijphart's favor. Rather than a "consociational democracy," it is an example of a successful ethnic control regime, with side-payments to the Chinese business elite, erected by suppressing democracy and free speech. Lijphart also counts India as an example of successful power sharing. Indeed, limited legal self-regulation by Muslims and linguistic federalism are power-sharing elements in the Indian political system. However, the main principle of the Congress system in its heyday was secularism, the opposite of representation along religious or communal lines. Congress's success in containing ethnic and religious conflict was precisely that it encompassed all cultural groups, so that communal groups were not mobilized in competition to each other. Finally, Lijphart used to claim Lebanon as the premier example of power sharing, but since the outbreak of the bloody civil war there in the 1970s, he now stresses the flaws in Lebanon's consociational arrangements (Lijphart 1991, 507–8). In fact, Lebanon, along with Yugoslavia, underscores the dangers of this approach: it locks in an ethnic definition of politics, which leads to disaster when the prospect of rising popular participation undercuts the moderation of elites, or when demographic shifts alter the ethnic balance of power.[3]

Horowitz's integrative approach pursues exactly the opposite strategy: it tries to depoliticize ethnicity by creating institutions that reward cross-ethnic alignments. For the most part, he suggests encouraging this through constitutional and electoral provisions. In federal systems, for example, he suggests that boundaries should not coincide with ethnic patterns of settlement, but cut across them or break them up into smaller units. He notes that Nigeria's three-province system, which corresponded with ethnic lines, broke up into bloody ethnic warfare. Afterwards, the new regime imposed a twelve-province scheme that successfully politicized local identities and subcleavages within the broader ethnic categories (Horowitz 1991b, 22–23). For similar reasons, Horowitz recommends electoral rules that require winning candidates to get at least some of their votes from voters of a different ethnicity. As several chapters in this book demonstrate, mere proportional representation does little by itself, since the handful of minority representatives in parliament will still be outvoted on every issue, unless some incentives can be created for cross-ethnic alliances, even in general elections or in parliamentary coalition-making. This can be done by requiring supermajorities larger than any single group could provide, or by requiring successful candidates to get a number of "second-preference" votes. Horowitz notes that such a scheme was instituted in Sri Lanka in 1978, but, he says, by then politics was so polarized that electoral rules were insufficient to induce moderation.

Horowitz is on the right track, but his institutional schemes are too mechanistic and insufficiently embedded in a broader supportive context. Cross-ethnic institutions are needed on more dimensions than just electoral and constitutional rules. Segmental boundaries in the marketplace of ideas need to be effaced by the development of media institutions that serve as a common forum for the presentation and rigorous evaluation of ideas for all the communities that comprise the state. That is, in addition to Horowitz's "vote pooling," multiethnic societies also need "idea pooling." Integrative institutions are also needed in the administrative realm. Whereas Lijphart wants ethnic representation in state bureaucracies, what is really needed are highly professionalized, ethnic-blind courts, police, and armed forces that will carry out state policy equally toward all individuals, regardless of ethnicity.[4]

The commitment to the creation of a dense web of such ethnic-blind institutions can serve as the basis for civic patriotism, based not on the co-existence of ethnic groups but on the civic rights and duties of individuals. Unlike the strategy of ethnic assimilation, the promotion of civic nationalism does not require citizens to alter that aspect of their identity that is rooted in traditional culture, but simply to depoliticize it. Thus, Genevans do not need to speak German or eat sauerkraut to be fully Swiss.

As a practical matter, a civic national identity can emerge in a number of ways. In the case of Switzerland, a long history of cross-cultural cooperation against outside threats created strong civic myths to underpin collective action. In a society of immigrants from many cultures, such as the United States, loyalty to state institutions based on equal individual rights can serve as a strong foundation for a common identity. In many states, however, civic nationalism is based on a broadened redefinition of a core ethnic identity (Smith 1986). British civic nationalism, for example, grew out of a redefinition of English patriotism that stressed the centrality of individual liberties and common struggles against foreign foes, thus creating a national identity in which Scots and Welsh could be full participants. French national identity, though based partly on the ethnic core of the Île de France, was broadened through the experience of the French Revolution to include civic principles of equality and the rights of man. As a result, immigrants have been able to become French by integrating themselves into French civic life much more easily than outsiders could become German in Germany, for example, where identity conception is more ethnic and exclusionary.

Despite the advantages in principle of the civic solution, some caveats are in order. In some cases, as in the regime of the Slovak nationalist prime minister Vladimir Meciar, the argument that group rights can be best guaranteed through the protection of individual rights was a rhetorical fig leaf rationalizing a policy of majority ethnic hegemony. While touting civic rights, Meciar tried to ban Hungarian street signs, gerrymandered districts to reduce political clout of the concentrated Hungarian minority in southern Slovakia, and shifted economic investment to the ethnically Slovak north. Even in such cases, however, the best strategy is not to promote minority group rights to defend against such encroachments but to insist that the majority regime implement its civic principles in an even-handed way.

However, the promotion of overarching civic identities is not a short-term possibility in circumstances where the mobilization of ethnic cleavages is already extremely intense. Civic nationalism is a non-starter in Bosnia today, no matter how much the promoters of the Dayton Accord cherish that ideal.

Nonetheless, short-run choices should, wherever possible, avoid expedients that make civic outcomes more difficult in the long run. Power sharing and ethnofederalism, by locking in ethnic identities, are in that sense a step in the wrong direction. Moderate, balanced ethnic control regimes, which contain ethnopolitical mobilization of the majority as well as minorities, may be a better strategy for the long run, so long as they are combined with the gradual fostering of civic institutions.

Multiculturalism and Co-optation of Groups

A final strategy, multiculturalism, tries to get simultaneously the advantages of power sharing and of civic nationalism. In this approach, society's basic form of organization is individual-rights democracy, supported by a civic nationalist commitment to liberal norms and democratic institutions. However, within this general framework, the norms of public discourse acknowledge that the achievement of the individual goals of some people is inherently tied to the prospering of the culture group with which they identify. Informal organization of public life through cultural groups is seen as legitimate, though individuals have the right to opt out of their nominal group. This approach has had successes not only in the United States, but also in the new democracies of Eastern Europe, where the political relevance of ethnic distinctiveness is taken for granted, and the assertion of group concerns is not necessarily considered to be in conflict with loyalty to the democratic state. In France, in contrast, multiculturalism of this kind has not made headway, since civic nationalism is seen to require assimilation to majoritarian norms of secularism (Shulman 2002).

SEQUENCING OF STRATEGIES

Political authorities are often tempted to resort to short-term expedients to stabilize an ethnically divided society as a first step toward a preferable long-term solution. In the wake of a civil war, for example, third party guarantors often urge the former belligerents to accept a power-sharing accord that purports to insure each of the belligerent groups a share of bureaucratic posts, legislative seats, and local administrative control (Walter 2002). This may indeed succeed in achieving short-term stabilization, but at the cost of locking in group politics in a way that hinders long-term integration. Provisional partition may have the same effect. The Dayton Accord for Bosnia, for example, relied heavily on the recognition of the de facto division of Bosnia into Serb and Croat regions, which hindered the subsequent integration of Bosnia on civic principles (Bose 2002).

In another example, we can see that by the 1920s and 1930s British colonial authorities typically tried to prepare their overseas possessions for a future transition to independence and democracy. While working on the strengthening of civic institutions in these colonies, however, the British needed to shore up their rule through whatever expedients were at hand. Often this included working through traditional, nondemocratic elites and adopting divide-and-rule tactics of privileging ethnic minorities who benefited from British rule. These temporary expedients often politicized ethnicity and encouraged antidemocratic elements in a way that complicated the eventual transfer of power on the basis of universal suffrage and majority rule.

Today in Lebanon, politics remains locked into a sectarian mode as the result of a decades-old pattern of power sharing, which guaranteed that all politics would be rooted in religious communities and hindered the development of a common Lebanese identity. This system kept the peace until the outbreak of civil war in 1975, when it was imbalanced by the influx of Palestinian refugees. Its restoration after the war was again a temporary expedient that prevented real change and left Lebanese policy hostage to the aims of its organized minorities, notably, Hezbollah and its armed standoff against Israel.

For this reason, if one's objective is to promote integrative, civic solutions, it is best to work on them directly, even if slowly, rather than take a detour through short-term expedients that have a different basic logic. This may not be possible, and if it is not, one should not be optimistic about the consequences of promoting democracy too quickly in a society that lacks the preconditions for it.

A common criticism of the implementation of the Dayton Accord is that the initial elections were held too soon, at a time when the ethnic nationalists remained the best organized groups in Bosnia. As a result, they swept the initial elections, giving them control over the levers of government and hindering the task of civic reintegration.

A similar dynamic unfolded in Iraq under U.S. occupation. The Americans hoped that secular, cross-ethnic political parties would prevail in the initial elections, thus unifying Iraq and setting it on a path to stable, tolerant democracy. At it turned out, about nine of ten votes went to ethnic or religious sectarian parties, and only one in ten to secular parties appealing across these groups. One reason is that when political institutions are new and weak, political networks tend to form along the lines of existing social or cultural networks, which in developing countries are often ethnic or religious. Holding elections too soon plays into the hands of these kinds of political forces, which (as in Iraq) are likely to include illiberal and divisive elements.

This confirms the point made decades ago by political scientists as diverse as Robert Dahl and Samuel Huntington: democratization goes most smoothly when the administrative, representative, and legal institutions needed to make it work already have at least a toe-hold before mass electoral competition begins. Figuring out how to foster the development of such institutions in societies on the brink of transition remains a vexed and important task (Carothers 2006).

Notes

1. For discussions of the definition of nationalism, see Snyder 2000, 21–25; and Hechter 2000, chap. 1.

2. Note also the list of conditions in Rothschild 1981, 162–64.

3. Banac 1984, 414, notes that the conditions for successful consociational power sharing were also absent in Yugoslavia.

4. Horowitz's own recommendations on the ethnic composition of military forces in South Africa are complex, taking into account both professionalism and representativeness (Horowitz 1991a, 227–31).

References

Anderson, Barbara, and Brian Silver, eds. 1996. "Population Redistribution and Ethnic Balance in Transcaucasia." In Ronald Suny, ed., *Transcaucasia,* 2d ed. Ann Arbor: University of Michigan Press. 490–91.

Anderson, Benedict. 1983. *Imagined Communities.* London: Verso.

Banac, Ivo. 1984. *The National Question in Yugoslavia.* Ithaca, N.Y.: Cornell University Press.

Bose, Sumantra. 2002. *Bosnia after Dayton: Nationalist Partition and International Intervention.* New York: Oxford University Press.

Brass, Paul. 1990. *The Politics of India since Independence.* Cambridge: Cambridge University Press.

Brubaker, Rogers. 1996. *Nationalism Reframed.* Cambridge: Cambridge University Press.

Byman, Daniel L. 2002. *Keeping the Peace: Lasting Solutions to Ethnic Conflicts.* Baltimore: Johns Hopkins University Press.

Carothers, Thomas, ed. 2006. *Promoting the Rule of Law Abroad.* Washington, D.C.: Carnegie Endowment for International Peace.

Cederman, Lars-Erik. 1997. *Emergent Actors in World Politics: How States and Nations Develop and Dissolve.* Princeton: Princeton University Press.

Dahl, Robert A. 1971. *Polyarchy: Participation and Opposition.* New Haven, Conn.: Yale University Press.

Deutsch, Karl. 1966. *Nationalism and Social Communication.* Cambridge, Mass.: MIT Press.

Gagnon, V. P. 1994–95. "Ethnic Nationalism and International Conflict: The Case of Serbia." *International Security* 19 (Winter): 130–66.

———. 2004. *The Myth of Ethnic War: Serbia and Croatia in the 1990s.* Ithaca, N.Y.: Cornell University Press.

Gellner, Ernest. 1983. *Nations and Nationalism.* Ithaca, N.Y.: Cornell University Press.

Gurr, Ted Robert. 1993. *Minorities at Risk.* Washington, D.C.: U.S. Institute of Peace.

Hechter, Michael. 2000. *Containing Nationalism.* New York: Oxford University Press.

Horowitz, Donald. 1991a. *A Democratic South Africa? Constitutional Engineering in a Divided Society.* Berkeley: University of California Press.

———. 1991b. "Making Moderation Pay." In Montville, *Conflict and Peacemaking.* 451–76.

Hroch, Miroslav. 2000. *Social Preconditions of National Revival in Europe.* New York: Columbia University Press.

Kaufmann, Chaim. 1996. "Possible and Impossible Solutions to Ethnic Civil Wars." *International Security* 20 (Spring): 136–75.

Kumar, Radha. 1997. "The Troubled History of Partition." *Foreign Affairs* 76 (Jan.–Feb.).

Laitin, David. 1996. "National Revival and Competitive Assimilation in Estonia." *Post-Soviet Affairs* 12 (Jan.–Mar.): 25–39.

Lijphart, Arend. 1977. *Democracy in Plural Societies.* New Haven, Conn.: Yale University Press.

———. 1991. "The Power-Sharing Approach." In Montville, *Conflict and Peacemaking.* 491–510.

Lipset, Seymour M., and Stein Rokkan, eds. 1967. *Party Systems and Voter Alignments: Cross-National Perspectives.* New York: Free Press.

Lustick, Ian. 1979. "Stability in Deeply Divided Societies: Consociationalism versus Control." *World Politics* 31 (April): 325–44.

Mansfield, Edward D., and Jack Snyder. 2005. *Electing to Fight: Why Emerging Democracies Go to War.* Cambridge: MIT Press.

Marx, Anthony W. 2003. *Faith in Nation: Exclusionary Origins of Nationalism.* Oxford: Oxford University Press.

McRae, Kenneth D. 1991. "Theories of Power-Sharing and Conflict Management." In Montville, *Conflict and Peacemaking.* 93–106.

Montville, Joseph, ed. *Conflict and Peacemaking in Multiethnic Societies.* New York: Lexington.

Nordlinger, Eric. 1972. *Conflict Regulation in Divided Societies.* Cambridge, Mass.: Center for International Affairs, Harvard Studies in International Relations. 21 33

Posen, Barry R. 1993. "Nationalism, the Mass Army, and Military Power." *International Security* 18 (Fall): 80–124.

Przeworski, Adam, Michael Alvarerz, José Cheibub, and Fernando Limongi. 2000. *Democracy and Development: Political Institutions and Well-Being in the World, 1950–1990*. Cambridge: Cambridge University Press.

Raun, Toivo. 1994. "Ethnic Relations and Conflict in the Baltic States." In W. Raymond Duncan and G. Paul Holman Jr., *Ethnic Nationalism and Regional Conflict*. Boulder: Westview. 155–82.

Roeder, Philip, and Donald Rothchild, eds. 2005. *Sustainable Peace: Power and Democracy after Civil Wars*. Ithaca, N.Y.: Cornell University Press.

Rothschild, Joseph. 1981. *Ethnopolitics*. New York: Columbia University Press.

Shulman, Stephen. 2002. "Challenging the Civic/Ethnic and West/East Dichotomies in the Study of Nationalism." *Comparative Political Studies* 35 (5) (June): 554–85.

Sisk, Timothy. 1996. *Power Sharing and International Mediation in Ethnic Conflicts*. Washington, D.C.: U.S. Institute of Peace.

Smith, Anthony. 1986. *The Ethnic Origins of Nations*. Oxford: Blackwell.

Snyder, Jack. 2000. *From Voting to Violence: Democratization and Nationalist Conflict*. New York: Norton.

Walter, Barbara F. 2002. *Committing to Peace: The Successful Settlement of Civil Wars*. Princeton: Princeton University Press.

Weber, Eugene. 1976. *Peasants into Frenchmen*. Stanford: Stanford University Press.

3

Citizens, Identities, and Democratic Dialogues

Opportunities and Challenges of Diverse Societies

MARK Q. SAWYER

The twentieth century began with W. E. B. Du Bois stating that the problem of the twentieth century would be "the color line." Du Bois's judgment was correct then and it is a safe bet that race and ethnicity will play an equally important role in the twenty-first century, particularly in the politics of democratic regimes. This essay addresses two critical concepts that will play a powerful role in determining the impact of racial and ethnic issues on democratic politics: citizenship and contention. Both concepts, when coupled with race and ethnicity, have the potential to plant the seeds for the refinement of democratic regimes. But they are equally capable of creating untenable conflicts that undermine democratic development. The reason for the uncertain effect of identity-based conflicts is that they do not have direct and simple effects on democratic politics. This point is lost on many because of the tendency to conflate race itself with the interactions between race, citizenship, and contention.

This conflation is problematic because, in order to understand the impact of identity-based conflicts on democratic development, one must unravel the interactions among identity, citizenship, and contention. Particularly important here are two issues. The first deals with the conception of citizenship held by the majority population: Is this conception supple enough to accommodate the aspirations of racial/ethnic minorities? The second issue involves the modes of contention pursued by minority groups: Despite differences, do the visions of the various groups include a sense of shared destiny?

This essay will develop the utility of distinguishing among the concepts of race, citizenship, and contention and will explore the analytical possibilities created by studying the interactions among them. The empirical examples I use to illustrate my argument draw primarily from the nations within the Americas, Europe, and Africa, which represent a wide range of possibilities for configurations of identity, the struggle for democracy, and institutional arrangements.

Difference in the Twenty-first Century

There has been a growing literature on questions of race and ethnic conflict (Horowitz 1985; Young 1990; Appiah 1994; Taylor 1994; Gutman 1996). The growing focus on the issue of difference is not because the problem is new.[1] Rather, it is because the decline of the Soviet Union and the forces of globalization have intensified the movement of citizens and made national identities central questions in the organization of the world (Laitin 1998; Sassen 1999). The former Soviet satellites, as well as countries in all regions of the world, are currently dealing with the problem of integrating or managing multiple racial and ethnic groups into nations. This problem is complicated by the ongoing phenomenon of transnational migration from developing countries to the Western industrialized world.

The growing real-world importance of incorporating subordinate or different ethnic and racial groups into nations and localities has become reflected in academia; it is a growing focus of emphasis in political science. Ongoing ethnic conflicts in Africa, accelerating migration from the underdeveloped world to Europe and the United States, and the growth of ethnic nationalism from the ashes of the former Soviet Union, have generated a new and profound interest in questions of identity. Also, social movements within the United States, such as the civil rights movement, the feminist movement and the struggle for gay and lesbian rights, have highlighted the complicated role of social and political identities in democratic politics and have captured the attention of many social scientists.

Scholars and activists like Frederick Douglass, W. E. B. Du Bois, Franz Fanon, and C. L. R. James had taken up questions of identity and its relationship to the political long ago (James 1963; Fanon 1967; Du Bois 1907, 1975; Fanon 1991). However, these questions, along with the insights of these scholars, have remained on the fringe of political science inquiry. Political science has been a discipline preoccupied with the movements of the powerful and one in which we see polities through color-blind liberal frames rather than the racial frames that so often inform everyday experiences (Young 1990; Mills 1997). These scholars and activists addressed deep questions related to identities and nationalism, including the nature of national identities, the expansiveness of citizenship, and the political systems that best produce just outcomes for outsiders.

Emanating from these scholarly insights, and reflecting the political movements that informed them, has been the scholarly and political debate over the question of multiculturalism. The concept of multiculturalism has created a new theoretical opening, one that allows us to explore questions of difference without resorting to simple, assimilation-based pluralist theory or modernization arguments.

Political theorist Barnor Hesse argues that

> [at] the end of the twentieth century, late western modern societies lived in the broadly uncharted relational terrain between multicultural and multiculturalism. Multiculturalism refers to particular discourses or social forms which incorporate marked cultural differences and diverse ethnicities. In this "substantive" sense, multiculturalism can be named, valued, celebrated and repudiated from many different perspectives. . . . However, constitutive of that political correlation is the colonial formation of the multicultural as a signifying relation. The multicultural is a signifier of the unsettled meanings of cultural differences in relation to multiculturalism as the signified of attempts to fix their meaning in national imaginaries. (2000)

What Hesse is alluding to is that, in many contexts, multiculturalism represents the fact of racially and ethnically diverse groups living within the same boundaries and embodies a contested political discourse around the meaning of that diversity.

The academic debate, much like the political debate, has focused on the normative and practical dimensions of recognizing alternative identities and their effects on democracy. Western theorists like Will Kymlicka, drawing from their own unique experiences, have largely created this literature (Kymlicka 1996). However, contestation over the meaning of diversity pervades not only Western countries but a variety of developing nations as well. In Western countries, critics of multiculturalism, like Arthur Schlesinger, Samuel Huntington, and Abigail Thernstrom, have argued that the focus on ethnic/racial identities in industrialized nations threatens cohesive civic identities (Schlesinger 1992; Huntington 2004). For these critics, the most prominent threats to narratives of common identity are race-specific programs and a perceived failure of immigrants to integrate.

In Europe, the focus is placed on Muslim and African immigrants, while in the United States the attention is turned toward the Latino/a population as a large threatening minority. These concerns recognize the multicultural but attack "multiculturalism" as a threat to national integrity and identity. Others have tended to see multiculturalism as the key to success for post-colonial states in the developing world (Horowitz 1985). In post-colonial states, managing ethnic, linguistic differences through governmental structures has been of paramount importance for scholars interested in promoting democracy in the developing world. Some of this literature rests on the idea that while there are flexible civic identities in the developed world, the developing world (Africa especially) is the place of primordial tribal identities that tend to trump modern identity formations around the nation-state. However, this essay rejects that division and points to a common set of problems encountered by all societies. All of these perspectives rest on the question of the importance and salience of identities rooted in the formation of national states.

It is impossible to talk about race and democracy without understanding the underlying concept of the nation-state. As Benedict Anderson notes, nations are "imagined communities," as are races and ethnicities (Anderson 1994). The creations of senses of peoplehood and nations draw their origins from European history and from colonization. Thus, in the West and the former colonized world there are struggles over the boundaries of the nation. The key is whether the recognized international boundaries constitute groups that imagine themselves as a single community, or whether those boundaries challenge the terms of inclusion of those people. Conflicts ranging from the Sunni insurgency in Iraq to the question of Mexican migrants in the United States all have their origins in the disjuncture between national boundaries and ethnic/racial identities. Since the two are not conterminous, tensions arise. Political scientist Anthony Marx argues that the origins of the nation-state involve the selective exclusion and inclusion of groups to generate a sense of national cohesion to support states (Marx 2003). The uneven inclusion and outright exclusion of groups within nations was itself the driving force behind the development of nations themselves.

Thus, again there is nothing new about the problems or conflicts. Rather, the tendency to avoid these dynamics is deeply rooted in the way in which American political science has tended to misread the American context and apply this misreading to the rest of the world. The tendency within scholarship to uncritically embrace American exceptionalism has in general seen racial difference as epiphenomenal to, rather than a constitutive part of, national development and liberalism. In a critique of Rogers Smith's work, political scientist Bonnie Honig articulates the problem with placing racism, sexism, xenophobia, and homophobia outside of liberalism:

> What is striking about Smith's reading of American liberalism is that its structure replicates the very mode of thinking that the author seeks to criticize. Out to discredit "ascriptive mythologies that can easily become demonologies," Smith produces an argument that is itself demonological in structure. The many violent crimes and injustices that mark American national history are not essential to its character as a partly liberal democratic regime. Those violences come from elsewhere, from other parts of the American polity. Ascriptive ideologies distinct from liberalism are responsible for nativist, sexist, and racist citizenship laws catalogued by Smith. Thus, liberalism is insulated from implication in the unsavory elements of American political history. (Honig 2001)

Citizenship and Modes of Contention

Reading the U.S. case in the way that Honig suggests it has been read creates a way of looking at race that assumes that race, liberalism, and democratic development are either inherently disconnected from one another or completely at odds. In contrast, Honig's argument points to a tension around the concept of citizenship that allows us to explore the limitations and possibilities that race poses for democratic development. I argue that these tensions are mediated through conceptions of citizenship and contention. It is citizenship as practiced both formally and informally that determines membership within the nation and mediates conflicts around identity. However, citizenship is not an on/off proposition. Rather, as T. H. Marshall and others have noted, it is a system of regulation that differentiates even among those who are formally citizens (Marshall 1950). Political theorist Raymond Rocco, commenting on Marshall and the application of his ideas to the situation of Latinos in the United States, states "[I] am arguing that a one-dimensional conception of citizenship fundamentally obscures its real political nature because it is incapable of capturing the contextual figurations that enable its essentially regulative function of controlling and containing societal membership" (Rocco 2004).

It is in the complex manifestations of gradations of citizenship within nation-states that we can find the context in which racial diversity may either drive or impede democratic governance.

CITIZENSHIP

Citizenship is a form of regulation that defines who is inside or outside of political communities (Rocco 2004). Thus, with the questions raised by mass migrations and redefinitions of national borders, it is not surprising that—along with concerns about nationalism and ethnicity—there has been a parallel interest in the concept of citizenship (Rocco 2004). A wide array of scholars has sought to define the contours of citizenship, as well as explore the problems raised by transformations in polities brought on by geopolitical changes. Theorists like Raymond Rocco, Iris Marion Young, Amy Gutman, Will Kymlicka, and Charles Taylor address economic, social, political, juridical, and cultural dimensions of citizenship. This level of interest derives from the fact that citizenship is a critical cultural mechanism that is part of the matrix that defines group membership. Contestation over race and identity politics generally involves challenges to definitions of citizenship.

These challenges include battles over the definition of the political community itself. However, they also include more micro-concerns, like access to public and private resources, respect, dignity, and freedom to practice cultural/linguistic activities. Thus, citizenship has social, cultural, economic, and legal dimensions that are regulated by the state and civil society. "Citizenship is interpreted here as a primary political strategy whose meaning changes over time as it is contested by a variety of claims" (Rocco 2004, 13). Therefore, it is only the inadequate ability of existing formations of citizenship to meet the demands of racial and ethnic groups that drives what we understand to be ethnic conflict. Groups seek to expand their social, cultural, political, and economic access to resources in both public and private spheres as citizens. Further challenges over the boundaries and definitions for citizenship provide opportunities for creative expansions of democracy through citizenship. Thus, citizenship is a changing concept that provides a vehicle for groups to challenge notions of inclusion, exclusion, and democracy. These challenges occur through social movements and other forms of contention that seek to transform conceptions of citizenship or destroy citizenship regimes altogether. In some cases these movements can expand notions of citizenship in ways that expand democracy; in other cases they can advance alternatives that make democracy improbable, if not impossible.

CONTENTION

Citizenship implies rights and access to the public sphere as well as to social, economic, and political resources. Moreover, what is encompassed by citizenship can frequently be expanded through contention. In all forms of political regimes, those who have fewer citizenship rights than others, or who are closed off from participation in public politics altogether, frequently challenge their exclusion through social movements. However, there are critical practical and theoretical differences between different forms of contention. The first is implicit in the concept of *contentious pluralism,* which asserts that democracy is expanded through resistance to power and exclusion. In practicing resistance, some groups imagine democracy in new and radical ways beyond the limitations presented to them: "In some cases, by demanding that democracy live up to its potential, people challenge and seek to change both the common practices of social interaction and the formal political institutions they encounter. For democracy to endure, contentious pluralism must continually subvert the relationships of power that emerge in public spheres. Democracy must keep reinventing itself and it does so through contentious pluralism" (Guidry and Sawyer 2003, 274).

It is also the case, however, that some groups pursue counterproductive strategies. In challenging their exclusion, they engage in politics and support ideas that are far from the goal of expanding citizenship in ways that open up democratic systems. Guidry and Sawyer contrast these situations as follows:

> The groups' actions and demands push the boundaries of the public sphere outward, sometimes in ways not imagined or anticipated by already established actors in public politics. There are other kinds of contentious popular politics that we have not included in this analysis. Demands to be heard frequently take on extremely undemocratic forms, such as populist movements that may have racist, fascist, or religiously intolerant aims. In these situations excluded groups seek to enter the public sphere not in order to expand public discussion but perhaps to exclude groups they do not like or to limit the debate in other ways. They are contentious without being pluralist. Illiberal popular movements illustrate the role of institutions and other actors (including elites) in mediating popular demands into democratic claims, underscoring the necessity of contentious pluralism in the sphere of democracies. (275)

The realization that contention interacts with citizenship calls upon us to expand our approach to understanding ethnic conflict. We need not understand identity politics as necessarily problematic. Nor can we assume ethnic conflict cannot, and does not, lead to democratic outcomes. Simultaneously, we must recognize potentially undemocratic outcomes of racial and ethnic contention. Thus, we must focus on the character of the politics and understand the circumstances in which challenges to limited citizenship can advance the norms of democracy. A deeper analysis of the contextual situations and forms of politics that either lead to expansion of democracy or destroy democracy are critical to enhancing our understanding of the interface between ethnic difference and democracy. In that context we can arrive at an understanding that neither sees a unidirectional effect of race and ethnicity on democracy nor sees them as epiphenomenal to democratic development.

Identity Conflicts and Democratic Outcomes

Understanding the limitations of identity politics and its implications for group conflict means exploring the nature of political groups formed around cultural identities. While the tendency may be to focus on the level of violence, this may not be the critical factor in determining whether the conflict generates a democratic outcome. I argue that the most critical variables are (1) the ability of minority groups to imagine their ethnic group as part of a broader polity; and (2) the ability of the dominant group to be flexible in allowing the minority group to be considered a part of the national project. Entirely exclusionary nationalist projects challenged by groups that see the debate in similarly zero-sum terms are not likely to produce democratic outcomes. In contrast, where there is basic recognition by all groups of legitimate claims and some common destiny, then there is a possibility for a democratic outcome. Here is where liberal norms and institutions can be critical factors. While liberalism is not a panacea, universal liberal citizenship provides at least a rubric for potential inclusion. At the same time, as noted by Honig, Young, and others, liberal democracy tends to universalize and thus obscure difference in a way that leaves inequalities intact. Iris Marion Young describes this as follows: "The problem with this conception of the unity of democratic discussion is that it may harbor another mechanism of exclusion. Assuming a discussion situation in which participants are differentiated by group-based culture and social position, and where some groups have greater symbolic or material privilege than others, appeals to a 'common ground' are likely to perpetuate such privilege" (Young 1996). Thus, many projects, though liberal, are fundamentally ethnic ones, as described by Charles Mills (Mills 1997). However, liberal norms and formal democratic practices provide access to the public sphere for protest and contention, thus giving racial and ethnic minorities opportunities to expand conceptions of citizenship.

Other political alignments and events can expand political opportunities in other ways. This is "captured" by social movements scholars who look for things like "political opportunity structures" (McAdam, Tarrow et al. 2001). That is, the alignments of institutions, organizations, and accidents of history at times create greater space for aggrieved groups to be successful in pressing their claims (Sawyer 2006). But it is the recognition of the basic political rights of the other group that determines the level of contention and the possibility for democratic expansion. For example, the mutual perceptions of Israelis and Palestinians militate against a solution to the conflict. In that case, the mutual nonrecognition of the rights and legitimacy of the other group constantly undoes the potential for anything more than a two-state solution. In contrast is the African American experience. While the struggle for strategic separation has generated some violent conflict, most conflicts have been filtered through the prism of a vision of equal incorporation in the American polity (Dawson 2001). This is accurately captured in W. E. B. Du Bois's classic work *The Souls of Black Folks,* in which he delineates a conception of double consciousness. Double consciousness provides an opportunity for simultaneous recognition of the African American stake in the American project and the recognition of the problems of racial inequality and attenuated citizenship. While the violent overthrow of Reconstruction and the implementation of Jim Crow in the South lead Du Bois to recognize the problems of the American national project, the 13th and 14th Amendments and the previous existence of Reconstruction provide the hope and possibility for a truly democratic America. Du Bois elucidated the notion of double consciousness in the statement,

> After the Egyptian and Indian, the Greek and Roman, the teuton and Mongolian, the Negro is a sort of seventh son, born with a veil, and gifted with second-sight in this American world,—a world which yields him no true self-consciousness, but only lets him see himself through the revelation of the other world. It is a peculiar sensation, this double-consciousness, this sense of always looking at one's self though the eyes of others, of measuring one's soul by the tape of a world that looks on in amused contempt and pity. One ever feels his two-ness, an American, a Negro; two souls, two thoughts, two unreconciled strivings; two warring ideals in one dark body, whose dogged strength alone keeps it from being torn asunder. (Du Bois 1907)

Du Bois's recognition of multiple consciousnesses or multiple overlapping and sometimes contradictory identities provides a tension for social movements but also a crucial space for reconciliation. Racial and ethnic conflicts can in some instances prove to be engines for democratic expansion and in other cases serve as intractable impediments to democratic development. The dual possibility is driven by the existent political culture of democratic norms and national identities that are more or less inclusive.

While the ethnic conflict literature tends to see racial diversity as a problem for democracy, this is true only when there is no shared identity or possibility for reconciliation (Horowitz 1985). Thus, more than being simply a problem of constitutional design, the problem is fundamentally about the imagination of those involved in the conflict. Therefore, even violent conflicts can result in democratic outcomes. The key for the future of political science in this area is to bring together studies of identity, citizenship, nationalism, and institutions. Social movements close this distance and provide the opportunity for transformations in regimes of citizenship. Parallel developments on theories of citizenship and the empirical literature on public opinion and ethnic conflicts must be brought into the conversation. Moreover, like Horowitz, we must continue to attend to the effects of institutional design on channeling conflicts and creating civic identities that comport with democratic values, principles, and norms.

Consider, for example, the current conflict in Iraq, in which both institutions and identities play a role. The conflict can be seen as both a challenge to U.S. occupation as well as a challenge to the creation of a Shiite-dominated government. A Shiite-dominated regime would rule out the possibility of a unitary Iraqi identity and democratic institutions that can aggregate across the interests of the major ethnic groups. Thus, beliefs, political trust, and institutions that are capable of channeling ethnic discord and contention are critical in formulating an effective Iraqi democracy. Furthermore, movements that place democratic norms and ideals at the center of their struggle can help create democracy. Groups that see no future together or who see the conflict in zero-sum terms are in many ways doomed to spiral further away from democracy. Finally, groups that do not imagine democracy as part of the opposition, or dominant groups who have no sense of the possibility of recognition for the "other," are also less likely to produce democratic outcomes. The following examples illustrate these assertions.

THE AMERICAS

The Americas, as the "new" world, have been a place of major transformation in both conceptions of citizenship and democracy. The transitions of societies in the Americas from slavery to democracy have not always fulfilled the promise of equality for racialized groups. People of African descent, and indigenous people most prominently, have frequently faced violence, social exclusion, and economic exploitation across the Americas. This has resulted, for the most part, in formal citizenship for all but radically uneven patterns of recognition and equality. Further, migrants from East and Southeast Asia have also experienced similar limitations throughout the Americas. The twenty-first century will provide a test for emergent and continuing democracies throughout the Americas, as well as raise new questions about the political incorporation of African and indigenous peoples.

The onset of formal democracy throughout Latin America and the 2001 World Conference on Racism loom large as watershed moments that will set the tone for Latin America. While the twentieth century was characterized by an often bloody transition to democracy in Latin America, the twenty-first century began by addressing the question of race and democracy. In many countries, such as Brazil, the twentieth century was characterized by declarations of "racial democracy," while there was little formal political democracy for persons of any racial background. Now that democracy has been realized, these communities have fought to overcome marginalization and hold leaders accountable to the concerns of the community. Landless black and indigenous peoples in Ecuador, Brazil, and other countries in Latin America have challenged governmental elites to provide land and basic means of existence. Just as international covenants and neoliberal economic reforms have continued to concentrate wealth, these groups have asserted that democracy is only viable in the context of a more equal distribution of wealth and recognition of the social and economic rights of minority groups. These groups are challenging given notions of citizenship to include long-denied economic and cultural rights. Practices of indigenous languages, Afro-Latin religious practices, and other cultural forms have been given greater formal recognition, as social movements have fought to challenge the exclusion of these practices from state recognition. In Mexico (Chiapas), the Zapatista movement elevated the issues related to the question of race contention and citizenship to new levels in the 1990s. The energy created by the Zapatista helped to expose the corrupt, anti-democratic practices of the PRI government and to open the door to a free and fair election.

In Venezuela, Bolivia, and other Latin American countries, the plight of racial minorities exposed the limitations of current neoliberal economic policies and current citizenship regimes. Contentious movements within the framework of democratic practices have challenged the social, cultural, and economic inequalities of these societies. However, it remains to be seen if the structure of neoliberal citizenship regimes connected to the international economy and free trade can accommodate the economic and social aspirations of these citizens. As the demands of citizens clash with the dictates of structural adjustment programs and free trade agreements that are sweeping the Americas, we are likely to see growing contention around issues of race across the Americas. However, one thing we do see in Latin America is contention that is being channeled through democratic norms. Furthermore, Latin America has generally produced flexible and inclusive notions of national belonging (Sawyer et al.; Sidanius et al.). These inclusive notions of national belonging that are shared by black and indigenous peoples, as well as ideologies of racial inclusion on behalf of whites and mestizos, do not prevent conflict. They do, however, help to channel conflict into an arena of shared recognition.

Canada and the United States face the issue of the ongoing struggle for full citizenship rights and social mobility. Both Canada and the United States have internal minority groups and immigrant populations all seeking greater rights and inclusion in society. Questions of citizenship, democracy, and incorporation include the salient questions of language, culture, and national identity. While these conflicts are channeled through constitutions and democracies, both the United States and Canada are struggling with persistent inequalities, despite being democracies. The struggles of indigenous peoples in Canada and the United States, such as the Quebecois in the former and African Americans in the latter, are evidence of long-standing issues of inequality for groups that have consistently challenged their status as unequal partners in national democratic projects. For the most part, these movements have used a range of activities, including protests, to challenge conceptions of citizenship that they feel either exclude them or are insufficient to meet their current circumstances.

In recent years, the United States and Canada have seen large-scale migration from Latin America, the Caribbean, Asia, Africa, Eastern Europe, and the Middle East. In the case of the United States, immigrants from the Middle East, Mexico, Central America, and the Caribbean have been the greatest source of controversy. Anti-immigrant sentiments at both the level of popular discourse and public policy have dogged the aspirations of these new Americans. While the above focuses on the Americas, these dynamics manifest themselves broadly in other parts of the world. If we think about the issue as one of accommodating racial and ethnic difference we can break down barriers between nations and think in truly comparative terms. Western and Eastern Europe, the Middle East, Asia, and Africa all face similar dynamics: struggles of minority groups against manifestations of political and economic inequality. Despite old and new democracies, and a significant worldwide rise in constitutionalism, many regions and countries still strain to accommodate the citizenship claims of minority groups. In every region, there are social movements and struggles; in many cases there are violent struggles. What circumscribes these struggles are limits to dominant-group power through constitutions, international norms, and local norms that, despite inequality, do not force minority groups into desperate situations. The relatively higher levels of racial violence in the United States, as compared to Canada and Latin America, reflect the exclusionary forms of nationalism in the United States, which struggle to see blacks, Latinos, and Asians as true parts of the nation. As Sidanius and Pratto note, in the United States, higher levels of patriotism for whites in public opinion surveys are correlated with higher levels of racism (Sidanius and Pratto 1999). As anti-immigrant movements like the "Minute Men" adapt patriotic discourse in the protection of the "homeland," it is not surprising that a surge in anti-immigrant violence has followed the September 11th attacks.[2] Thus, while minorities and immigrants in the United States see themselves as part of the nation, or struggle for incorporation, the problem posed for democracy is that significant portions of the majority do not see a common destiny with ethnic racial minorities.

EUROPE

Europe has struggled continually with issues of diversity. These struggles have traditionally been around incorporating internal minorities like Jews, the Roma, the Basque, and the Irish. Recently, Europe has also faced growing migration from the underdeveloped world to fill labor market positions. The political, social, economic, and cultural incorporation of these minorities raises deep questions about the flexibility of democratic norms and constitutionalism in Europe. For new and old democracies, these groups raise questions about the limits and boundaries of democratic norms and citizenship regimes. Reactionary right-wing parties that preach racial intolerance have emerged in recent years in places like France and Austria. These manifestations show us that, as in the United States, democracy is no automatic antidote for racism and intolerance. Societies will continue to struggle with cultural differences and their implications for democracy. This struggle will continue, especially when cultural practices by immigrants do not fit what are perceived to be liberal or democratic norms. In France, this has been characterized by the struggle over the ability of women to wear Islamic headscarves where concerns about secularism clash head-on with democratic principles of free expression.

Across Europe, concerns about immigration and terrorism have produced difficult problems. Addressing security concerns while maintaining rights and civil liberties poses a challenge. In addition, the acceleration of immigration and the growing integration of the European Union have increased anxieties among members of the public about the sanctity of national identities and cultures. One example of this is popular expressions of racism that have been focused at black international football players in places like Italy, France, Germany, and Poland. Racism in football demonstrates that popular struggle for commitments to democracy and citizenship requires a constant reinforcement of the value of tolerance. Exclusionary conceptions of democracy and national identity militate against tolerance and challenge democratic development. Only through expanding notions of citizenship through managed contention will democratic ideas overcome forces of intolerance and come to incorporate the aspirations of citizenship for newcomers in Europe.

At the same time, many internal minority groups in Europe also do not envision themselves as part of the nation. The Northern and Southern Irish struggle with a sense of shared destiny. In general, neither sees a common destiny, and significant portions of each group prefer separation rather than some form of common future. Similarly, the Basque in Spain and groups like ETA consistently use terror and other tactics to emphasize a separatist agenda that, while expressing legitimate grievances, questions the historical connections between the two groups. Finally, the Balkans have proven to be a place where none of the groups or states see a common destiny; thus, it has been the site of various forms of genocide and ethnic cleansing that have deeply divided it. In the Balkans, it is not so much the existence of difference but difference without a sense of shared destiny, along with forms of contention that see struggle in zero-sum terms, that tear at the fabric of democratic development. Immigrant groups pose problems and concerns about national culture and language, while internal minorities with long-held grievances challenge the configurations of European nations themselves. Thus, expanding citizenship to incorporate immigrants may solve these nations' problems, while groups with territorial aims represent a unique and distinct problem because there is no shared conception of citizenship or nation.

AFRICA

Africa has long struggled with race, ethnicity, and democracy. Since Africa's colonial experience created African nations, there have been moments of severe ethnic and racial conflict. Further, struggles with the white minority governments in South Africa and Zimbabwe lasted until quite recently. Thus, Africa has struggled both to overcome colonial racism in the search for autonomy and to overcome internal conflicts with groups that have racial, ethnic, linguistic, and religious differences. In terms of regions of the world, Africa is perhaps the most variable. It is the home to everything from promising constitutional multiracial democracy (South Africa) to brutal ethno-racial genocide (Sudan and Rwanda). While this huge variability causes considerable analytic challenges, it also makes Africa perhaps the best laboratory for the promise and problems of multiethnic democracy in the twenty-first century.

Africa faces basic struggles with poverty and underdevelopment. In addition, Africa must cope with linguistic, cultural, and racial differences within nations. Almost all of the world's major differences can be found within and across African nations. Here future success depends not only on managing difference within institutions but on overcoming major crises that destroy civil society, such as AIDS, civil wars, and extreme poverty. These are all engines that generate the worst forms of conflict. At the same time, countries like South Africa and Nigeria are attempting to forge an internal democratic consensus that manages diversity, thus hoping to influence other African nations in ways that enhance stability. However, it will take resources from outside the continent to alleviate the dire material consequences that make conflicts truly a zero-sum game—with few opportunities for winners or losers. Further, while African identities, like all identities, are far more mutable than one might imagine, the resource battles are severe and militate against moderating these conflicts. In many cases, ethnic identities in Africa trump senses of shared destiny in ways that are more similar to the Balkans than to Canada and Latin America. Thus, in some closed African political systems the lack of mutual recognition and the dire material conditions create the possibility for extreme violence and undemocratic movements.

Conclusion

While political science has tended to shy away from discussions of ideology, ideologies are critical. Ideologies, identities, and institutions are critical points that transform and shape ethnic conflict. They are also where we should look to identify ethnic conflicts that drive democratic development and conflicts that stifle it. Moreover, it is important to think of ideologies and democracy as dynamic, interactive, and transnational. While this collection covers arguments about diffusion in the development of democracy, it is not only diffusion of elite practices and institutions that shape the interactions between race and democracy.

It is also important to examine conceptions of citizenship and modes of contention. The substantial borrowing and interchange between African Americans in the United States and black South Africans is such a case. That is, the nature and development of cultures that include forms of contention, ideologies, institutions, and conceptions of citizenship are interacting and borrowing from one another. Thus, diffusion works on many levels, as the more globalized world raises questions about democracy through the migration of peoples and ideas. Diffusion can operate from above and below and inform the challenges racial groups pose to inadequate citizenship regimes.

Social movements that generate norms like the World Social Forum, which challenges corporate globalization, or the World Conference on Racism (Durban, South Africa, 2001), and which seek to expand citizenship for ethnic/racial minorities, are reinforced by these institutions and international interchanges. But the torture scandals in Abu Ghraib, groups like Al-Qaeda, and the conflict in Darfur, Sudan, illustrate modes of contention that do not seek to expand citizenship rights and democracy. Rather, they destroy those conceptions and replace them with their own more limited politics. At the same time, we see evidence that things can change. Difference does not mean destruction and can mean positive things for democratic development—if proper norms, values, and political institutions are in place. Democratic openness and flexible notions of national identity breed more of the same. The United States, in this account, falls in the middle. We are neither exemplars nor the worst, but are yet another country attempting to deal with varying levels of racial and ethnic inequality while struggling to perfect democracy.

Notes

Special thanks to John Guidry, who helped develop the concept of "contentious pluralism" and also to Raymond Rocco for reading an early draft of this paper. I would also like to thank Michael Hanchard, Michael Dawson, Dianne Pinderhughes, Dorian Warren, Christopher Parker, and Celia Lacayo. Conversations with them inspired central parts of this chapter. Please do not quote without permission from the author.

1. I use the term "difference" because it encompasses dimensions of race, gender, ethnicity, sexual orientation, religion, and language.

2. The Minute Men are a group of Arizona "patriots," who in 2005 patrolled the Arizona border to capture undocumented immigrants seeking to enter the United States from Mexico.

References

Anderson, B. 1994. *Imagined Communities: Reflections on the Origin and Spread of Nationalism*. New York: Verso.

Appiah, K. A. 1994. "Identity, Authenticity, Survival: Multicultural Societies and Social Reproduction." In A. Gutman, ed., *Multiculturalism*. Princeton: Princeton University Press.

Dawson, M. C. 2001. *Black Visions: The Roots of Contemporary African-American Political Ideologies*. Chicago: University of Chicago Press.

Du Bois, W. E. B. 1975. *Dusk of Dawn*. New York: Harcourt.

———. 1907. *The Souls of Black Folk*. New York: A. C. McClurg.

Fanon, F. 1967. *Black Skin, White Masks*. New York: Grove Weidendfeld.

———. 1991. *The Wretched of the Earth*. New York: Grove.

Guidry, J., and M. Q. Sawyer. 2003. "Contentious Pluralism: The Public Sphere and Democracy." *Perspectives on Politics* 1 (2): 273–89.

Gutman, A. 1996. "Democracy, Philosophy, and Justification." In S. Benhabib, ed., *Democracy and Difference*. Princeton: Princeton University Press.

Hesse, B. 2000. "Introduction: Un/Settled Multiculturalisms." In B. Hesse, ed., *Un/settled Multiculturalisms: Diasporas, Entanglements, Transruptions*. London: Zed Books.

Honig, B. 2001. *Democracy and the Foreigner*. Princeton: Princeton University Press.

Horowitz, D. L. 1985. *Ethnic Groups in Conflict*. Los Angeles: University of California Press.

Huntington, S. P. 2004. *Who Are We? The Challenges to American's National Identity*. New York: Simon & Schuster.

James, C. L. R. 1963. *The Black Jocobins*. New York: Vintage.

Kymlicka, W. 1996. *Multicultural Citizenship: A Liberal Theory of Minority Rights*. New York: Oxford University Press.

Laitin, D. 1998. *Identity in Formation: The Russian Speaking Populations in the Near Abroad*. Ithaca, N.Y.: Cornell University Press.

Marshall, T. H. 1950. *Citizenship and Social Class*. Cambridge: Cambridge University Press.

Marx, A. W. 2003. *Faith in Nation: Exclusionary Origins of Nationalism*. New York: Oxford University Press.

McAdam, D., S. Tarrow et al. 2001. *Dynamics of Contention*. Cambridge: Cambridge University Press.

Mills, C. W. 1997. *The Racial Contract*. Ithaca, N.Y.: Cornell University Press.

Norton, A. 2004. *95 Theses on Politics, Culture, and Method*. New Haven: Yale University Press.

Rocco, Raymond. 2004. "Transforming Citizenship: Membership, Strategies of Containment, and the Public Sphere in Latino Communities." *Latinos* 2: 4–25.

Sassen, S. 1999. *Globalization and Its Discontents: Essays on the New Mobility of People and Money.* New York: New Press.

Sawyer, M. 2006. *Racial Politics in Post-Revolutionary Cuba.* New York: Cambridge University Press.

Sawyer, M, Y. Peña, and J. Sidanius. 2004. "Cuban Exceptionalism: Group-Based Hierarchy and the Dynamics of Patriotism in Puerto Rico, the Dominican Republic, and Cuba." *DuBois Review* 1 (1): 93–114.

Schlesinger, A. M. 1992. *The Disuniting of America.* New York: Norton.

Sidanius, J., Y. Peña, and M. Sawyer. 2001. "Inclusionary Discrimination: Pigmentocracy and Patriotism in the Dominican Republic." *Political Psychology* 22 (4): 827–51.

Sidanius, J., and F. Pratto. 2001. *Social Dominance: An Intergroup Theory of Social Hierarchy and Oppression.* Cambridge: Cambridge University Press.

Taylor, C. 1994. "The Politics of Recognition." In A. Gutman, ed., *Multiculturalism.* Princeton: Princeton University Press.

Young, I. M. 1990. *Justice and the Politics of Difference.* Princeton: Princeton University Press.

———. 1996. "Communication and the Other: Beyond Deliberative Democracy." In S. Benhabib, ed., *Democracy and Difference.* Princeton: Princeton University Press.

4

Democracy, Diversity, and Leadership

PAUL M. SNIDERMAN

The problem of "diversity" was once thought to be a distinctively American problem—*An American Dilemma,* Myrdal called it. It was not, of course, that intolerance was thought to be peculiarly American. Hitler, after all, was in his heyday as Myrdal wrote. The issue of race was a peculiarly American problem precisely because of the American commitment to equality. It was the contradiction between the commitment to equality and the intolerance, not the intolerance itself, that set America apart.

There has been a loss of moral innocence—or more exactly, the loss of a sense of moral superiority—since the civil rights movement stalled in the 1960s. This loss has been the result of a scissors change: on the one side, elevation of the standards of tolerance; on the other, exacerbation of the problem of intolerance. As Nardulli observes in the preface to this volume, "democracy enjoyed unparalleled prestige at the close of the twentieth century." One result is that a commitment to tolerance and inclusion of ethnic and immigrant groups has become a pledge of liberal democracy generally, not merely the American variant. Like all pledges, observance has been uneven. But, at least in the first world, it has become a standard to which governments expect to be held.

Expecting more is one blade of the scissors; needing to do more is the other. Democratization has meant the collapse of alternative forms of rule as much as the establishment of new ones. One consequence has been incentives for emigration; another has been a loss of control over immigration. The results have been profound socio-demographic change in the first world, including Western Europe.

The waves of immigration have raised a series of diversity challenges. Western Europe is not the only area confronting these challenges; it's just the most obvious. Most countries in Western Europe have no tradition of immigration. Indeed, rather the reverse: most have been homogenous over many dimensions and many years. Against this homogenous background, immigrants are more distinctive than they otherwise would be—not so distinctive as blacks in America, but strikingly so all the same. Differences in dress, language, publicly visible social practices—even, for many, color—set them apart, as does the practice of a religion at odds with established, dominant religions. Even more so than the practice of religious difference, the establishment of a secular culture sets such groups apart from the mainstream.

My objective is to see what light issues of diversity in Western Europe throw on the dynamics of democratic responsiveness. In particular, I want to explore two ideas. The first is quite general; the second, quite specific.

The general idea has to do with the direction of influence in liberal democracies. Politics works bottom-up—at any rate democratic politics does just so far as it is democratic. Citizens have problems that concern them and objectives they wish to accomplish. Politicians respond under the pressure of electoral incentives, choosing policies that match public preferences. Electoral responsiveness is coarse, not fine-grained, to be sure. It would be unreasonable to suppose that politicians match the electorate's policy preferences detail-by-detail; unreasonable, for that matter, to suppose that the public has policy preferences worked out in detail. But there is a public mood—a broad orientation to the dominant set of issues[1] of the time—and politicians can track changes in it.[2]

It is worth emphasizing that the bottom-up story of democratic politics is not necessarily a story of politicians as passive agents. They must anticipate changes in the public mood and produce policies to capitalize on them. Moreover, the bottom-up story does not necessarily rest on a view of politicians as blank ciphers. They have preferences of their own. But the engine driving the process is the need of politicians to win votes, hence their need to advance policies they anticipate will match the public's mood. Thus, influence in democracy runs from the electorate to politicians, at least in the long run.

I believe that one version of the bottom-up story is likely to be correct in the long run. But it does not follow that the bottom-up story is correct over the short run. On the contrary, I want to suggest that democratic politics also works "top down," with influence running from political leaders to the public as well as the other way around.[3] I am obviously not the first to offer a top-down model of democratic politics.

Hypotheses, like medicines, come in various dosages—and most of the top-down models that have drawn interest and support by political scientists have been "weak" versions. In these weak versions of top-down models, politicians can exercise influence on public opinion (i.e., help set the public agenda),[4] but they cannot change it. By contrast, the version of a top-down model of politics I discuss here is a "strong" version. In this version, politicians can influence the opinions that citizens hold—or, to be more precise, the positions that they take on issues of the day.

The general idea I am interested in is thus quite general; the specific idea is correspondingly quite specific. If politicians do influence the opinions of citizens, the question is, *how* do they exercise this influence—what is the *mechanism* at work?

I mean to focus here on just one mechanism—conformity effects. A focus on just one mechanism is narrow, and still more so is a focus on conformity effects. They certainly are not the principal mechanism for the exercise of elite influence. But they bear directly on the politics I most wish to understand—the politics of tolerance.

Within the politics of tolerance a revealing paradox follows from two propositions, each innocuous taken by itself. On the one hand, the more importance people attach to conformity, the more likely they are to be intolerant.[5] On the other, the more importance they attach to conformity, the more susceptible they are to situational pressure.[6] Hence the paradox: the very same factor that underlies prejudice—and therefore opposition to diversity—also increases susceptibility to social pressure—and therefore to pressure to inhibit opposition to diversity.

The two ideas I want to explore—the general and the specific—are connected. The specific hypothesis—about conformity and pliability—can be seen as a story about political psychology. But the specific hypothesis bears on the general notion of top-down politics. If the conformity hypothesis is true, political leaders have more freedom to maneuver on issues of tolerance than has been supposed. Ironically, the segment of their constituency most opposed to immigrants and, therefore, to policies that help them is the segment most susceptible to the influence of political leaders—not political leaders in the abstract, however, but political party leadership. Political leadership in competitive politics is organized around political parties.

My focus is on Western Europe and specifically on the Netherlands. Party leadership counts for more in parliamentary than presidential systems, and still more in proportional representation than in plurality systems. The Netherlands' system is both parliamentary and based on proportional representation (P.R.).

Political parties were established to organize electoral competition.[7] And so they do. But the party system can also be an instrument of cooperation in the form of cross-party coalitions. Multiculturalism is less popular on the right than on the left, but is not highly popular on either side. Yet, so far as party leaders have the power to moderate their adherents' opposition to multiculturalism, party leaders on the left can advance multicultural policies; those of the right tacitly acquiesce. This tacit cross-party coalition is a key to the politics of multiculturalism—collusion in the service of tolerance.

My plan is to proceed in three steps: to start with a puzzle; then to turn to a paradox; then to consider some of the dynamics of democratic ideals.

The Puzzle

In 1968, Enoch Powell made his "rivers of blood" speech.[8] The popular response was immediate and overwhelmingly favorable. Edward Heath, the leader of his party, was less popular than Powell at the time, and the Conservative party as a whole was trailing the Labour Party in election polls. Yet Heath repudiated Powell and dismissed him from the Shadow Cabinet. As it happened, Heath and the Conservative Party won the election. Through one of those ironies of democratic politics, voters thought Powell's position on immigrants, not Heath's, was the position of the Conservative Party. Irony is not an electoral strategy; hence the puzzle: Heath knew his party was running behind. He also knew immigration was an issue his party could exploit, even possibly ride to victory. Why did the logic of the situation not induce him to take advantage of the issue of immigration that Powell had brought to the fore?

The puzzle is not why mainstream political elites would be reluctant to be, or appear to be, exploiting bigotry. Rather, the puzzle is *how* mainstream political leaders have maintained their hold on their supporters notwithstanding the unpopularity of policies they have either supported or acquiesced in. The avoidance of xenophobic stances is not hard to understand. Public figures who appeal to anti-immigrant sentiments—or give the appearance of doing so—risk being stigmatized as racist, and thus marginalized politically. Moreover, and quite apart from sanctions they themselves may suffer, there is a widely shared fear among mainstream elites of letting a genie out of the bottle, of legitimizing xenophobia and intolerance. What is difficult to understand is why mainstream political leaders have not suffered for failing to reflect popular views on some immigrant groups.

The reach of this puzzle should not be overstated. If there is a tacit cross-party consensus in some countries, there is not in others—Germany, for example.[9] Moreover, in response to public resentment of immigrants, mainstream parties on the left and right have put forward tougher policies that restrict immigration and reduce assistance for immigrants.[10] Furthermore, politically consequential parties on the extreme right have emerged in a number of countries—among them, the National Front in France, the Freedom Party in Austria, and the Alleanza Nazionale in Italy. Nonetheless, in many places and many elections, mainstream parties on the right have not pressed their advantage on these issues to anything like the extent they could, allowing mainstream parties on the left to initiate "rights-based" policies unpopular among many of their following without electoral risk.

Cross-party cooperation in the service of electorally unpopular policies is a puzzle in itself; still more of a puzzle is cooperation in the service of unpopular policies dealing with ethnic and immigrant minorities. The standard story of the politics of tolerance is thoroughly bottom up. Opposition to policies to assist minorities is driven by deeply rooted factors. These include the desire to defend one's dominant position,[11] early socialization,[12] and the frustration and anger generated by inner psychological conflicts,[13] among others.[14] The positions citizens take on issues regarding minorities are thus well grounded and, accordingly, they are fixed in place. Ordinary citizens may not know what they think about many of the issues of the day,[15] but they know what they think about policies to help minorities. They know what they think precisely because they need know nothing about the policies themselves, only that they dislike minorities and therefore dislike help being awarded to them.[16]

I have drawn a stylized picture here. But it represents the thrust of scholarship on race and public opinion. To a first approximation, the politics of public opinion on issues of group tolerance is the politics of fixed positions. I do not believe that political leadership has the power to change the minds of citizens on issues of race and ethnicity. I do believe it has the capacity to influence the positions they take.[17] There is a politics of multiculturalism precisely because the choices that citizens make on issues of the day are, in part, a function of the strategic choices that political elites make.

Conformity

I want to put my argument forward in two steps. My strategy is this. In the first presentation of the argument, everything works just as a thoughtful person would expect it to work. And just so far as the argument has plausibility on the first go around, when things work as they should, I trust it will have plausibility on the second, when things don't work as a thoughtful person would expect them to work.

Politics, at its core, is about influence. How many citizens favor one side of an issue over another matters; how many can be brought over from one side to the other when push comes to shove matters more.

Some people are more susceptible to influence than others, obviously enough. But what makes them susceptible? Stanley Feldman (2003) has called attention to a specific mechanism: conformity. Feldman hypothesizes, and provides evidence, that the more importance people attach to conformity as a social value, the more responsive they are to situational pressures. The question is, how large a constituency is there for extremist policies? A portion of the public is willing to support punitive policies toward minorities, even highly punitive policies. But previous research suggests that this constituency is a small one: as a rule no more than one in ten. But previous studies have followed the rules of the standard public opinion survey. Questions are written to be balanced; interviewers trained to be neutral; interviews carried out with the aim of minimizing pressure on respondents to take one side of an issue rather than another.

This is exactly the right way to proceed for many purposes but not the right thing to do to understand the politics of tolerance and multiculturalism. The question we need to understand is, how many will support an extremist policy *when an effort is made to induce them to do so?* To answer this question, we need to make an effort to induce them to support an extremist policy.

For evidence, I draw on a study of multiculturalism in the Netherlands done in collaboration with Professor Louk Hagendoorn of the University of Utrecht.[18] The reflexive desire to celebrate the uniqueness of every country notwithstanding, an encyclopedia analysis of public opinion data (Coenders, Lubbers, and Scheepers 2003)[19] reveals that the Netherlands hovers at the median for Western European democracies on a large array of indicators of resistance to immigrants and multiculturalism. A more relevant point is that the findings I rely on are based on experiments conducted for the first time; the need for replication should be underlined in red ink.

One of our experiments in the Dutch Study, the Segregation Experiment, addressed this question. The purpose of the experiment was to see how many could be induced to support an extremist policy. Accordingly, the experiment focused on a policy proposal that is beyond the social pale: creating an officially segregated education system. One set of schools would be restricted as a matter of law to Dutch children; another would be restricted to ethnic minority children. This is an extreme proposal by any standard. The mere idea of suggesting the possibility of an officially segregated school system made our interviewers blanch.

How much popular support does such an extreme proposal enjoy? That very much depends on how you go about gauging support. Measured in the standard way, a segregated school system enjoys the support of only a veritable handful: just slightly over one every ten, to be more precise. What needs to be known, however, is how many will support an extremist policy *if an effort is made to win their support*. Therefore, the Segregation Experiment includes an appeal to authority. Respondents are told that studies have established that Dutch children do not do as well when minority children are also in the classroom; they are also informed that the Ministry of Education will carefully develop and implement a plan to carry out this proposal. After being presented with this appeal to authority, one out of every four in the Dutch population expressed support for a segregated school policy.

These results suggest there is a latent constituency in Western Europe for extreme policies on immigration. It is a constituency larger by orders than previous studies have suggested. Let me be clear about what I am—and am not—saying. I am not saying that people can be *persuaded* to support extreme policies. No doubt they can. What I am saying is that it is not necessary to persuade them, that is, to change their minds.

Under all but unusual circumstances it is difficult to change the minds of a substantial number of the public on some political issue. And just so far as it is difficult, things will continue more or less as they have. But no one's mind was changed in the Segregation Experiment; no one's beliefs about right and wrong were transformed. All that happened was that they were given some information: and believing what they did, the information they received was quite sufficient to change their responses. From being a policy at the political fringes, official segregation became a policy favored by a significant portion of the public—a minority, to be sure, but a substantial one.

Of course, it is not a matter of a politician snapping his or her fingers and support instantly materializing for extreme policies. In the actual play of politics there will be debate: arguments against as well as for. Still, looking at the *manipulation* in the Segregation Experiment, we ourselves are struck by how minimal it is: one or two bits of information. All the same, the one or two bits are sufficient to change the politics of the issue.

Hence our puzzle. Immigration, multiculturalism, and government assistance to minorities are all issues on which there are strong bottom-up pressures. And as the Segregation Experiment shows, there is even more bottom-up pressure that could be generated. What makes it possible for elites to resist these pressures from below?

The Paradox

Finding that the more importance people attach to conformity as a value, the more likely they are to yield to an appeal to authority is perfectly obvious. In truth, it is precisely its obviousness that I am counting on to bring to light a paradox. The paradox is this. The very same factor—conformity—that underlies the prejudice of many also makes them susceptible to social pressure to inhibit their prejudice.

For two decades, my colleagues and I have been carrying out studies of prejudice. By "prejudice" we mean plain old bigotry—a systematic readiness to respond with hostility to members of a group merely by virtue of their membership in the group.[20] I appreciate that it has become unfashionable to pay attention to old-fashioned prejudice. It has become fashionable to claim either that it has virtually disappeared,[21] or at any rate cannot put in a public appearance given the societal norms now in place. The claim of course is not that prejudice itself no longer exists. It is rather that it has gone underground. Prejudice is now subtle, covert.

Prejudice can be expressed in subtle ways. But the idea that there are no longer large numbers of people in liberal democracies who are ready to express, systematically and openly, derogatory judgments about minorities is simply false. We have studied prejudice against African Americans; against Jews; against immigrant minorities white and black, Christian and Muslim. We have studied prejudice in the United States and Canada, and in Italy, France, and the Netherlands. We find no shortage of prejudice anywhere.

What we also have found is that one particular value is closely tied to prejudice. The more importance that people attach to social conformity as a value, the more prejudiced they are likely to be against ethnic, cultural, and religious minorities. This finding may be stated more strongly. In all of our studies in which both prejudice and conformity have been measured, the importance attached to conformity as a value is the single best predictor of intolerance of minorities. I do not mean to suggest that a large array of other factors, economic, social, and psychological, do not also underlie prejudice. Quite the contrary; we have developed an explanatory model of prejudice—the "Two-Flavors" Model—expressly designed to integrate realistic conflict and psychological theories of intolerance. And it is their impact on the importance attached to conformity that brings these two flavors of explanatory factors together. Conformity, in our theoretical set up, is the proximate cause of prejudice. But the paradox is that just so far as conformity makes people susceptible to influence, it can operate to decrease the likelihood that they will act on their prejudice.

To show how this process works, consider two experiments included in the Dutch Study. The first one, the End-of-the-Interview Experiment, dealt with social influence; the second one, the Party Leader Compliance Experiment, dealt with political influence.

THE END-OF-THE-INTERVIEW EXPERIMENT

This experiment focuses on views toward ethnic minorities. Its design is decidedly unusual, but for a good reason. We wanted to observe how people react when they are not being interviewed, which created significant challenges in an interview process! But thinking about the dynamics of an interview suggested a possibility that was exploited. Well-conducted interviews promote a bond of trust and familiarity between the interviewer and the person being interviewed. Our objective was to take advantage of this interpersonal bond to test the expression of interpersonal influence. Our strategy was to have the interviewer tell the respondent that the interview was over—*before* it was actually over.

More specifically, in the experimental condition, the interviewer announces: "The interview is at an end"; then, reading from a script, goes on to say: "I would like to add that I enjoyed talking to you and that your answers will be very useful to us." The phrase "I would like to add that I enjoyed talking to you" confirmed that the interview had ended and implicitly conveyed the appreciation of the interviewer for the views of the respondent. The interviewer then goes on to say: "Wouldn't you also agree that ethnic minorities are responsible for *many fewer* social problems than is usually supposed?" The phrasing, "Wouldn't you also agree," is intended to convey the impression that the interviewers are expressing their personal views. The word "also" is included to reinforce the expectation that the interviewer expects that views of the person he or she is interviewing to match their own. In the control condition, by contrast, the interviewer merely says: "One last question"; then asks: "Do you think that ethnic minorities are responsible for *many fewer* social problems than is usually supposed?" The End-of-the Interview Experiment thus offers an opportunity to assess the exercise of interpersonal influence.

The bar should be set high in order for an experiment like this to yield useful results. The test item thus requires that respondents agree with a *positive* assessment of immigrants: that is, to do just the opposite of what conformists are predisposed to do. Specifically, the question reads: "Do you think that ethnic minorities are responsible for *many fewer* social problems than is usually supposed?"

Figure 4.1 displays our findings. The vertical axis in figure 4.1 indexes the probability of a negative response to immigrant minorities; the horizontal axis is the amount of importance respondents attach to social conformity as a value. The dotted line tracks the probability of a negative response to minorities in the baseline condition, when respondents are not exposed to the experimental condition. In contrast, the solid line in figure 4.1 reports the probability of a negative response when the respondents are exposed to the experimental treatment. Finally, the shaded areas around the line depict confidence intervals.

Figure 4.1 shows two things. The first finding is a matter of common sense. In both the baseline and the treatment condition, the two lines rise as you

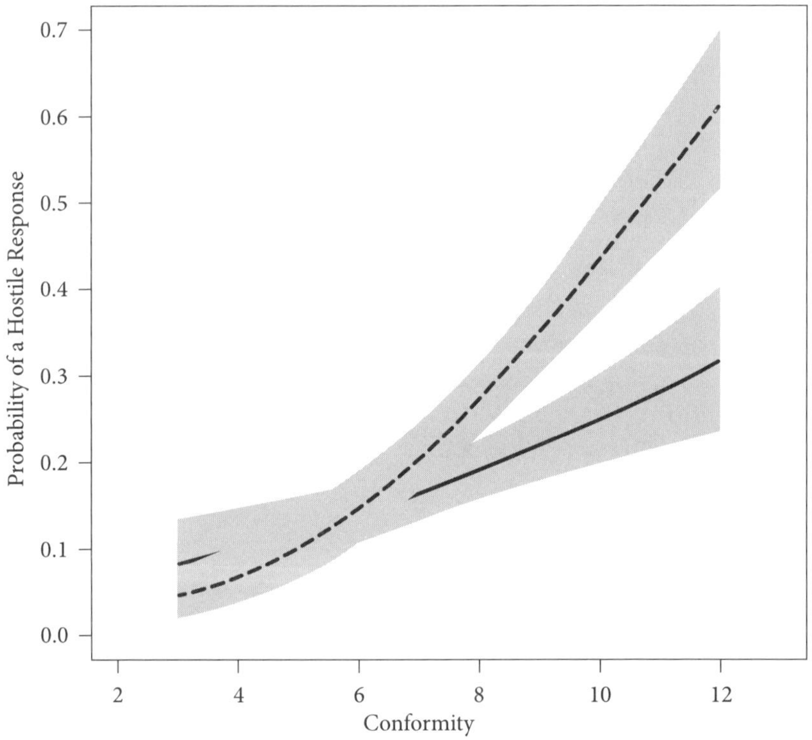

Figure 4.1. End of experiment results

move from left to right. What that means is that the more importance respondents attach to conformity as a social value, the more likely they are to emit a hostile response to immigrants. And of course that is just what we should expect to observe; as noted earlier, the importance attached to conformity as a value is one of the strongest predictors of hostility to immigrants.

The second finding is the one of interest. Compare the slopes of the two lines. They lie on top of each other on the left-hand side of the figure. Taking account of the confidence intervals, the two are indistinguishable. What this means is that the intervention of the interviewer has no impact on people who do not attach a great deal of importance to conformity as a social value. Whether the interviewer attempts to sway them or not, they are equally likely—which is to say overwhelmingly unlikely—to blame immigrant minorities for creating social problems. What happens as people attach progressively more importance to conformity as a value? The dotted line, which shows reactions in the treatment conditions, rises steeply; the solid line, which shows reactions in the baseline condition, only modestly. The result is that the two lines increasingly diverge. What this means is that those who are most strongly predisposed to respond negatively are strikingly inhibited from doing so by the intervention of the interviewer. Moreover, the strength of the experimental effect is striking. Without the restraint of the interviewer, the probability of someone who attaches high importance to conformity responding negatively is approximately six out of ten. By contrast, when the interviewer implicitly suggests that he disagrees with this view, the probability of responding negatively is only slightly more than one out of five. Thus, the results of the End-of-the-Interview Experiment show that, although those who most value conformity are most likely to respond negatively to immigrant minorities, they also are the most susceptible to social pressure to moderate negative responses to immigrant minorities.

THE PARTY LEADER COMPLIANCE EXPERIMENT

The issue this experiment focuses on is multiculturalism and the effect that party leaders can have on citizens' views toward it. Multiculturalism comes in many versions: among them, a demand that public life be stripped of procedures, symbols, and norms that embody the values of the previously dominant group; that traditional social practices—for example, the subordination of women—be affirmed; that minorities have veto power over policies affecting them; that "cultural" defenses against otherwise criminal acts—kidnapping, for example—be authorized as a matter of law.[22] Little is to be gained by focusing on such extreme versions of multiculturalism. We therefore focus on a moderate version of multiculturalism, the principle of cultural pluralism. The survey item that was at the core of this experiment was the following: "Since the Netherlands is a free country, Turks and Moroccans who have come here should be free to follow their own way of life."[23]

The assertion this experiment tests is that political elites can reduce, to a degree that matters politically, overt opposition to controversial policies designed to aid immigrants. An important source of the elite political influence posited here, one that enhances the political relevance of the experiment, is the ability of party leaders to influence the views of their party's loyalists most hostile to these policies (i.e., conformists). The top-down influence that party leaders can assert over their constituents (i.e., political leadership) makes possible the type of cross-party consensus that can curb xenophobic sentiments aroused by large influxes of immigrants. This, of course, makes the results of this experiment particularly useful to democratic politics in the twenty-first century.

This experiment fit nicely with the contemporary history of Dutch partisan politics. The Party for Freedom and Democracy (Partij Voor Vrijheid en Democratie, VVD) and the Labour Party (Partij van de Arbeid, PvdA) have been the main antagonists in post–World War II Dutch politics. In the 1990s, the VVD and PvdA broke tradition by forming a coalition (the so-called Purple coalition). In spite of their tradition of disagreement, the leadership of the VVD and PvdA agreed that immigration and ethnic minorities should not become a political issue. This consensus, at the elite level, was based on the deeply felt conviction that a politics that appealed to intolerance risked democracy and social stability. The result was a collective political taboo on appeals that might arouse prejudice. Prejudice, it was widely agreed in leadership circles, is a genie that must be kept in the bottle: if it escapes, it may never be bottled up again.

The specific hypothesis tested here is that conformity increases readiness to inhibit a negative response in the face of pressure from partisan elites to do so. Accordingly, in one condition, respondents are told that "an important VVD politician has spoken out in support of cultural pluralism"; in another, that "an important PvdA politician" has done so. Since it is only the two major parties that are part of the experiment, the analysis is only of their adherents.

As a general proposition, the more importance people attach to social conformity as a value, the more likely they are to oppose cultural pluralism. This is equally true whether they belong to the PvdA, the party of the left, or the VVD, the party of the right.[24] The question, then, is what difference it makes—if, indeed, it does make a difference—whether their party or its competitor supports the policy.

Focusing on views about the legitimacy of cultural pluralism provides a reasonable test of the inhibition hypothesis. On the one hand, issues of national identity are highly charged. Moreover, two of the minority groups are mentioned by name, Turks and Moroccans. People may well have a fixed position on the issue of multiculturalism, even if they are ready to adjust their positions on other issues. Or they may be fixed in place by the reference to Muslim groups, even if they would be ready to adjust their position on multiculturalism with regard to other groups. On the other hand, the issue of multiculturalism is pitched in terms of the principle of cultural pluralism, and they are given a positive reason—the Netherlands is a free country—to support it. The test of the hypothesis that political influence can restrain expression of negative responses to immigrants accordingly is this: Are VVD supporters who attach the most importance to conformity less likely to express opposition to cultural pluralism when *their* party supports it than when the PvdA does? Conversely, are PvdA supporters less like to express opposition to it when *their* party supports it?

Table 4.1a shows mean levels of opposition to cultural pluralism for PvdA adherents conditional on their level of conformity and whether their party or its principal opponent supports it. Table 4.1b reports a parallel set of results for VVD adherents. In both analyses, the dependent variable is scored from 0, which reflects the most support for the principle of cultural pluralism, to 1, which reflects the most opposition to it.

Table 4.1a. Elite counter-persuasion experiment

VVD Followers (ANOVA)	Party of Elite Actor	
Conformity	VVD	PvdA
Low	.47	.58
Middle	.53	.57
High	.53	.84

Table 4.1b. Elite counter-persuasion experiment

PvdA Followers (ANOVA)	Party of Elite Actor	
Conformity	VVD	PvdA
Low	.24	.25
Middle	.54	.37
High	.86	.52

Consider first responses of VVD supporters (table 4.1b). When the VVD advocates cultural pluralism, opposition sharply increases with conformity—from .24 for the lowest third on the Conformity Index to .86 for the highest third. By contrast, when their own party advocates cultural pluralism, although opposition does increase with conformity, it increases far less sharply—from .25 for the lowest third on the Conformity Index to .52 for the highest. Not surprisingly, the interaction between the level of conformity and the experimental treatment is highly significant. The results are very nearly (though not precisely) the same for PvdA supporters (table 4.1a). When the PvdA advocates cultural pluralism, opposition increases with conformity. The increase is not linear.

The small difference in patterns between the parties reflects the difference in base-rate opposition for cultural pluralism. Opposition is more pronounced among the party of the right, the VVD, than among the party of the left, the PvdA, as one would expect. Nonetheless, the highest third on conformity among the VVD are just as opposed to cultural pluralism when the opposing party advocates it as are their counterparts in the PvdA in similar circumstances. By contrast, when *their* party advocates cultural pluralism, opposition does not significantly increase with conformity. Thus, the results of the Party Leader Compliance Experiment support those of the End-of-the-Interview Experiment. Both show that those who prize conformity are prone to follow the lead of others they esteem even when doing so requires *not* doing what they are predisposed to do.

I do not want to give the impression that conformity is the only operative mechanism of top-down politics. Political leaders have a number of resources on which to draw. Sometimes they can put an issue on the public agenda, thus bringing it to the fore of citizens' thinking. Sometimes they can keep it off the public agenda, thus pushing it to the margins of citizens' thinking.[25] Sometimes they can contest an issue, with one party offering one policy alternative, another a competing alternative. Sometimes they can choose not to contest an issue, leaving citizens no opportunity to express their preferences on it.[26] Sometimes they can choose to contest an issue, giving the impression that citizens have changed their preferences on an issue when in fact all that has happened is they now have an opportunity to express them.

I have chosen to focus on the mechanism of conformity here because it brings to light a potentially pivotal feature of the politics of diversity. The thesis I have offered is composed of three premises. First, a substantial opposition to diversity is driven by prejudice. Second, the more prejudiced people are, the higher the value they place on conformity. Third, the higher the value people place on conformity, the more susceptible they are to situational pressures. The Dutch study provides good evidence for all three premises.

This trio of premises suggests a conclusion that throws new light, I believe, on the dynamics of the politics of diversity, an issue that is likely to be an important component of democratic politics in polities in many parts of the world throughout most of the twenty-first century. Many policies to promote diversity evoke opposition, often intense opposition, from the majority. People may oppose such policies on a number of grounds. But one of them is out of prejudice (premise one). And just so far as the intolerant fall disproportionately on one side of issues of diversity, so, too, do those who value conformity (premise two). Finally, the more people value conformity, the more susceptible they are to situational pressures (premise three). Taking all three premises together implies that there is a fundamental asymmetry to the politics of diversity. Opponents of diversity can more readily be diverted from their position on issues of diversity by social and political influence than supporters.

I turn now to a consideration of the broader implications of our findings for understanding the interplay of democratization, democratic ideals, and political leadership.

Limits on Leadership: Multiculturalism and Democratic Ideals

Political leaders have more freedom to maneuver than is commonly recognized on hot-button issues like multiculturalism. Public opinion influences their positions. But they can also influence public opinion—so our results suggest. They also suggest that one mechanism of influence is conformity: party adherents take positions that conform to those of party leaders. Conformity effects are not the most important mechanism of top-down politics, nor the most typical. The heart of a conformity effect is the capacity to induce people to take a different position than they otherwise would—without giving them a relevant reason for doing so. But politics is about giving reasons. Politicians make the best case they can for the policies they advance (and still more for themselves). They make arguments—often compressed, sometimes no more than "sound bites," but arguments all the same. They convey relevant reasons to support one political choice or reject another.

Because of their paradoxical political dynamic and their relevance to the politics of diversity, I have focused on conformity effects, although they are neither the most important nor the most common way politicians influence public opinion. The more importance people attach to conformity as a value, the more likely they are to be intolerant of ethnic minorities. Yet the more they value conformity, the more likely they are to be susceptible to pressures to inhibit expression of their intolerance. The result, our experiments suggest, is that political leaders who wish to promote multiculturalism can most readily influence the positions of their supporters who oppose it.

Leadership, then, has been my theme, hence the need to consider limits on it. Political leaders may have more freedom to maneuver than has been supposed; but they do not have unlimited freedom. Of the many limits on leadership, I want to focus on one—the contestability of democratic values. Their contestability was responsible for the rise of diversity as a democratic ideal; it may turn out to be responsible for its fall. The inherent contestability of democratic ideals also throws light on the larger theme of this book—democratization.

Democratization is normally taken to mean one thing, albeit it is a complex thing. I believe it means two things, both of them complex. Democratization in the first sense refers to the complex of processes by which a state that was not democratic becomes democratic. Democratization in the second sense refers to the dynamics of change in the understanding of democratic ideals, even the most fundamental of democratic ideals.[27] Democratization in the first sense has generated a large research literature;[28] democratization in the second sense has generated a comparatively small body of research literature (one more reason for me to concentrate on it).[29]

Multiculturalism is offered—by multiculturalists—as an example of democratization in the second sense. So it is, though not in the sense multiculturalists mean. The sense that they mean is that the thrust for change comes from outside liberal democracy. In this view, the new ideal of diversity is at odds not merely with the dominant culture of a particular country but with liberal democracy as it has been understood in all liberal democracies. Multiculturalism requires a fundamental reworking of democratic understandings. Minorities and the majority must renegotiate mutually the institutions and values of liberal democracies.[30]

This "outside-in" view is based on a flawed conception of the dynamics of multiculturalism in democratic societies. True, the fact of social heterogeneity creates a pressure for change. But the arguments and terms for change—and the very conception of diversity as a democratic ideal—have come from members of the majority, not those in the minority.[31] The resonance of diversity as a political ideal among the politically aware and engaged has come from the continuing power of equality as a moral idea,[32] not from any newly sprung commitment to diversity per se. And the political success of diversity as a democratic ideal has come from the support of the politically influential in the dominant society, not from the political power of minorities.

Thus, diversity as a democratic ideal is not an alternative to liberal democracy; it is a product of it—a critique of the practices of liberal democracy premised on the critical ideals of liberal democracy itself.[33] The "outside-in" view misses this internal critique. Democratic ideals are not merely open to revision; they invite it. Revision is inevitable because democratic ideals are inherently contestable—every one of them without exception. They are inherently contestable because there are competing democratic ideals, so each of them can be challenged in the name of another. What is more, there are competing conceptions of each democratic ideal; thus, each can be challenged in its own name as well as in the name of another.[34] And the clash among and between conceptions is genuine: getting more of one means getting less of another. The inherent contestability of democratic ideals means that there are built-in grounds for appeal against the status quo. Which is to say that diversity as a democratic ideal, having become part of the status quo, has itself become contestable.

The events of September 11, 2001, seized the attention of us all, so much so that it is nearly irresistible to explain what happens next in terms of 9/11 and what followed it, not what happened before it. It is irresistible—and wrong. There was already an intractable conflict. The political leadership of the day needed a policy to cope with social heterogeneity, hence multiculturalism. But they assumed that minorities were to be part of their society only on a temporary basis—"guest workers" in the phrase of the day. The purpose of multiculturalism was to facilitate the temporary stay of immigrant minorities, not to inaugurate a diverse society. From the perspective of immigrant minorities, however, the purpose of multiculturalism was not to accommodate their temporary residence and facilitate eventual departure, but just the opposite: to guarantee the legitimacy of their separate status in their new country—an understandable view on their part, not least because social theorists assured them that the larger society had to go beyond mere tolerance and "recognize" the intrinsic worth of their way of life. And not least, the public at large, who had been told in their turn that the aim of multiculturalism was to promote inclusion, discovered it was instead a device to justify separatism. The collision of understandings—and misunderstandings—guaranteed conflict with—or without—9/11.

Notes

1. Stimson 1999, 1.

2. The phrase is Stimson's (1999).

3. For a formal statement of our version of top-down politics, see Sniderman 2000, and Jackman and Sniderman 2002.

4. Iyengar and Kinder is the classic work on agenda setting and priming. For a recent, important extension, see Druckman, Jacobs, and Ostermeier 2004.

5. Sniderman, Peri, de Figuerido, and Piazza 2000.

6. I follow here Feldman's (2003) pioneering argument, discussed later in this chapter.

7. Aldrich 1995.

8. I am indebted to McLean's (2001) account of the clash between Heath and Powell and follow it here.

9. See Green 2004.

10. Schain 1987.

11. Sidanius and Pratto 1999.

12. For example, Kinder and Sears 1981.

13. Adorno et al. 1950.

14. For a remarkably thorough, intellectually independent, and impartial review of the array of theories about prejudice, see Duckitt 1992.

15. Zaller 1992.

16. Converse 1964.

17. See Sniderman and Carmines 1997.

18. We are grateful for support from the National Science Foundation (grant SR-9515006 and SES-grant 510–50–805), the Dutch National Science Foundation, and the Dutch Ministry of Public Health, Welfare, and Sports.

19. This is an exceptional work of analysis, clear and comprehensive to an unusual degree.

20. See Sniderman, Peri et al., for an overview of different conceptions of prejudice.

21. Kinder and Sears 1981.

22. The examples given are reproductive rights policy for women and land use policy for Indian reservations. See, for example, Miller 2000 and Renteln 2004.

23. The response format was modified Likert: strongly agree, somewhat agree, somewhat disagree, strongly disagree.

24. The zero-order correlation between the Index of Conformity and opposition to cultural pluralism is .33 for the VVD and .48 for the PvdA.

25. Two distinguishable effects—agenda setting and priming—can be at work. See Iyengar and Kinder 1987.

26. Fiorina (2004) draws attention to a scenario of deep importance: electorates may give an appearance of holding extreme preferences, not because they actually do, but because they are offered a choice only between extreme candidates.

27. A paradigmatic example is the First Amendment. What it is now taken to mean, as an inviolable commitment, is the work of the Supreme Court in the last seventy years. See Shapiro and Tresolino 1983.

28. See, for example, Przeworski et al. 2000; also Elkins 2000.

29. The major work in my view is Rae 1981.

30. For a representative example, see Young 2000.

31. There are, of course, important exceptions. See, for example, the work of Parekh (2000).

32. Frankfurt 1988.

33. In politics, attention to the regulative role of democratic ideals has come at the expense of attention to their critical role.

34. Rae 1981.

References

Adorno, T. W., Else Frankel-Brunswick, Daniel Levinson, and R. Nevitt Sanford. 1950. *The Authoritarian Personality.* New York: Harper & Row.

Aldrich, John H. 1995. *Why Parties?: The Origin and Transformation of Political Parties in America.* Chicago: University of Chicago Press.

Coenders, Marcel, Marcel Lubbers, and Peer Scheepers. 2003. *Majority Population's Attitudes towards Migrants and Minorities.* Report for the European Monitoring Centre on Racism and Xenophobia.

Converse, Philip E. 1964. "The Nature of Belief Systems in Mass Publics." In David E. Apter, ed., *Ideology and Discontent.* New York: Free Press. 206–61.

Druckman, James N., Lawrence R. Jacobs, and Eric Ostermeier. 2004. "Candidate Strategies to Prime Issues and Image." *Journal of Politics* 66:1180–1202.

Duckitt, John. 1992. *The Social Psychology of Prejudice.* New York: Praeger.

Elkins, Zachary. 2000. "Gradations of Democracy? Empirical Tests of Alternative Conceptualizations." *American Journal of Political Science* 44:293–300.

Erikson, Robert S., Michael B. Mackuen, and James A. Stimson. 2002. *The Macro Polity.* New York: Cambridge University Press.

Feldman, Stanley. 2003. "Enforcing Social Conformity: A Theory of Authoritarianism." *Political Psychology* 24:41–74.

Fiorina, Morris P. 2004. *Culture War? The Myth of a Polarized America.* New York: Pearson Longman.

Frankfurt, Harry. 1988. *The Importance of What We Care About.* New York: Cambridge University Press.

Green, Simon. 2004. *The Politics of Exclusion: Institutions and Immigration Policy in Contemporary Germany.* Manchester: Manchester University Press.

Iyengar, Shanto, and Donald R. Kinder. 1987. *News That Matters: Television and American Opinion.* Chicago: University of Chicago Press.

Jackman, Simon, and Paul M. Sniderman. 2002. "The Institutional Organization of

Choice Spaces: A Political Conception of Political Psychology." In Kristen Monroe, ed., *Political Psychology.* Mahway, N.J.: Lawrence Erlbaum. 272–83.

Kinder, Donald R., and David O. Sears. 1981. "Prejudice and Politics: Symbolic Racism versus Racial Threats to the Good Life." *Journal of Personality and Social Psychology* 40:414–31.

McLean, Ian. 2001. *Rational Choice and British Politics: An Analysis of Rhetoric and Manipulation from Peel to Blair.* Oxford: Oxford University Press.

Miller, David. 2000. "Group Identities, National Identities, and Democratic Politics." In *Citizenship and National Identity.* Cambridge: Polity Press. 62–80.

Parekh, Bhikhu. 2000. *Rethinking Multiculturalism: Cultural Diversity and Political Theory.* Cambridge, Mass.: Harvard University Press.

Przeworski, Adam, Michael E. Alvarez, Jose Antonio Cheibub, and Fernando Limongi. 2000. *Democracy and Development: Political Institutions and Material Well-being in the World, 1950–1990.* Cambridge: Cambridge University Press.

Rae, Douglas, 1981. *Equalities.* Cambridge, Mass.: Harvard University Press.

Renteln, Alison Dundes. 2004. *The Cultural Defense.* New York: Oxford University Press.

Schain, Martin A. 1987. "The National Front in France and the Construction of Political Legitimacy." *West European Politics* 10:229–52.

Shapiro, Martin, and Rocco J. Tresolini. 1983. *American Constitutional Law.* New York: Macmillan.

Sidanius, Jim, and Felicia Pratto. 1999. *Social Dominance: An Intergroup Theory of Social Hierarchy and Oppression.* New York: Cambridge University Press.

Sniderman, Paul M. 2000. "Taking Sides: A Fixed Choice Theory of Political Reasoning." In Arthur Lupia, Mathew D. McCubbins, and Samuel L. Popkin, *Elements of Reason: Cognition, Choice, and the Bounds of Rationality.* New York: Cambridge University Press.

Sniderman, Paul M., and Edward G. Carmines. 1997. *Reaching Beyond Race.* Cambridge, Mass.: Harvard University Press.

Sniderman, Paul M., Louk Hagendoorn, and Markus Prior. 2003. "De Moeizame Acceptatie Van Mosilims in Nederland." *Mens and Maatschappij* 78:199–218.

Sniderman, Paul M., Pierangelo Peri, Rui de Figuerido, and Thomas Piazza. 2000. *The Outsider: Prejudice and Politics in Italy.* Princeton: Princeton University Press.

Stimson, James A. 1999. *Public Opinion in America: Moods, Cycles, and Swings.* Boulder, Colo.: Westview Press.

———. 2004. *Tides of Consent: How Public Opinion Shapes American Politics.* New York: Cambridge University Press.

Young, Iris Marion. 2000. *Inclusion and Democracy.* New York: Oxford University Press.

Zaller, John. 1992. *The Nature and Origins of Mass Opinion.* Cambridge: Cambridge University Press.

5

Electoral Engineering, Social Cleavages, and Democracy

BERNARD GROFMAN
AND JON FRAENKEL

This chapter focuses on the potential for electoral engineering to serve as a tool to foster democracy, with a central concern being the role of electoral systems in mitigating ethnic conflict.[1] With democracy's "third wave" having produced a large number of new (or "renewed") democracies, and numerous countries aspiring to become democracies, electoral systems are presently an especially hot topic in the study of democratization. They promise to remain so for a good part of the twenty-first century. As a potential lever of political and social change, electoral systems possess two important features. The first is that they can be changed without totally changing the nature of the political system. While electoral systems tend to be "sticky," they are still certainly easier to modify than other central aspects of constitutional design—such as presidential versus parliamentary systems or unitary versus federal systems. This is true because, in most countries, the structure of electoral systems is not constitutionally embedded; this allows for change by legislative action.[2]

The second reason is that changes in electoral systems may be expected to have important effects on political behavior. A large body of literature claims that electoral systems impact such things as party proliferation; the balance of intraparty versus interparty electoral competition; incentives for legislative parochialism and pork-barrel politics; and the likelihood of extremist parties achieving representation, cabinet durability, political stability, and the like. Moreover, a newer literature argues for specific policy consequences of electoral rules in areas such as size of government, budget deficits, and policies affecting income inequality. There are also strong theoretically grounded reasons to expect choice of electoral systems to have especially important consequences for descriptive representation and ethnic accommodation in plural or divided societies.[3]

While what we have to say in this chapter will generally be relevant to the study of electoral systems as a democratizing force, our special concern will be for the relationship between electoral systems and ethnic accommodation. As Williams (2003, 36–37) observes, few countries are essentially monoethnic or monoreligious in character. Ethnic and religious diversity arises from many causes. These include

- Conquests of native peoples by outsiders who settle/colonize a territory;
- Multiple waves of settlement within the same territory by non-native groups prior to the definition of present state boundaries;
- Shifting of boundaries as a result of war or the breakup of empires that redefine boundaries in ways that create multiethnic composite nations and/or irredentist residues;
- Individual migrations of refugees or job-seekers (either legal or illegal), many of whom do not leave and who, together with their descendants, cumulate into a substantial minority presence;
- Importation of slaves;
- Change of religious affiliation by a ruler that affects the religious affiliations of some, but not all, of his subjects; and
- Religious proselytizing.

In the post–World War II period, transnational migration, including an influx of people into the home countries of their former colonizers (e.g., Algerians into France, Indians and West Indians into Britain), international refugees (whose recent impact, relative to total population, has been especially marked in Scandinavia and the Netherlands), and economic migrants (including those from the former Soviet Union) has led to significant changes in the ethnic composition of a number of industrialized nations. Perhaps even more important, the ending of colonial empires, including most recently the breakup of the Soviet Union, has created a multiplicity of states whose borders do not coincide neatly, or at all, with ethnic territorial boundaries, but where powerful former colonial regimes are no longer in place to suppress ethnic conflict.[4] Thus, it is increasingly important that countries find ways to accommodate their ethnic and religious diversity. Electoral rules are often proposed as tools for institutional engineering in multiethnic societies to assure fairness of treatment across groups, to reduce the potential for ethnic conflict, and to promote or strengthen democracy.

We begin with some introductory material on each of the two research areas, electoral systems and ethnic conflict, whose intersection lies at the heart of this chapter. These two sections situate electoral system choices in the broader literature on ways to mitigate ethnic antagonisms in multiethnic societies. We then turn to a set of more specific questions about the possibility of institutional design ameliorating ethnic tensions, the appropriateness of Western political institutions for tribal societies, and the likely effects of different electoral rules. We conclude with a discussion of electoral system reform issues in two of the small island nations of the South Pacific, Fiji and Papua New Guinea. These Melanesian nations are deeply divided societies—the former because of permanent settlements of guest-worker populations, the latter due to ethnolinguistic hyper-fractionalization and tribal rivalries across language groups.

Approaches to Electoral Systems in Political Science: A Brief Overview

Most early literature on electoral systems was couched in terms of a dichotomy between first-past-the-post (plurality or majoritarian) rules and proportional representation (PR). There are two main forms of proportional representation. In one, citizens vote for a given party and party elites completely control the nominating process. In the other, voters rank candidates and can directly determine which candidates of a given party are elected. In the pure form of *list PR,* parties present a list of candidates and voters must choose to vote for a single party. Each party is then entitled to elect the k highest candidates on its list, where k is determined by the level of voter support for that party. In contrast, the *single transferable vote* form of proportional representation requires voters to rank order the candidates. Initially, any candidate who has at least one quota of first place votes (where a quota is defined by the fraction, 1/(m+1) of the electoral turnout, with m the number of seats to be filled) is elected. If fewer than m candidates are elected in this fashion, the candidate with fewest first-place votes is dropped, and ballots that listed that candidate first are then reallocated to the next highest nonelected candidate still eligible for office. This process continues until m candidates are chosen. Ballots "used up" in electing a candidate (exactly one quota's worth) are, in effect, discarded. We omit the technical details of how to reallocate the votes a winning candidate may receive in excess of quota.[5]

The publication in 1967 of Douglas Rae's Ph.D. dissertation, *The Political Consequence of Electoral Laws* (2d ed., 1971) marked a sea change in the study of electoral systems. Its theoretically grounded and far-ranging empirical analysis largely supplanted the more polemic approaches characteristic of an earlier generation of research.[6] With this book, the study of electoral systems moved into the mainstream of comparative politics research, making first steps in drawing on analytic tools from game theory, and making use of quantitative analyses. For example, it showed how electoral systems could be characterized in terms of thresholds of representation and exclusion,[7] thus allowing us to replace nominal classifications in terms of the names of electoral rules with quantitative continua along which different rules could be arrayed.

In the 1980s, the growing maturity of the electoral systems field was signaled by the publication of a number of important books offering summaries and syntheses of data-oriented research findings as well as new analytic perspectives: for example, Katz (1980); Bogdanor and Butler (1983); Lijphart (1984); Lijphart and Grofman (1984); Grofman and Lijphart (1986); and Taagepera and Shugart (1989). Much of this work concerned three empirical issues: the impact of electoral rules on the proportionality of seats-votes relationships for political parties; the link between electoral system choice and party proliferation; and the consequences of electoral rules for political stability. Moreover, there was important work on seats-vote issues and redistricting done by political geographers such as R. J. Johnston, M. Taylor, G. Gudgin, and F. Shelley (Johnston, Shelley, and Taylor 1990; Taylor and Johnston 1979; Gudgin and Taylor 1979; see review in Grofman 1982b). Also, and perhaps even more important, during this period the international journal *Electoral Studies* was founded. In addition to de-polemicizing the debate, this new research cast doubt on the simplistic notion that the only relevant electoral choice is based on a dichotomy between plurality and proportional representation systems (see, e.g., Taagepera 1984; Rose 1984; cf. Sartori 1968). It also cast strong doubt on the empirical claims made about the inherent political instability of PR systems as compared to plurality systems (see esp. Lijphart 1984).

The renaissance of the electoral systems field continues. In the past decade or so we have seen the publication of Lijphart's *Electoral Systems and Party Systems* (1994), Cox's *Making Votes Count* (1997), and numerous detailed studies of particular electoral systems and their effects (e.g., Davidson and Grofman 1994; Reynolds 1999; Grofman, Lee, Winckler, and Woodall 1999; Bowler and Grofman 2000; Shugart and Wattenberg 2001; Lijphart and Grofman 2002), with various of the essays in Colomer (2004) forcing us to rethink claims often made about the causal impact of changes in electoral systems.[8] Electoral system research has moved into the political science mainstream and established itself as an important subfield. A host of authors, many of them young scholars only recently attracted to the field, publish lively and important research in the pages of *Electoral Studies* and other major journals, including the *American Political Science Review,* the *American Journal of Political Science, Comparative Politics, Party Politics,* the *British Journal of Political Science,* and the *European Journal of Political Research.* What had been a dearth of work on electoral arrangements has recently become a flood.

Moreover, strong links have been forged between electoral systems research and the study of party systems, on the one hand, and constitutional design, on the other (see e.g., Shugart and Carey 1992). The most important aspect of this body of work is that electoral systems and their consequences are seen as embedded in a larger political and institutional framework (see Grofman 1999). For example, Shugart and Carey (1992) and others have begun to look at how the presence of a presidential system, the rules for electing the president, and the timing of parliamentary and presidential elections interact with choice of electoral system for parliamentary elections to produce political consequences.

Another important very recent change is the entry of economists into the comparative politics field, where they have examined electoral systems and constitutional design in terms of their impact on public policy. Major contributions to understanding the electoral system effects on political economy (e.g., overall size of government and size of the welfare state component, incentives for pork-barrel politics, political corruption, budget deficit levels, rates of inflation and unemployment, levels of economic inequality, rate of economic growth) have been made by economists associated with the "new public economics," such as Alberto Alesina, Torsten Persson, Gerard Roland, and Guido Tabellini (Alesina 1994, 1995; Persson and Tabellini 1999, 2000; Persson, Roland, and Tabellini 2000). These topics are also being investigated by political scientists such as Arend Lijphart (Lijphart 1999) and his students (see esp. Crepaz 1996a, 1996b, 1998, 2001; Birchfield and Crepaz 1998; Crepaz and Moser 2004). However, there remain ongoing controversies about, for example, whether PR systems are more conducive to high overall levels of government spending, and high ratios of both welfare expenditure and pork-barrel spending to total spending, than are single-member district systems. While such positive correlations are well established, and even validated in multivariate modeling, skeptics doubt the causal nature of the linkages, arguing that they may be explained by selection bias connected to variations in cultural patterns and economic development that cannot be fully addressed with only cross-sectional data.

Mathematical modeling of voting rules has also grown apace, exemplified best in the ever-expanding literature on social choice springing primarily from the earlier work of pioneering scholars such as Anthony Downs (1957), Kenneth Arrow (1962), and Robin Farquharson (1969). The neo-Downsian literature deals with questions such as the nature of the incentives different electoral rules provide to vote-share maximizing parties to pick policy platforms that are similar to/differentiated from one other. The Arrowian literature deals with issues like axiomatic characterizations of the "normative" properties of different voting rules, while Saari (1994, 1995) has shown how to generate preference profiles that will give us all possible differences in outcomes across a wide class of voting rules. The literature inspired by Farquharson makes use of game theoretic tools to look at strategically motivated choices, e.g., voters, parties, and sometimes interest groups as well (see e.g., Cox 1997, 2000). Finally, we have the sui generis modeling work of Taagepera (see e.g., Taagepera and Shugart 1989, 1993; Taagepera 1999a, b), which makes use of ideas from statistical thermodynamics based on expectations under a principle of insufficient knowledge. This work offers a rich network of interlinked statistical propositions about electoral system effects based on only a handful of key institutional variables. For example, in a constituency from which m legislators will be elected under a proportional representation rule, Taagepera's work shows why we might expect that the number of seat-winning parties will be roughly proportional to the square root of m (see review in Grofman 2004).

Institutional Design and Ethnic Antagonisms in Multiethnic Societies

The most common dichotomy in the ethnic accommodation literature is that between recognizing differences across ethnic groups by various forms of multicultural recognition and accommodation, and policies that encourage assimilation and control. Our preferred approach (see esp. Grofman and Stockwell 2003) has three components. First, rather than a dichotomy between assimilation and recognition of communal difference, we prefer to think of options in terms of two crosscutting dimensions of choice, giving rise to a four-fold (2 x 2) categorization. The horizontal axis represents communalist versus integrative perspectives and the vertical axis is the degree of emphasis on institutional mechanisms that primarily affect representation as compared to institutional arrangements that affect general social and legal arrangements (see table 1, taken from Grofman and Stockwell 2003, 110). Second, following the perspective of Buchanan and Tullock (1962) on optimal institutions, we do not believe that, in general, the best solution is one that is "all of a piece," i.e., one all of whose elements are located within a single cell of table 1. In other words, we are open to the possibility of arrangements that mix different options. Third, we do not see institutional design for ethnically divided societies as one size fits all, that is, we believe very strongly that institutional arrangements for ethnic accommodation must be tailored to the specific historical circumstances that brought different ethnics together within the same polity and to their history of interaction.

We make no effort to plumb the depths of the vast literature on ethnicity and ethnic conflict in this overview. Rather, in what follows we briefly address three topics that bear directly on the relevance of electoral system design to ethnic accommodation.[9] The first has to do with the possibility of sustaining democracy in deeply divided societies. A second issue has to do with the applicability of Western models of representation to more tribal societies. A third important area of disagreement in the ethnic relations literature involves both sharply contrasting normative perspectives and an ongoing empirical debate about the likely consequences of different electoral systems.

PROSPECTS FOR DEMOCRACY IN DEEPLY DIVIDED SOCIETIES

"Is democracy possible in deeply divided societies?" This debate is alive and well and living in Iraq and Afghanistan, among numerous other places. One camp argues that democracy is inherently unstable in plural societies because conflicts over division of resources will inevitably be fought primarily along ethnic lines, and thus will be inherently irresolvable, especially if the ultimate question is "Who owns the state?"

Pessimism about plural societies is empirically grounded in the large number of ethnically or religiously divided societies that have failed to sustain democracy, or suffered repeated crises: an abbreviated list includes Burundi, Fiji, Guyana, Lebanon, Nigeria, Northern Ireland, Pakistan, Rwanda, Sri Lanka, Suriname, and Sudan, and now, of course, several of the parts of the former Yugoslavia. Quantitative research examining the link between ethnic diversity and degree of democracy often suggests a negative relationship (Bollen and Jackman 1985; Diamond 1992; Hannan and Carroll 1981; Muller and Seligson 1994; Powell 1982). Recent investigations under the auspices of the United Nations Research Institute for Social Development have suggested,

Table 5.1. Categorizing institutional approaches to fostering stable democracy in plural societies

	Institutions that perpetuate the importance of ethnicity but seek to minimize its negative consequences (communal institutions)	Institutions that seek to minimize the importance of ethnicity and/or foster a multi-ethnic character to the state (integrative institutions)
Mass-oriented	• Separate (communal) legal systems • Specific provisions for group rights • Separate (communal) school systems • Ethnically based allocative rules for jobs, etc. that draw on the norm of proportional representation	• A legal system with a strong emphasis on individual rather than group rights • Political distributions that are not tied to ethnicity • Requiring a single common language or requiring multilingualism of all citizens • Forbidding certain markers of group distinctiveness (e.g., the veil) • Bans on ethnically based political parties or rules requiring a given regional spread of voter support • STV in multi-ethnic constituencies (Reynolds & Reilly 1999) • The alternative vote in multi-ethnic constituencies (Horowitz 1985) with optional ranking of preferences and without above-the-line ballots
Representational	• Ethnically rooted (territorial) federalism with considerable autonomy for subunits • Mono-ethnic electoral constituencies (or, in the extreme, communal rolls), or full or partial quota systems for the nomination of electoral representatives • Elite power-sharing mechanisms (e.g., grand coalitions, minority veto, ethnically based political or in the extreme, ethnically based office holding) • Electoral rules that foster centralized elite control (e.g., list PR) • Use of a parliamentary rather than presidential system	• Forms of federalism that either do not coincide with ethnicity or that divide up ethnic blocs into multiple units so as to diminish prospects of ethnic solidarity • The alternative vote in multiethnic constituencies (Horowitz 1985) with above-the-line ticket options in lodging ballots • First-past-the-post electoral systems—where used to promote stable governments via seats/votes bonuses parties, and discouraging third party contestants

however, that it is not ethnically multi-polar or hyper-fractionalized states (such as India, Tanzania, or Papua New Guinea) that face the greatest difficulty in sustaining democracy, but rather ethnically tripolar or bipolar states (such as Fiji, Guyana, Malaysia, or Bosnia) where two or three large ethnic groups compete for control over the state.[10] Even here, the trajectory is not inexorably downhill, as the examples of Fiji and Malaysia indicate (Bangura 2004).[11] Of course, a correlation between ethnic diversity and state failures and violence does not mean that positive outcomes cannot ever occur in the presence of ethnic heterogeneity. Indeed, Thomas, Ramirez, Meyer, and Gobalet (1979) find no statistically significant linkage between state failure and ethnic diversity once other factors are controlled.

Another troubling claim is that democracy, or at least *attempts* at democracy, might exacerbate conflicts in deeply divided societies, as for example with the dispute over the timing of the first post-Saddam election in Iraq. As the distinguished student of ethnic conflict, Brendan O'Leary, observed in a panel broadcast on BBC radio in April 2000: "Democracy can cause conflict because it nationalizes territories, suggesting exclusive rights for one people, the *Staatsvolk,* the nation. . . . Unchecked democracy . . . can drive conflict." Ultimately, as Sisk (1996, ix) observes, "democratic practices offer greater promise for long-term peaceful conflict management," even where articulating grievances through democratic channels threatens in the short term to jeopardize stability.

In defense of a more optimistic appraisal, one can directly point to multiethnic societies that have achieved long-term democratic accommodation (e.g., Belgium, Canada, India, and Switzerland), and others that seem well on their way (e.g., South Africa and Mauritius). The case for at least partial optimism is bolstered by the fact that the latter set of countries lacks the level of wealth that is often held to be a prerequisite of stable democracy.[12]

But, most important for present purposes, those who hold out hope for democracy in divided societies are virtually unanimous in their belief that constitutional engineering is the key to avoiding disaster (see, e.g., Reynolds and Reilly 1999).[13] There are three choices that are most often identified as critical: parliamentary versus presidential system, federal versus unitary systems, and choice of electoral system.

Prominent scholars of comparative politics (perhaps most notably Juan Linz) have asserted that *presidential* (as opposed to *parliamentary*) systems are not suited to plural societies and must be replaced. The existence of a president and the inevitable winner-take-all conflict for that office allegedly exacerbates ethnic tension, on the one hand, and provides a power base to the winner to use for ethnic subordination, on the other (Linz and Valenzuela 1994). Because, in plural societies, ethnic issues are likely to be "trump" cards in the quest for votes, and radical outbidding on divisive ethnic issues is pervasive (Rabushka and Shepsle 1972; Sisk 1996, 32), majority rule in such societies often ends up in permanent control over the political process by the largest (or most warlike) ethnic group, and permanent exclusion of minority ethnic groups. The issue of whether presidentialism is, per se, a destabilizing force has triggered an ongoing debate in the comparative politics literature that would take us beyond the scope of this essay (see e.g., Lijphart 1992; Horowitz 1985).

Another key issue (see table 1) is federalism (Filippov, Ordeshook, and Shvetsova 2004). Elsewhere, one of us (Grofman and Stockwell 2003) has argued that useful lessons can be learned from Nigeria's experiments with federalism, despite its failures, and from federalist practices in India. The view that federalism is highly desirable for multiethnic societies is widely held but not without dissenters; space limitations make it impossible for us to pursue this topic here. Instead, our concern in the remainder of this chapter will be limited to electoral system choice.

Conflict between Traditional and Imported Forms of Representation

In most colonial states, the choice of electoral laws for legislative assemblies was initially strongly influenced by the model bequeathed by the colonial power. Hence, most British colonies adopted plurality (aka first-past-the-post) systems, and the U.S. territories also embraced plurality or plurality bloc voting, while the French colonies used double ballots or list proportional representation for territorial elections. But there are also some intriguing anomalies. In particular, if we focus on the South Pacific, whose island nations have been characterized as "natural laboratories for constitutional and electoral experimentation" (Reilly 2002), we find some interesting exceptions.[14]

For example, Nauru's unique voting method is in the same family of scoring rules as the Borda rule,[15] involving a ranked ballot with successive preferences counted as a diminishing fraction of the first-choice vote (Reilly 2002), while Vanuatu is one of the few remaining countries in the world with a single-non-transferable vote (SNTV) system.[16] Papua New Guinea (PNG) initially copied practices of its Australian neighbors in adopting the alternative vote[17] and, although that method was abandoned at independence in favor of a British first-past-the-post system, PNG is now returning to use of a variant of the alternative vote. The alternative vote has also recently been implemented in Fiji, another former British colony.[18]

In some island nations (Samoa, Tonga), indigenous forms of authority provided the bases for the postcolonial order. Tonga's monarchical system, in which the king appoints twelve members of parliament, thirty-three nobles select nine representatives, and nine are elected by a common suffrage, is a legacy of the nineteenth century, although significant reforms occurred in 1914, strengthening the power of the king against the nobility (Campbell 2004). Samoa's system initially restricted both suffrage and office holding to those holding matai-titles.[19] Since 1990, the Samoan franchise is no longer restricted to matai alone; although it remains the case that only matai may stand as candidates for parliament. In other cases (the Marshall Islands, Fiji), customary leadership was initially incorporated by way of establishment of bicameral legislatures that provided a special role for chiefs in the upper chamber.

In recent years, in different Pacific countries, ambitious reform efforts have aimed at strengthening political parties, stabilizing governments, and encouraging moderation and compromise amongst competing ethnic groups. Much recent concern with electoral reform in the South Pacific has centered on Melanesia, because of coups in Fiji (1987, 2000) and the Solomon Islands (2000), and high turnover of incumbent MPs and government instability in Papua New Guinea, the Solomon Islands, and Vanuatu (see e.g., Steeves 1996; Roughan 2004).

Thirty or so years after independence, the issue of the appropriateness of "imported" institutions still plays a significant role in discussions of electoral reform in many Pacific Islands, as do claims that democracy may be a "foreign flower" unsuitable in the Pacific context (Larmour 1994). In some states, voting rules that draw on European practices that eliminate or downplay the role of chiefs and the importance of communal consensus have been challenged by indigenous groups as inappropriate given Pacific Island traditions. In particular, states with British-influenced Westminster-style systems of parliamentary government have been widely and frequently criticized.

Nonetheless, customary chiefs have less political or institutional power than they had during the earlier postwar years, and (especially in Micronesia) are less likely to hold elective office (Crocombe 2001, 490). For example, reserved parliamentary seats for chiefs set up during the Trust Territory era have been abandoned, although the Marshall Islands retains a rather inactive Council of Iroij (chiefs) as its upper house (Crocombe 2001, 507–9). The Marshallese 1999 and 2003 elections both saw a "commoner" president, Kessai Note, and his United Democratic Party (UDP), elected in preference to a coalition centered around support for high chiefs. Even in Vanuatu, where the role of chiefs is often extolled in dealing with grassroots social discontent, customary leaders have fared poorly in postindependence elections (Patterson 2004). Moreover, the incorporation of indigenous forms of authority into the postcolonial era forms of government has sometimes been discarded. For example, in the Solomon Islands, initial efforts to establish a more communally oriented system of representation were abandoned under local pressure despite the belief of the British colonial government that the Westminster system was unsuitable in the Solomon Islands due to exceptional ethnic diversity and the absence of party-based politics (Ghai 1983, 27).[20] Thus, even for tribal societies we think it reasonable to focus on representational choices that come from the standard "Western" kit-bag.

Electoral Engineering for Mitigation of Ethnic Conflict: Minority Accommodation and Representation

When we turn back to table 1 to look at the repertoire of electoral rules we have identified that might help us mitigate ethnic conflict and foster democracy, there are two interlinked critical choices: (1) choice about the degree of ethnic homogeneity in electoral constituencies, with communal rolls or ethnic quotas anchoring one end of this continuum, and (2) choice of electoral rules. A key choice is between multi-seat constituencies using some form of proportional representation (PR), on the one hand, and single-seat constituencies, on the other.

If we opt for single-seat constituencies there are two quite distinct routes that have been identified for ethnic accommodation. One requires manipulation of constituency boundaries to achieve ethnic homogeneity within constituencies as a means of guaranteeing at least some ethnic representation in situations where voting is polarized along ethnic lines; the other requires use of the so-called alternative vote in constituencies with a multiethnic composition, with the aim of encouraging cross-ethnic coalitions. In most societies where achieving proportional ethnic representation is a concern, methods such as list PR or the single transferable vote are employed. In the United States, because of the long tradition of first-past-the-post voting, while there have been limited uses of PR and semi-PR methods (such as the cumulative vote), the common remedy for minority vote dilution is the creation of single-member districts in which the minority population has been concentrated.

The exact expected impact of simple-plurality voting in single-member districts on the descriptive representation of ethnic minorities is hard to characterize, since expected effects are mediated by how geographically concentrated the minority is, by how polarized along racial or ethnic lines is the electorate, and by whether drawing districts in which the minority population has a realistic chance to elect candidates of its choice is favored or disfavored by those doing the construction of constituency boundaries. Nonetheless, a rough generalization is that, *ceteris paribus,* minorities can achieve substantial (even near proportional) descriptive representation under single-member district plurality elections, if the following three conditions are met: (1) their voting-eligible population is substantial, (2) they are highly geographically concentrated, and (3) if districts are deliberately drawn to preserve those concentrations (or at least, not intentionally fragment them).[21] However, absent extreme geographic concentration, single-member district plurality methods will systematically underrepresent minorities—with the degree of underrepresentation greatest when the minority population is small and dispersed (see Grofman 1982b).

For PR systems, the greater the number of seats to be filled, m, the easier it is, in principle, for a party to nominate a diverse array of candidates rather than only candidates from the dominant group among a given party's activists—a group that may be predominantly male or predominantly of one racial or ethnic or religious persuasion (Grofman and Reynolds 2001). Arend Lijphart, for example, advocates the use of pure-list PR in divided societies because it facilitates proportional descriptive representation for minorities at the same time as it allows strong party leaders (perhaps from ethnically based parties) to broker interethnic deals. Lijphart (1968, 1969, 1977, 1991, 1996) also argues that stable democracy in plural societies requires power-sharing arrangements, where by power sharing is meant "practices and institutions that result in broad-based governing coalitions generally inclusive of all major ethnic groups in society" (Sisk 1996, vii). To achieve this end, the most clearly articulated form of power-sharing arrangements, consociationalism (Lijphart 1977), has a particular constellation of institutional features as its hallmarks/defining characteristics: in addition to PR-based elections, "(1) grand coalition arrangements that include representatives of all major linguistic and religious groups, (2) cultural autonomy for these groups, (3) proportionality in political representation and civil service appointments, and (4) a minority veto with regard to vital minority rights and autonomy" (Lijphart 1996, 258). Lijphart (1991, 503) mentions "the inseparability of these four characteristics: Power-sharing is not complete unless all four are included, and it cannot work well—and certainly not optimally—if one or more are missing."[22]

However, the claim that PR (especially pure-list PR) is the best method for divided societies has been disputed. An important alternative view is that list PR encourages ethnically based voting and tends to encourage ethnic entrepreneurs to divide amongst themselves the spoils of office. Among mainstream political scientists, the most forceful critic of consociationalism is Donald Horowitz (see e.g., Horowitz 1985, 1991a, b, 1993). Horowitz questions the consociational focus on accommodation at the elite level and is concerned that consociational arrangements reinforce the importance of ethnic or religious cleavages. He argues for an integrative approach that seeks to deal with ethnic conflict potential through fostering political arrangements that will lead to bridging or transcending ethnic group differences. The goal of the integrative approach is to structure politics in such a way as to provide incentives for interethnic cooperation and the creation of pre-election coalitions between ethnic parties or broad multiethnic parties based on interests (e.g., region or common economic interests) that transcend ethnic identities (Sisk 1996, 5).[23] In particular, Horowitz wishes to create incentives for pan-ethnic coalitions and/or candidates who make cross-ethnic appeals. To achieve these ends, Horowitz (1985, 1991a, b, 1997) has been rather insistent that the alternative vote is the best electoral rule to foster voting patterns that will cross ethnic lines and coalitions that will adopt accommodative or moderate policies designed to solicit support across the ethnic divide.[24]

Where Horowitz and Lijphart would agree, however, is in rejecting plurality, and especially plurality bloc voting methods (i.e., plurality in multi-seat constituencies, with each voter given as many votes as there are seats to be filled (m), and the m candidates with highest votes elected). In the United States, in elections at all levels of government, plurality bloc voting rules (the extreme form of which, the at-large election, makes use of a jurisdiction-wide election) have been shown to be especially pernicious to minority electoral success in areas where there is a substantial minority presence (Davidson and Grofman 1994). The reason for this is that African Americans, Hispanics, or other minority groups that are sufficiently concentrated so as to constitute a majority in at least one single-member district, were such smaller constituencies to be drawn, may end up having their voting strength swamped by white/Anglo voters in larger multi-member districts that use plurality bloc voting in situations where voting is polarized along racial or ethnic lines.

Now we turn to two mini-case studies on the choice and impact of electoral rules in the South Pacific: Fiji and Papua New Guinea.

FIJI

Fiji is a society divided between its native Fijian population and a very substantial settler population largely descended from Indians brought in by the British to work on plantations. In Fiji in 1965, the British colonial authorities introduced a so-called cross-voting system. This was a grand plan to reconcile Indo-Fijian calls for a common roll with ethnic Fijian attachment to separate ethnically reserved constituencies. The system was extended at independence in 1970 and survived until the 1987 coup. As a result, we can examine a run of six elections over twenty-two years.

In this system, all registered citizens could cast four votes. Each chose a "communal" candidate, but in addition cast a further three votes in common franchise constituencies. Ethnically demarcated electorates selected the communal candidates. In the "cross-voting" or "national" electorates, all registered voters regardless of race cast ballots for candidates whose ethnicity was "Fijian," "Indian," or "general." In these contests, it was the ethnicity of the candidates, rather than the voters, that was legally predetermined. After 1970, twenty-five MPs were returned from cross-voting/national constituencies, and twenty-seven from communal constituencies.

The "cross-voting" system, influenced by similar colonial experiments in Tanzania and elsewhere, was intended to encourage the emergence of national statesmen (or, infrequently, women) who could successfully appeal across the ethnic divide. In the Fiji context, the system was no doubt thought to advantage the Alliance Party, which had been founded on a common political front forged by Fijian and European members against the more narrowly Indian-backed Federation Party.

But the cross-voting system did not work as expected. After a period of adjustment, the larger political parties all became adept at finding candidates from other ethnic groups whom they could field in the ethnically reserved seats. The Federation Party, although it at first faced difficulties in securing reliable allies, soon found sufficient "Fijian" and "general" candidates to stand on its platform and renamed itself the National Federation Party (NFP). Yet its support always remained solidly Indo-Fijian. The NFP won elections in April 1977 and, in coalition with the Fiji Labour Party, in 1987. In the first case, a constitutional crisis and in the second case a coup halted the largely Indo-Fijian-backed parties from assuming or retaining office.

In nearly all constituency contests between 1965 and 1987 (when the system was abolished), it was the ethnic composition of the national constituencies that determined outcomes under cross-voting. In other words, a seat with a majority Indian electorate returned an MP associated with the NFP (or NFP-FLP in 1987), whereas a similar seat with a majority European or indigenous Fijian electorate tended to return an MP from the Alliance Party (see further details in Fraenkel 2003). Moreover, as NFP leader A. D. Patel had predicted, the system encouraged the emergence of "Uncle Tom" or "stooge" type Fijian and Indo-Fijian politicians, whose legitimacy relied on party affiliations with the other community.[25] The cross-voting system did not facilitate the emergence of national leaders able to appeal across the ethnic divide. Nor, as it turned out, did it guarantee the Alliance Party's hold on office. Rather, its main effect was to strengthen political party organization in Fiji and encourage ethnic loyalties to become expressed via votes for ethnically defined parties and policy platforms, rather than votes for individuals on account of their ethnicity.

Where this system might have been expected to best promote moderation or greater cooperation across the ethnic divide was in seats where registered voters from the two main ethnic groups appeared in more or less equal proportions. In Fiji, these were the regions around the capital, Suva, in eastern Viti Levu. Everywhere else, the cross-voting constituencies were either overwhelmingly ethnic Fijian or Indian. Yet eastern Viti Levu has, since independence, been the area of the sharpest racial antagonism in Fiji.

In the light of this history, Fiji's mid-1990s Constitutional Review Commission suggested that postindependence electoral institutions possessed a "divisive effect" and set out to "break down the barriers which force ethnic parties to take a narrow, communal view of their best interests" (Reeves, Vakatora, and Lal 1996, 277, 20). Changes in electoral laws were identified as the "main stimulus for the emergence of a multi-ethnic political culture" (ibid., 9–10). A new electoral system, it was hoped, would facilitate greater cooperation and moderation among leaders of the 44 percent Indo-Fijian and 52 percent indigenous Fijian communities. The commission eventually recommended the alternative vote system (AV). By requiring victors, in single member electorates, to obtain 50 percent +1 of the vote, it was hoped that politicians would adopt more moderate stances on ethnically divisive policy issues to appeal across the ethnic divide. With its provisions for parties to swap preferences, AV, it was claimed, would offer stronger "electoral incentives to moderation and compromise" (ibid., 11–12, 312, 317).

As part of the new 1997 constitution, Fiji introduced the alternative vote system. Fiji's choice of the alternative vote system was strongly influenced by debates in the international political science literature about appropriate electoral institutions for ethnically divided societies, as well as by the use of that system in elections to the lower house in neighboring Australia (see e.g., Horowitz 1997, 2000). The new constitution also had some provisions for mandatory power sharing. All parties with more than 10 percent of seats in the house were entitled to cabinet portfolios.

Yet, as with its predecessor, the system did not work as proponents hoped it might.[26] At the May 1999 polls, the centrist coalition that initiated the constitutional compromise found itself heavily defeated. Instead, the Fiji Labour Party (relying mainly on first preference support from the 44 percent Indo-Fijian community, coupled with transfers of lower-order preference votes from closely or loosely allied parties) found itself with an absolute majority. The country's first ever Indo-Fijian prime minister, Mahendra Chaudhry, took office, at the head of a coalition including several small Fijian-backed parties. Precisely a year later, that government was overthrown in a coup perpetrated by indigenous Fijian extremists—a coup supported by many rank-and-file members and backbench MPs from parties whose leaders had joined the coalition government.

After the May 2000 coup, the constitution was restored by a decision from Fiji's Court of Appeal, paving the way for fresh elections, again held under the alternative vote system. At the 2001 polls, two exclusively ethnic-Fijian-backed political parties, the *Soqosoqo ni Duavata ni Lewenivanua* (SDL) and *Matanitu Vanua* (CAMV) secured the largest number of seats and formed a coalition government. Ironically, given the hoped for pro-moderation effects of the electoral system, the self-styled "Moderates Forum" obtained only a single seat in the 2001 election.[27]

Even strong enthusiasts for the adoption of AV have acknowledged that Fiji's system proved faulty, although they hold the continued use of a large number of communal seats and curious provisions governing split-format ballot papers responsible (see e.g., Reilly 2001a, 2001b; cf. Horowitz 2000). Some still argue for the retention of that system, no longer upholding enthusiastically its supposed moderating effect on ethnic divisions, but rather on the thinner grounds that electoral systems should rarely be changed lightly. Others, however, argue that Fiji's alternative vote system is likely to continue to generate disproportionate results and ethnically based governments (e.g., Arms 2004) and propose that it be replaced.[28]

In our view, Fiji's electoral system has shown itself to be an odd and unwieldy construct, which generates outcomes very different to those envisaged by its architects or supporting theorists. Combining a majoritarian electoral system with a proportional multi-party cabinet is unlikely to yield either sturdy government (one of the key supposed benefits of majoritarian systems) or governments that proportionally represent different strands and alignments within the electorate (the intended advantage of proportional systems). Moreover, the continued usage of a large number of communal constituencies alongside a minority of open or "common roll" constituencies has done little to assist ethnic accommodation.

PAPUA NEW GUINEA (PNG)

Prior to independence, Papua New Guinea briefly made use of the alternative vote system at elections in 1964, 1968, and 1972, before switching to plurality voting in single-member districts at independence (Reilly 1996; 1997; 2001a, 2001b). When the alternative vote system was abandoned in 1975, the PNG Electoral Commission argued, in line with the experience in Ireland and some of the Canadian provinces,[29] that with optional marking of preferences, outcomes differed little from those under first-past-the-post systems.[30]

Papua New Guinea is a hyper-fractionalized society, with over 850 separate ethno-linguistic groups, and lacks a truly political party–based system. As a result, under the post-1975 first-past-the-post electoral law, increasing numbers of candidates contested elections and victors emerged with a continually declining share of the vote. Over the period from 1977 to 2002, the average number of candidates contesting each constituency rose from eight to twenty-seven, and the number of constituency victories obtained on the basis of less than 20 percent of the vote rose from 9 percent to 58 percent (see Fraenkel 2004). In past decades, Papua New Guinea's so-called unbounded politics (Steeves 1996) has been associated with a weak party system, a high degree of government instability, and an extraordinarily high rate of incumbent MP turnover. Some 70 percent of sitting parliamentarians failed to get reelected at the 2002 PNG elections. In PNG (and the Solomon Islands as well), so-called yo-yo or rubber band politicians frequently switch parties while serving in office, and parliamentary proceedings become engulfed in perpetual "no-confidence" conspiracies. Under perpetual threat, beleaguered prime ministers restrict parliamentary sittings to a minimum to avoid no-confidence votes, in the process frustrating the needed initiating and reviewing of legislation. The result is gridlock and political paralysis (see Okole 2002).

Politicians in PNG, and elsewhere in Melanesia, behave as the "big men" of politics much like the traditional "big men" within localized, clan-based Melanesian society. That is, they compete by dispensing favors (Steeves 1996). Kaima (2004) argues that candidates obtain support by direct distribution to voters, rather than offering alternative policy platforms likely to promote local or national development. Moreover, cash-strapped MPs in PNG face extraordinary pressures to recoup expenses involved in their elections, which include payments to their supporters, which in turn leads to corruption.

In PNG, recent electoral reforms have aimed at addressing perceived defects in the inherited Westminster system. These reforms have attempted to strengthen political party organization through funding provisions for campaigns and by outlawing party switching by incumbent legislators. The goal of avoiding continual government instability has led to efforts to restrict parliamentary "no-confidence" challenges. Also, a form of preferential voting within single-seat constituencies has been adopted for future elections. It requires voters to mark their top three preferences; the objective of this reform is to encourage candidates to broaden their support and appeal to voters outside their immediate clan. It remains to be seen whether this form of limited preferential voting will generate a more moderate and broadly acceptable genre of MPs, or whether feverishly competitive and highly fractionalized elections in PNG will simply assume new forms.

The current transition to limited preferential voting in PNG is intended to arrest the proliferation of candidates and vote splitting, particularly in the Highlands of PNG. Yet accurately assessing the repercussions of that reform requires a key question to be addressed: Why do so many candidates currently stand in PNG elections (an average of twenty-six candidates contested each constituency in 2002)? Why do some not stand aside to allow ideologically like-minded allies to defeat powerful adversaries?

The answer is surely that there is (or perhaps there is as yet) no ideologically unifying dimension(s) to the political process encouraging candidates to group themselves along a left-right or any other such ideological axis. Little at present restrains candidate proliferation. If so, the response to the introduction of a limited form of the alternative vote may, if no new organizing dimension to the political process emerges, simply be to *further* increase the number of candidates contesting elections. Indeed, a contestant may choose simply to add to his campaign two closely allied "dummy" candidates from other geographic areas within the constituency to gather preferences that are then redistributed towards them later in the count. Dummy candidates may also be used to split rival candidates' votes.[31]

Conclusion

Stemming from Arrow's (1962) "Impossibility Theorem," it has become one of the clichés of the literature on social choice theory that "no voting rule is uniformly best" with respect to all plausible normative criteria. Ethnic impact is only one aspect of electoral system choice; there are other competing desiderata that may lead us in different directions than the approaches favored by either Horowitz or Lijphart. Also, in general, choice of electoral rules raises questions of what will happen, and not just normative issues of what should happen. Frequently, normative and empirical considerations are hard to separate. Beliefs about what should be done may be highly contingent on what the expected consequences of any choice will be. Further, no change is likely to have just one consequence. Thus, we would emphasize that, in judging an electoral rule, we must look not merely to its abstract theoretical properties, but how it is likely to operate "on the ground" in the historical and socio-political context in which it is being embedded.

Much of the attraction of modern electoral engineering formulae arises from claims that they might provide mechanisms for (1) challenging the power of vested interests and/or the elite; (2) mitigating ethnic tension or promoting moderation; and/or (3) forcing aspiring parliamentarians to keep their promises or reduce corruption. Yet these are political tasks, which are unlikely to succeed unless popular support can be mobilized behind them. Furthermore, electoral systems may also matter in ways that differ from those envisaged by their architects—as we saw when we considered the history of electoral reform in Fiji. Also, we would emphasize that "the devil is in the details." Rules that seem identical when viewed in terms of their large-scale properties may operate quite differently from one another when we consider more fine-tuned details. These details include such things as the nature of the candidate selection process, the number of seats per constituency, and, for preference-based rules such as the alternative vote and STV, whether complete rankings of all preferences must be submitted. Still, despite these important caveats, electoral systems do matter. They do have important direct and indirect impacts on voter loyalties, alliances, and coalitions, party strategy, and the composition of legislative chambers.[32] Political culture is not "everything."

Notes

Table 1 is taken from Bernard Grofman and Robert Stockwell, "Institutional Design in Plural Societies: Mitigating Ethnic Conflict and Fostering Stable Democracy," in *Economic Welfare, International Business and Global Institutional Change,* edited by Ram Mudambi, Pietro Navarra, and Giuseppe Sobbrio (New York: Edward Elgar Publishers, 2003).

1. A much different, singly authored version of the first half of this paper was presented at the "Conference on Democracy in the Twenty-first Century: Prospects and Problems," University of Illinois, Urbana-Champaign, October 2004. The discussion of Pacific Island states in the second half of the paper draws heavily on the insights of participants at the conference "Political Culture, Representation, and Electoral Systems of the South Pacific" in July 2004, organized by the second author of this chapter, sponsored by the University of the South Pacific and held on its Vanuatu cam-

pus. It also draws heavily from the paper presented at that conference, and expands on ideas in Fraenkel and Grofman (2005). We are indebted to Peter Nardulli for a number of specific editorial suggestions, to an anonymous reviewer for some ideas about structuring our arguments, and to Clover Behrend-Gethard for bibliographic assistance. The first-named author is indebted to helpful discussions over the years with his long time co-authors/co-editors/friends Rein Taagepera, Arend Lijphart, and Chandler Davidson, but the views expressed are solely those of the authors.

2. In some countries, however, while electoral details are not fixed, there may be constitutional language about a "principle" of proportionality.

3. Following Williams (2003) and the work of other sociologists, we use the term "ethny" or "ethnic group" to designate groups that are viewed both by themselves and by nongroup members as having a defined identity that allows members of the group to be clearly distinguishable from other citizens in terms of genotype, or phenotype, or language, or religion, or other cultural markers. Nations with more than one ethny but in which ethnic differences have been minimized in importance are commonly referred to as *pluralistic*. In contrast, *deeply divided* societies are those where politics is organized largely or entirely along ethnic lines, and two or more ethnies compete for power at the center of the political system. Of course, individuals may have multiple ethnic identities and part of the political struggle will be to determine which of these becomes the most politically salient (see e.g., Posner 2004, 2005).

4. Here we paraphrase Grofman and Stockwell 2003.

5. See Tideman 2000 for a consideration of alternative methods for this purpose.

6. Other early important work on electoral system effects includes that of Giovanni Sartori (see esp. Sartori 1968) and Stein Rokkan (see esp. Rokkan 1968).

7. The *threshold of exclusion* is the *maximum* support that can be attained by a party while still failing to win even one seat in a district; the *threshold of representation* is the *minimum* support that can be attained by a party while winning at least one seat in a district (Loosemore and Hanby 1971).

8. See also Boix 1999.

9. The discussion here is adapted from Grofman and Stockwell 2003. See also Sisk 1996.

10. Cf. Collier and Hoeffler 2002.

11. Unfortunately, much of the literature suffers from inadequate awareness of the difficulty of measuring ethnic cleavages and/or from circularity. The conflicts may fuel the perceptions of ethnic difference. For example, Somalia was often considered ethnically homogeneous until it collapsed; from then onwards, it was categorized as hyper-fractionalized.

12. In its classic articulation, Seymour Martin Lipset (1959, 75) writes, "The more well-to-do a nation, the greater the chances that it will sustain democracy." The mechanism proposed is that high levels of wealth provide resources that mitigate the tensions produced by political conflicts. Also, economic development brings about

higher rates of literacy and education, urbanization, and the development of mass media, factors conducive to democracy. A large number of empirical studies have generally supported Lipset's thesis (Diamond 1992; Lipset 1994). The strength of the association led Robert Dahl (1971, 65) to conclude that it is "pretty much beyond dispute" that the higher the socioeconomic level of a country, the more likely that it would be a democracy," but recent work has suggested the need to restate this claim as: "If a rich country becomes democratic, it is likely to stay that way." Moreover, recent work by various scholars (e.g., Przeworski et al. 2002; Boix and Stokes 2003) has suggested the need for important modifications of the argument about the impact of wealth to reflect factors such as the tax base of the state and the nature of resource distribution. Indeed, unpublished work by one of the present authors (Grofman) on this topic argues that the degree of inequality in the distribution of wealth (and related factors such as high levels of citizen literacy) are far more important in predicting sustainable democracy than mean GDP per capita, per se. Such results help explain some otherwise puzzling cases of unsuccessful democracies, as well as why oil-rich Arab countries are not democracies despite high *average* wealth.

13. The present authors are rather less certain of this point.

14. See Levine and Roberts 2005. These nations exhibit both a wide range of electoral system choices and a wide range of levels of democratization and of inter-ethnic harmony. While we briefly consider whether the cultural distinctiveness of these societies implies that modes of representation drawn from Western practices are undesirable, space considerations prevent more than touching on other important topics, such as spillover effects of past cultural practices into new institutions ("old wine in new bottles"); and the way in which both cultural practices and situational realities affect both institutions chosen and how they work once in place ("political embeddedness").

15. The Borda rule requires voters to rank-order their choices. In each voter's preference ranking of the alternatives, one point is awarded to an alternative for each choice to which it would be preferred. For each alternative, these points, summed over all voters, give us the *Borda count* of that alternative. The *Borda rule* is to pick the alternative with the highest Borda count.

16. SNTV has been abandoned in Jordan and Japan, but continued to be used in Taiwan (see Grofman et al. 1999) until its use was ended very recently; it has recently been adopted in Afghanistan. In SNTV elections, each voter has one vote and the candidates with the most votes win, just as in plurality, but there is more than one legislator elected from each district. Thus, SNTV, although sometimes called a semi-proportional system, can be viewed as operating as a type of proportional method, with its threshold of exclusion the same as the most common form of list PR, the D'Hondt method.

17. The *alternative vote* is the single transferable vote restricted to single seat election. Thus the quota is one half (see the preceding note), and this procedure will operate analogously to a majority runoff. Indeed, in the United States the alternative vote is known as the "instant runoff."

18. See further discussion of Fiji and PNG below.

19. *Matai* is often translated as "chief," although the expression "chief" means very different things across the Pacific. In Samoa, many adult males (but very few women) carry matai titles, whereas Tongan nobles are very much a minority in the population.

20. For many long-time observers of the South Pacific, the important issue is not finding new ways to institutionalize customary authority. Rather, it is that the conduct of contemporary elected Melanesian politicians and prime ministers is unworkably modeled on the customary feast-giving "big man," thus diverting assets and financial resources from the state into the dispensing of personal favors to associates, clients, and clan folk.

21. Among the *ceteris* that would need to be *paribus* would be suffrage eligibility and turnout levels across ethnies (Brace, Grofman, Handley, and Niemi 1988).

22. In a particular polity, some consociational features, e.g., group autonomy and minority veto, may not be desired by any of the various ethnies. It is critical to distinguish between imposed and voluntary/negotiated forms of power sharing.

23. The debate between Horowitz and Lijphart parallels an earlier and still ongoing debate about whether it is best for political compromises to take place at the constituency level (by choosing rules that will make it more likely that ideological moderates will be elected) or in the legislature itself (with the legislature intended to be a microcosm of the society, mirroring the full range of political viewpoints, including extreme ones).

24. Relatedly, various authors (e.g., O'Leary et al. 1993; Reynolds 1999) familiar with the use of the single transferable vote in Northern Ireland have argued for its use in preference to list forms of PR. The single transferable vote, in addition to opening up the possibility of proportional representation of an ethny's voting strength, also has been posited by some scholars to provide incentives for cross-ethnic choices by voters and the formation of cross-ethnic pre-electoral alliances by parties.

25. "The idea uppermost in the voter's mind when he considers the candidates of other races is which one is likely to help his racial group most, so that instead of erasing the racial outlook it will intensify it. Every race will be looking for the stooge or puppet from other communities who is likely to help their race" (A. D. Patel, NFP leader, cited in *Pacific Review,* Aug. 25, 1965, p. 7). The Alliance lacked "in any district the chance of creating a firm base for continuing interaction between a leader and his community. Trying to achieve rapport with Indians through Indian parliamentarians elected on national seats with Fijian support and utilizing them in building a party with an ardent Indian following was like attempting to build an edifice roof first" (Ali 1977, 195). This author, Ahmed Ali, was one such MP. He was an Indo-Fijian parliamentarian regularly elected by ethnic Fijian voters in the Lau noncommunal constituency.

26. We will only briefly summarize the story here (see Fraenkel 2001, 2003; Fraenkel and Grofman 2006)

27. At the close of counting in August 2001, it had obtained two seats, but one was reversed on appeal, after a recount and a determination of invalid votes.

28. For Fiji, one of us, Fraenkel, has suggested that an MMP system with a mix of single-seat constituencies and proportional representation ought to be preferred to pure-list PR.

29. See Punnett 1987, Jansen 2004.

30. Papua New Guinea Electoral Commission (1983, 78; cited in Reilly 1996, 45).

31. However, as Ron May (2004) shows, using ballot box data from a portion of PNG, even under the about-to-be-replaced plurality system, victors apparently do successfully widen their support across regions. It is rather the losers whose support is confined to own-clan. Also by-elections under the new system have already occurred, and do seem to show evidence of cross-village alliances.

32. We can illustrate this point with a few examples from the South Pacific. For one, there can be no doubt about the effect of Tonga's appointment-based institutions in propping up the monarchy. Under Samoa's *matai*-only system, political power remains closely tied to the customary hierarchy. Electoral laws in French Polynesia and New Caledonia, including recently the requirement that party lists alternate men and women (the parity law), have ensured that the French territories have the highest share of women members of parliament in the region.

References

Alesina, Alberto. 1994. "Political Models of Macroeconomic Policy and Fiscal Reforms." In Stephan J. Haggard and Steven B. Webb, eds., *Voting for Reform: Democracy, Political Liberalization, and Economic Adjustment*. New York: Oxford University Press. 37–60.

———. 1995. "Elections, Party Structure, and the Economy." In Jeffrey Banks and Eric Hanushek, eds., *Modern Political Economy*. London: Cambridge University Press. 145–70.

Ali, A. 1977. "The Fiji General Election of 1977." *Journal of Pacific History* 12 (3–4): 189–201.

Arms, David. 2004. "The Alternative Vote System in Fiji—Options for the Future." Paper presented at conference on "Political Culture, Representation, and Electoral Systems in the Pacific." University of the South Pacific, Port Vila, Vanuatu, July 10–12.

Arrow, Kenneth J. 1962. *Social Choice and Individual Values* (1st ed., 1951). New York: John Wiley and Sons.

Bangura, Y. 2004. *Ethnicity, Inequality, and the Public Sector: A Comparative Study*. Geneva, Switzerland: United Nations Research Institute for Social Development (UNRISD).

Birchfield, Vicki, and Marcus M. L. Crepaz. 1998. "The Impact of Constitutional Structure and Collective and Competitive Veto Points on Income Inequality in Industrialized Democracies." *European Journal of Political Research* 34:175–200.

Bogdanor, V., and D. Butler, eds. 1983. *Democracy and Elections: Electoral Systems and Their Political Consequences*. Cambridge: Cambridge University Press.

Boix, Carles. 1999. "Setting the Rules of the Game: The Choice of Electoral Systems in Advanced Democracies." *American Political Science Review* 93 (3): 609–24.

Boix, Carles, and Susan Stokes. 2003. "Endogenous Democratization." *World Politics* 55 (July): 517–49.

Bollen, K. A., and R. Jackman. 1985. "Political Democracy and the Size Distribution of Income." *American Sociological Review* 50:438–57.

Bowler, Shaun, and Bernard Grofman, eds. 2000. *Elections in Australia, Ireland, and Malta under the Single Transferable Vote.* Ann Arbor: University of Michigan Press.

Brace, Kimball, Bernard Grofman, Lisa Handley, and Richard Niemi. 1988. "Minority Voting Equality: The 65 Percent Rule in Theory and Practice." *Law and Policy* 10 (1): 43-62.

Buchanan, James M, and Gordon Tullock. 1962. *The Calculus of Consent: Logical Foundations of Constitutional Democracy.* Ann Arbor: University of Michigan Press.

Campbell, I. 2004. "The Quest for Constitutional Reform in Tonga." Paper presented at conference on "Political Culture, Representation and Electoral Systems in the Pacific." University of the South Pacific, Port Vila, Vanuatu, July 10–12.

Collier, Paul, and Anke Hoeffler. 2002. "On the Incidence of Civil War in Africa." *Journal of Conflict Resolution* 46 (1): 13–28.

Colomer, Joseph, ed. 2004. *Handbook of Electoral System Design.* New York: Palgrave.

Cox, Gary. 1997. *Making Votes Count: Strategic Coordination in the World's Electoral Systems.* New York: Cambridge University Press.

———. 2000. "Rational Choice Models in Electoral Studies: Coordination, Persuasion, and Mobilization." Prepared for delivery at the Eighteenth World Congress of the International Political Science Association. Quebec City, Canada, August 1–5.

Crepaz, Marcus M. L. 1996a. "Consensus vs. Majoritarian Democracy: Political Institutions and their Impact on Macroeconomic Performance and Industrial Disputes." *Comparative Political Studies* 29:4–26.

———. 1996b. "Constitutional Structures and Regime Performance in 18 Industrialized Democracies—A Test of Olson's Hypothesis." *European Journal of Political Research* 29:87–104.

———. 1998. "Inclusion vs. Exclusion: Political Institutions and the Welfare State." *Comparative Politics* 31:61–80.

———. 2001. "Veto Players, Globalization, and the Redistributive Capacity of the State: A Panel Study of 15 OECD Countries." *Journal of Public Policy* 21 (1): 1–22.

Crepaz, Marcus M. L., and Ann Moser. 2004. "The Impact of Collective and Competitive Veto Points on Public Expenditures in the Global Age." *Comparative Political Studies* 37:259–85.

Crocombe, R. 2001. *The South Pacific.* Institute of Pacific Studies, University of the South Pacific: Suva, Fiji.

Dahl, Robert. 1971. *Polyarchy: Participation and Opposition.* New Haven: Yale University Press.

Davidson, Chandler, and Bernard Grofman, eds. 1994. *Quiet Revolution in the South: The Impact of the Voting Rights Act, 1965–1990*. Princeton: Princeton University Press.

Diamond, Larry. 1992. "Economic Development and Democracy Reconsidered." *American Behavioral Scientist* 35:450–99.

Downs, Anthony. 1957. *An Economic Theory of Democracy*. New York: Harper & Row.

Farquharson, Robin. 1969. *Theory of Voting*. New Haven: Yale University Press.

Filippov, Mikhail, Peter C. Ordeshook, and Olga Shvetsova. 2004. *Designing Federalism: A Theory of Self-Sustainable Institutions*. New York: Cambridge University Press.

Fraenkel, Jon. 2001. "The Alternative Vote System in Fiji; Electoral Engineering or Ballot-Rigging?" *Journal of Commonwealth & Comparative Politics* 3 (2): 1–31.

———. 2003. "Electoral Engineering and the Politicisation of Ethnic Frictions in Fiji." In S. Bastian and R. Luckham, eds., *Can Democracy Be Designed? The Politics of Institutional Choice in Conflict-Torn Societies*. Institute of Development Studies, Sussex: Zed Books.

———. 2004. "Electoral Engineering in Papua New Guinea: Lessons from Fiji and Elsewhere." *Pacific Economic Bulletin* 19 (1): 122–33.

Fraenkel, Jon, and Bernard Grofman. 2004. "A Neo-Downsian Model of the Alternative Vote as a Mechanism for Mitigating Ethnic Conflict in Plural Societies." *Public Choice* 121:487–506

———. 2005. "Editors' Introduction: Minisymposium on Electoral Systems and Democracy in the South Pacific." *Commonwealth and Comparative Politics* 43 (3): 261–75.

———. 2006. "Does the Alternative Vote Foster Moderation in Ethnically Divided Societies?: The Case of Fiji." *Comparative Political Studies* 39 (5): 623–51.

Ghai, Y. 1983. "The Making of the Independence Constitution." In P. Larmour and S. Tarua, eds., *Solomon Islands Politics*. Suva, Fiji: Institute of Pacific Studies, University of the South Pacific.

Grofman, Bernard. 1982. "For Single-Member Districts, Random Is Not Equal." In Bernard Grofman, Arend Lijphart, Robert McKay, and Howard Scarrow, eds., *Representation and Redistricting Issues*. Lexington, Mass.: Lexington Books 55–58.

———. 1999. "Preface: Methodological Steps toward the Study of Embedded Institutions." In Grofman et al., *Elections in Japan*. ix–xvii.

———. 2004. "Rein Taagepera's Approach to the Study of Electoral Systems." *Journal of Baltic Studies* 35 (2): 167–85.

Grofman, Bernard, Sung-Chull Lee, Edwin Winckler, and Brian Woodall, eds. 1999. *Elections in Japan, Korea, and Taiwan under the Single Non-Transferable Vote: The Comparative Study of an Embedded Institution*. Ann Arbor: University of Michigan Press.

Grofman, Bernard, and Arend Lijphart, eds. 1986. *Electoral Laws and Their Political Consequences.* New York: Agathon Press.

———, eds. 2002. *The Evolution of Electoral and Party Systems in the Nordic Countries.* New York: Agathon Press.

Grofman, Bernard, and Andrew Reynolds. 2001. "Electoral Systems and the Art of Constitutional Engineering: An Inventory of the Main Findings." In Ram Mudambi, Pietro Navarra, and Giuseppe Sobbrio, eds., *Rules and Reason: Perspectives on Constitutional Political Economy.* New York: Cambridge University Press. 125–63.

Grofman, Bernard, and Robert Stockwell. 2003. "Institutional Design in Plural Societies: Mitigating Ethnic Conflict and Fostering Stable Democracy." In Mudambi et al., *Economic Welfare.* 102–37.

Gudgin, G., and P. J. Taylor. 1979. *Seats, Votes, and the Spatial Organisation of Elections.* London: Pion.

Hannan, Michael T., and Glenn P. Carroll. 1981. "Dynamics of Formal Political Structure: An Event-History Analysis." *American Sociological Review* 46:19–35.

Horowitz, Donald L. 1985. *Ethnic Groups in Conflict.* Berkeley: University of California Press.

———. 1991a. "Ethnic Conflict Management for Policymakers." In Montville, *Conflict and Peacemaking.* 115–30.

———. 1991b. "Making Moderation Pay: The Comparative Politics of Ethnic Conflict Management." In Montville, *Conflict and Peacemaking.* 451–76.

———. 1993. "Democracy in Divided Societies." *Journal of Democracy* 4 (4): 18–38.

———. 1997. "Encouraging Electoral Accommodation in Divided Societies." In Brij V. Lal and Peter Larmour, eds., *Electoral Systems in Divided Societies: The Fiji Constitutional Review.* Canberra: Australian National University Press.

———. 2000. "Constitutional Design: An Oxymoron?" In Ian Shapiro and Stephen Macedo, eds., *Designing Democratic Institutions, Nomos XLII.* New York: New York University Press. 253–84.

Jansen, Harold. 2004. "The Political Consequences of the Alternative Vote: Lessons from Western Canada." *Canadian Journal of Political Science* 37 (3): 647–69.

Johnston, R. J., F. M. Shelly, and P. J. Taylor, eds. 1990. *Developments in Electoral Geography.* New York: Routledge.

Kaima, Sam. 2004. "'Bigman' and 'Cult' Legacies Continue: Villager Perceptions of Elections in Markham Open." Paper presented at conference on "Political Culture, Representation, and Electoral Systems in the Pacific," University of the South Pacific, Port Vila, Vanuatu, July 10–12.

Katz, Richard S. 1980. *A Theory of Parties and Electoral Systems.* Baltimore: Johns Hopkins University Press.

Larmour, P. 1994. "A Foreign Flower: Democracy in the South Pacific." *Pacific Studies* 17 (1): 45–77.

Levine, Stephen, and Nigel Roberts. 2005. "Proportionality in Paradise? A Comparative Evaluation of the Electoral Systems of the South Pacific." *Commonwealth and Comparative Politics* 43 (3): 276–95.

Lijphart, Arend. 1968. *The Politics of Accommodation: Pluralism and Democracy in the Netherlands.* Berkeley: University of California Press.

———. 1969. "Consociational Democracy." *World Politics* 21 (2): 207–25.

———. 1977. *Democracy in Plural Societies: A Comparative Exploration.* New Haven: Yale University Press.

———. 1984. *Democracies: Patterns of Majoritarian and Consensus Government in Twenty-One Countries.* New Haven: Yale University Press.

———. 1991. "The Power Sharing Approach." In Montville, *Conflict and Peacemaking.* 490–510.

———. 1992. *Parliamentary versus Presidential Government.* Oxford: Oxford University Press.

———. 1994. *Electoral Systems and Party Systems: A Study of Twenty-Seven Democracies, 1945–1990.* Oxford: Oxford University Press.

———. 1996. "The Puzzle of Indian Democracy: A Consociational Interpretation." *American Political Science Review* 90 (2): 258–68.

———. 1999. *Patterns of Democracy.* New Haven: Yale University Press.

Lijphart, Arend, and Bernard Grofman, eds. 1984. *Choosing an Electoral System.* New York: Praeger.

Linz, Juan, and Arturo Valenzuela, eds. 1994. *The Failure of Presidential Democracy.* Baltimore: Johns Hopkins University Press.

Lipset, Seymour Martin. 1959. "Some Social Requisites of Democracy: Economic Development and Political Legitimacy." *American Political Science Review* 53:69–105.

———. 1994. "The Social Requisites of Democracy Revisited." *American Sociological Review* 59:1–22.

Loosemore, John, and Victor J. Hanby. 1971. "The Theoretical Limits of Maximum Distortion: Some Analytic Expressions for Electoral Systems." *British Journal of Political Science* 1:467–77.

May, Ron. 2004. "Why Do Winning Candidates Win in Papua New Guinea Open Elections? Looking at Data from Angoram." Paper presented at conference on "Political Culture, Representation, and Electoral Systems in the Pacific." University of the South Pacific, Port Vila, Vanuatu, July 10–12.

Montville, Joseph, ed. *Conflict and Peacemaking in Multiethnic Societies.* Lexington, Mass.: Lexington Books.

Mudambi, Ram, Pietro Navarra, and Guiseppe Sobbrio, eds. *Economic Welfare, International Business, and Global Institutional Change.* New York: Edward Elgar Publishers.

Muller, Edward N., and Mitchell A. Seligson. 1994. "Civic Culture and Democracy: The Question of Causal Relationships." *American Political Science Review* 88 (3) (Sept.): 635–52.

Okole, Henry. 2002. "Institutional Decay in a Melanesian Parliamentary Democracy: Papua New Guinea." *Development Bulletin* 60:37–40.

O'Leary, Brendan, Tom Lyne, Jim Marshall, and Bob Rowthorn. 1993. *Northern Ireland: Sharing Authority.* London: Institute for Public Policy Research.

Patterson, D. 2004. "Customary Chiefs in Vanuatu's Electoral Politics." Paper presented at the conference on "Political Culture, Representation, and Electoral Systems in the Pacific." University of the South Pacific, Port Vila, Vanuatu, July 10–12.

Persson, Torsten, Gerard Roland, and Guido Tabellini. 2000. "Comparative Politics and Public Finance." *Journal of Political Economy* 106:1121–60.

Persson, Torsten, and Guido Tabellini. 1999. "The Size and Scope of Government: Comparative Politics with Rational Politicians." *European Economic Review* 43:699–735.

———. 2000. *Political Economics: Explaining Economic Policy.* Cambridge: MIT Press.

Posner, Daniel. 2004. "The Political Salience of Cultural Difference: Why Chewas and Tumbukas Are Allies in Zambia and Adversaries in Malawi." *American Political Science Review* 98 (Nov.): 529–45.

———. 2005. *Institutions and Ethnic Politics in Africa.* New York: Cambridge University Press.

Powell, G. Bingham, Jr. 1982. *Contemporary Democracies: Participation, Stability, and Violence.* Cambridge, Mass.: Harvard University Press.

Przeworski, Adam, Michael E. Alvarez, Jose Antonio Cheibub, and Fernando Limonge. 2002. *Democracy and Development: Political Regimes and Material Well-Being in the World, 1950–1990.* New York: Cambridge University Press.

Punnett, R. M. 1987. "The Alternative Vote with Optimal Use of Preferences: Some Irish Lessons for Britain and Australia." *Journal of Commonwealth and Comparative Politics* 25 (1): 26–43.

Rabushka, Alvin, and Kenneth A. Shepsle. 1972. *Politics in Plural Societies: A Theory of Democratic Instability.* Columbus, Ohio: Merrill.

Rae, Douglas. 1967. *Political Consequences of Electoral Laws* (2d ed., 1971). New Haven: Yale University Press.

Reeves, P., T. Vakatora, and Brij V. Lal, eds. 1996. *Report of the Fiji Constitutional Review Commission: The Fiji Islands—Towards a United Future.* Suva, Fiji: Parliamentary Paper 34.

Reilly, Ben. 1996. "The Effects of the Electoral System in Papua New Guinea." In Y. Saffu, ed., *The 1992 Papua New Guinea Election: Change and Continuity in Electoral Politics.* Canberra: Australian National University. 43–76.

———. 1997. "The Alternative Vote and Ethnic Accommodation: New Evidence from Papua New Guinea." *Electoral Studies* 16 (1): 1–11.

———. 2001a. *Democracy in Divided Societies: Electoral Engineering for Conflict Management.* New York: Cambridge University Press.

———. 2001b. "Evaluating the Effect of the Electoral System in Post Coup Fiji." *Pacific Economic Bulletin* 16 (1): 58–94.

———. 2002. "Social Choice in the South Seas: Electoral Innovation and the Borda Count in the Pacific Island Countries." *International Political Science Review* 23 (4): 355–72.

Reynolds, Andrew. 1999. *Electoral Systems and Democratization in Southern Africa.* New York: Oxford University Press.

Reynolds, Andrew, and Ben Reilly. 1999. *Electoral Systems and Conflict Management in Divided Societies.* Washington, D.C.: National Research Council/National Academy Press.

Rokkan, Stein. 1968. "Elections: Electoral Systems." *International Encyclopedia of the Social Sciences.* New York: Crowell-Collier, Macmillan. 6–21.

Rose, Richard. 1984. "Electoral Systems: A Question of Degree or of Principle?" In Lijphart and Grofman, *Choosing an Electoral System. 73–81.*

Roughan, J. 2004. "Social Unrest and Electoral Institutions in the Solomon Islands." Paper presented at the conference on "Political Culture, Representation, and Electoral Systems in the Pacific." University of the South Pacific, Port Vila, Vanuatu, July 10–12.

Saari, Donald. 1994. *Geometry of Voting.* New York: Springer-Verlag.

———. 1995. *Basic Geometry of Voting.* New York: Springer-Verlag.

Sartori, Giovanni. 1968. "Political Development and Political Engineering." In J. D. Montgomery and Albert. O. Hirschman, eds., *Public Policy,* vol. 17. Cambridge, Mass.: Harvard University Press. 261–98.

Shugart, Matthew Soberg, and John M. Carey. 1992. *Presidents and Assemblies: Constitutional Design and Electoral Dynamics.* New York: Cambridge University Press.

Shugart, Matthew, and Martin Wattenberg, eds. 2001. *Mixed Member Electoral Systems: The Best of Both Worlds.* Oxford: Oxford University Press.

Sisk, Timothy. 1996. *Power Sharing and International Mediation in Ethnic Conflict.* Washington, D.C.: United States Institute of Peace.

Steeves, J. 1996. "Unbounded Politics in the Solomon Islands: Leadership and Party Alignments." *Pacific Studies* 19 (1): 115–38.

Taagepera, Rein. 1984. "The Effect of District Magnitude and Properties of Two Seat Districts." In Lijphart and Grofman, *Choosing an Electoral System.* 137–56.

———. 1999a. "Ignorance-based Quantitative Models and Their Practical Implications." *Journal of Theoretical Politics* 11 (3): 421–31.

———. 1999b. "The Number of Parties as a Function of Heterogeneity and Electoral Systems." *Comparative Political Studies* 32 (5): 531–48.

Taagepera, Rein, and Matthew Shugart. 1989. *Seats and Votes: The Effects and Determinants of Electoral Systems.* New Haven: Yale University Press.

———. 1993. "Predicting the Number of Parties—A Quantitative Model of Duverger Mechanical Effect." *American Political Science Review* 87 (2): 455–64.

Taylor, P. J., and R. J. Johnston. 1979. *Geography of Elections.* New York: Holmes & Meier Publishers.

Thomas, G. M., F. O. Ramirez, J. W. Meyer, and J. Gobalet. 1979. "Maintaining National

Boundaries in the World System: The Rise of Centralist Regimes." In J. Meyer and M. Hannan, eds., *National Development and the World System*. Chicago: University of Chicago Press. 187–206.

Tideman, Nicholas. 2000. "A Comparison of Improved STV Methods." In Shaun Bowler and Bernard Grofman, eds., *Elections in Australia, Ireland, and Malta under the Single Transferable Vote*. Ann Arbor: University of Michigan Press. 248–64.

Williams, Robin. 2003. *The Wars Within: People and States in Conflict*. Ithaca, N.Y.: Cornell University Press.

PART II

Technology and Democracy

Mass-Elite Linkages in the Twenty-first Century

6

Technological Advances and Individual Liberties

Privacy and the Reach of the State in the Twenty-first Century

WAYNE V. McINTOSH
AND STEPHEN A. SIMON

Privacy is a core component of a democracy, especially one whose governing structure is built upon notions of self-government and self-determination. Although the U.S. Constitution does not articulate it specifically as a corollary of democracy, individual privacy represents an important aspect of several rights itemized in the Bill of Rights; these include the freedoms of speech and religion, the privilege against self-incrimination, and protection against unreasonable searches and seizures by government authorities. Indeed, we generally understand a free and open society to be one in which each individual is granted autonomy to pursue his or her own personal interests and to develop and express his or her own conception of the common good without undue restriction. Moreover, meaningful decision making by the people lies at the heart of democratic self-government, and this requires a free flow of information between the government and the citizenry, as well as among the citizens themselves. According to the vision of the founders (see especially Madison's Federalist no. 10), individuals will naturally disagree and coalesce with others holding similar points of view. Thus, a republican form of governing fosters reconciliation of differences through a process of reasoned reflection and deliberation. A responsive and responsible government must convert the disparate preferences of the governed, expressed through elections and other means, into coherent public policies for the common good. A considerable stream of literature addresses these and related issues (e.g., Mills 1956; Dahl 1956; Schattschneider 1960; Lowi 1969; Delli Carpini and Keeter 1996; Lupia and McCubbins 1998; Macedo 1999).

Thus, a primary set of responsibilities of democratic government includes protecting individual integrity (including privacy interests) and providing mechanisms for free exchange of ideas and information. This assumes that individuals' policy preferences are fluid (rather than static) and are subject to change as new information is obtained, filtered, and absorbed. A second equally important bundle of government responsibilities includes providing for the general welfare and protection of national security.

Pubic policy must balance the need for free expression and exchange of ideas with providing for general protection and security. Resolving the tension between these primary functions of government represents an ongoing public policy challenge, in which information is a key ingredient. In a number of ways, free flow of information (in both directions between government and private sector, as well as between private individuals and institutions) is essential to a well-functioning democratic society. Indeed, all of the processes we associate with democracy—for example, representation of constituent interests by decision makers who are accountable for their actions, an informed citizenry free to express individual policy preferences and political beliefs, an unrestricted press—assume open information exchange. Similarly, free market economics, in which production and consumption decisions are rational, driven by efficiency and preference considerations, assumes that choices are informed ones. These considerations all place a premium on the free flow of information.

Enter technology. In order to make sound and informed decisions, both government and economic actors have always relied heavily on existing communications systems to accumulate and exchange essential information. Indeed, development of a fully functioning postal system that would connect everyone, no matter how distant and removed from the central and regional hubs, was among the first priorities of the new nation as the founders hoped to promote a cohesive society and growing economy (e.g., John 1995). Moreover, taking a census of the population, although somewhat intrusive on individual privacy (requiring an accounting of employment, housing status, number of children, and the like), is essential to useful public policy and good planning.

In at least two major ways, however, the government's demands concerning information give rise to ongoing tensions with the imperatives of constitutional democracy. First, government data aggregation may infringe upon individual privacy rights; second, the government's attempts to keep certain kinds of information secret may hinder democratic accountability. In this essay, we turn our attention to the ongoing inherent tensions created by the dual responsibilities of government—to obtain accurate and extensive information and to enhance individual privacy rights. We will be concerned particularly with the extent to which this tension is heightened by technological advances. Recent years have seen the development of information technologies that pose serious challenges to privacy. These technologies enhance not only the methods of information collection, but also the manner in which it is analyzed, stored, manipulated, and transmitted. At the same time, the horrific events of 9/11 have shifted anti-terrorism to the top of the public agenda and altered perceptions of the stakes involved in matters of domestic security. After briefly describing recent technological advances, we examine the existing privacy paradigm, relying heavily upon U.S. Supreme Court decisions. Indeed, judges, in the final analysis, are called upon to mediate inevitable conflicts. Within this context, we explore a range of issues that lie on the technology-privacy horizon.

Advanced Technologies and Privacy Concerns

Recent technological advances have considerable public appeal and provide significant benefits. The advantages apply to a wide spectrum of activities, from everyday commercial exchanges to the most serious concerns over health and safety. For example, the range of products and services purchased over the Internet is already significant, and is growing rapidly.[1] The storage of information by corporations, including, for example, specific detailed travel itineraries, purchasing trends, and product preferences, facilitates consumer transactions in general. The benefits of Global Positioning System (GPS) capabilities run from relatively frivolous conveniences—finding the closest coffee house—to assisting in the location of lost persons, stolen cars, and stray cattle (e.g., Anderson 2000). Aggregation of a person's medical records, quickly accessible to attending physicians from almost anywhere, holds the promise of a sounder approach to medical care and fewer surgery errors due to incorrect chart entries or miscommunication, and pharmacists can utilize a centralized database to minimize mistakes and adverse reactions. DNA testing may enable early treatment for medical conditions not yet outwardly manifested, as trends and correlations are best detected by assessment of data accumulated from large numbers of people over a period of time. By maintaining a close watch over our spending patterns, credit card companies can detect an unusual purchase and alert the cardholder to the possibility of theft. The installment of RFID (Radio Frequency Identification Technology) chips may allow us to purchase gasoline without fumbling for a credit card and pass through the toll both without having to stop—zipping by the Luddites stuck in an ancient ritual of long lines and manual coin-tosses. Cameras at the ATM make us feel safer withdrawing cash at night, and surveillance systems in convenience stores, subway stations, and trains have helped to identify criminals. In short, we experience life as easier and more secure in numerous ways thanks to recently developed technologies.

Many of the conveniences associated with advanced technologies depend on voluntary disclosure of information, important for both practical and legal reasons. The fact that information disclosures are voluntary, market-driven phenomena indicates robust demand and argues for continued investment in ever more sophisticated technologies. The pervasiveness of the Internet and other communication technologies, and their relentless diffusion throughout "high tech" societies, make it increasingly difficult to opt out without seriously downgrading one's social connectedness and lifestyle. From a legal perspective, voluntary disclosure limits the remedies available to those adversely affected by technology's encroachments into private spaces.

Voluntary information disclosure poses problems that were unforeseen in the early stages of privacy doctrine development. Among the most significant are expanded monitoring and surveillance activities and the databases created in the process. Credit card companies do not know that a particular purchase is unusual unless they monitor individuals' buying patterns. GPS technology can determine location at any given time and log the information for later reference. The supermarket chain discount card that provides coupons for future purchases also keeps a running record of consumption and brand preferences.

The storage of isolated bits of voluntarily disclosed information of the kind illustrated above may not, in itself, generate meaningful privacy concerns. How threatening, for example, is the digital encoding of the fact that a person passed through Massachusetts exit nine on Interstate 95–S on Saturday, May 9, at 9:12 p.m.? A privacy threat is more apparent, however, when the disparate data threads are connected to create a revealing personal profile. The rapidly advancing technology of digitization and relational databases facilitates data aggregation and analysis on a massive scale, thus presenting reasons for privacy concerns. The next two sections address the crucial questions of data collection and dissemination.

INTEGRATED DATA AGGREGATION

Development of relational database analytical software that allows merging of multi-sourced information was an important milestone in commercial technologies. Employing a model originated by Edgar F. Codd (1970), Larry Ellison and several associates marketed the first commercial software in the late 1970s and launched Oracle Corporation, a company that has pioneered the improvement and expansion of relational database management systems. This capability is particularly important to businesses, allowing information collected for differing purposes to be accessed by multiple users and cross-referenced to assess relationships among data housed in different archives. These tools are essential, for example, to compare and balance wholesale purchases, employee location and compensation records, and retail sales, each of which is typically collected independently and kept in different files. Integrating them allows greater efficiency and more rational decision making (see e.g., Rosen 2004, 108–17).

There is also a vast natural market for aggregated and cross-referenced information regarding consumption activities of individuals. A number of companies like Acxiom and ChoicePoint combine and organize information from a wide range of sources into individual preference profiles (e.g., Nissenbaum 2004, 121), and store them in electronic "warehouses" from which they can be analyzed and distributed for marketing purposes (Whitaker 2003, 55). Similar data-mining techniques have also become important tools in political fund-raising and election campaigns to identify a party's most likely supporters. Indeed, while the Republican effort has become legendary in its effectiveness, both parties used the approach to create individual voter profiles in the 2004 presidential campaign (the Republican program is called Voter Vault, and the Democrats' project is DataMart). Aggregating voter registration data, turnout information, and census data, the parties are able to pinpoint their concentrations of strength and vulnerability with a high degree of accuracy. In addition, these caches of voter profile data allow party operatives to identify undecided voters and map blocks of voters with specific issue preferences (Farhi 2004).

The breadth and depth of information that may be gathered and stored in such databases is staggering. Due largely to the growth of online activity and electronic forms of payment, individuals increasingly leave transactional digital markers relating to their financial and medical situations, travel and leisure activities, and many other aspects of their personal lives. In a recent interview with Jeffrey Rosen, Larry Ellison (CEO of Oracle) stated:

> The Oracle database is used to keep track of basically everything. . . . The information about your banks, your checking balance, your savings balance, is stored in an Oracle database. Your airline reservation is stored in an Oracle database. What books you bought at Amazon is stored in an Oracle datable. Your profile on Yahoo! is stored in an Oracle database. . . . We already have this large centralized database to keep track of where you work, how much you earn, where your kids go to school, were you late on your last mortgage payment, when's the last time you got a raise. . . . I don't understand [concerns about privacy]. Central databases already exist. Privacy is already gone. (Rosen 2004, 113)

Moreover, individuals often leave locational footprints evidencing their whereabouts and activities. ATM and credit card transactions are generally traceable to a specific location, and the evolution of increasingly sensitive tagging and tracking devices, including RFID chips and GPS, promises to escalate this trend. RFID chips, which can be attached to almost any object (including library books, store merchandise, automobiles, livestock, and even human beings, as in the case of conditionally released parolees) emit signals that can be picked up by scanners some distance away (Nissenbaum 2004). Many cell phones allow the service provider to track the location of the phone user. In recent years there has also been a significant increase in the use of surveillance cameras. For example, cameras have been installed to patrol red lights at busy intersections, and closed-circuit cameras monitor places of employment, commerce, parking lots, and the like.

Several recently developed programs demonstrate the expansive potential of surveillance technologies. In the wake of a violent incident in East Newark, New Jersey (approximate population, 2,000), for example, the locality installed enough surveillance cameras with rotating eyes to cover every street twenty-four hours a day (Whitaker 2003, 82–83). This kind of blanket approach to surveillance has been far more common in the United Kingdom as part of a larger strategy to deal with the challenges presented by Northern Irish separatists (Whitaker 2003, 83). The potential for combining the use of surveillance cameras with the technology of biometric identification (e.g., face-recognition programs) suggests an even greater capacity for tracking individuals as they go about their daily activities. In addition, the development of related technologies, such as DNA profiling and iris and brain recognition techniques, expands the potential for data aggregation from the bureaucratic and transactional to the biological.

As noted previously, any single bit of information about a person's activities and movements, in the hands of the company that originated it, may not be troubling. What alters the situation is database exchange and aggregation. A scattering of piecemeal gibberish, maintained as completely separated data entries, can be transformed into a very revealing individual life portrait when combined to create an electronic profile.

ACQUISITION OF INFORMATION BY "THIRD PARTIES" AND GOVERNMENT

The tension between technology and privacy is compounded by the potential that integrated databases will be marketed to third parties, including government. Indeed, companies like Acxiom collect and integrate data precisely for the purpose of distributing it to others for profit.

Individuals routinely provide private information under an assumption that it will be used only for legitimate purposes and without realizing that it may be redistributed to third parties (see generally, Nissenbaum 2004). Very often, consumers provide intimate data about themselves and their family members quite willingly, in exchange for something of small value, for sheer convenience, and in the interest of efficiency. For example, merchant discount cards are quite popular even though they associate us with our buying habits.

Convenience and efficiency come with a price—often trivial, but potentially very significant. Indeed, corporations already rely upon data collected from various sources to determine credit worthiness and reliability, as well as to identify potentially fraudulent purchases. Compounding the threat posed by the unauthorized dissemination of personal information is the fact that when these data are bought, sold, merged, and stored in multiple locations, they take on a perceived reality and permanence that can be very difficult to alter.

While the unauthorized dissemination of information in the private sector can cause injury, a unique set of concerns is raised by the possibility that information initially provided to private sector agents will find its way into the hands of government agencies. These concerns are magnified in a post-9/11 environment. Public officials are under considerable pressure to enhance domestic security, thus increasing their propensity to acquire information that might be useful in counter-terrorism activities. Indeed, the demands of responding to 9/11 spurred governmental agencies to begin utilizing a number of capabilities that previously had been largely untapped (Whitaker 2003, 56).

Government already maintains numerous databases in a variety of agencies, including the FBI, IRS, state DMVs, licensing boards, and agencies that maintain personnel files. Recent attempts to produce mega-databases as contemplated by the Total Information Awareness (TIA) program (e.g., Solove 2004)[2] render the prospect that information held by government agencies could be combined with privately gathered data a more likely scenario. Furthermore, the existence and prospective expansion of governmental eavesdropping activities, such as those represented by ECHELON,[3] Carnivore,[4] and the Bush administration's implementation of a warrantless wiretapping program,[5] serve as a reminder that data collection and aggregation may take place secretly and without knowledge of those under surveillance. Government has the ability to create its own aggregated database or, perhaps more easily, to purchase existing databases from the private sector. Once in possession of such a comprehensive information system, the government could also employ data-mining techniques for any number of purposes, including identification of possible terrorist threats.

Government agencies are already deploying these analytical techniques. From May 2003 through April 2004, the U.S. General Accounting Office (GAO) investigated data mining by 128 offices in the federal government.[6] For purposes of the study, the GAO defined data mining as "the application of database technology and techniques—such as statistical analysis and modeling—to uncover hidden patterns and subtle relationships in data to infer rules that allow for the prediction of future results" (U.S. General Accounting Office 2004). According to the GAO survey, 52 agencies reported that they are using or planning at least one such program, amounting to 199 in total. Of these, 131 were already underway, and 122 rely on personal information. The most commonly reported purposes for the programs include detection of fraud, waste, and abuse, increasing tax compliance, intelligence analysis, detection of criminal behavior, and uncovering terrorist activity. It is also notable that 54 of the programs obtain data from the private sector (such as credit reports or credit card transactions); of these 54, 36 involved personal information. Moreover, the survey revealed 77 projects by federal departments to mine data from other government agencies. Of these 77 projects, 46 included personal information such as student loan applications and bank account, credit card, and taxpayer identification numbers (U.S. General Accounting Office 2004).

These are technologies that the private sector has been developing for some time; only the scale and comprehensiveness of the venture are new. For example, HNC Software has created methods to wade through vast quantities of disparate information across independently archived databases, revealing both "normal" and "aberrant" trends. Consumer buying patterns are important to retailers so that they can efficiently target their customers. Wal-Mart reputedly used this approach to discover that customers, particularly young fathers shopping late at night, tend to buy a consistent combination of items. Thus, on the basis of observed correlations, they placed beer and diapers on adjacent shelves (Rosen 2004, 103). Moreover, HNC has determined that credit card thieves and deadbeat dads tend to follow discoverable patterns, information that might interest law enforcement. Indeed, the company has boasted that its technology is capable of discerning such things as unusual airline ticket purchases that could be of interest to anti-terrorist investigators (O'Harrow 2002).

Analytical mining of private-sector databases by government agencies is of particular concern for a number of reasons. Constitutional restrictions do not apply to the acquisition of information by private entities. This is true even though individuals may not realize that their disclosures to a private entity could find their way into a government database to be sifted for patterns that trigger closer assessment. Moreover, statutory restrictions on government's use of data obtained from the private sector are far from comprehensive. There is no all-inclusive law governing privacy and the use of commercial data. Without violating existing laws, government can acquire vast quantities of information either by simply purchasing it or through voluntary submission (Dempsey 2003, 2). Even when private agencies are not technically required to supply information to the government, they may feel pressured to do so when subjected to agency requests. Indeed, the USA Patriot Act (PL 107–56) authorized collection of a range of data, including financial records and even transaction data from public libraries. While a number of privacy laws restrict use of information by corporations, few apply to government. Nonetheless, even those that do restrict government use generally provide exceptions for sharing data with law enforcement and intelligence agencies (Dempsey 2003, 2). It should also be noted that there is nothing to stop government agencies from acquiring information through their own Internet searches (Dempsey 2003, 3).

Such activities present a range of concerns. Given the nature of data-mining techniques, there is a high likelihood of producing many false positives, thus misidentifying individuals as suspects. A common example is a simple Google web search. The search engine sifts through millions of sources, with results listed in order of likely relevance. But anyone who has used this approach knows that many "misses" are generally listed among the "hits." From a policy perspective, this, of course, is not an entirely new problem. Reliance upon jailhouse snitches and street informants is a proven risky proposition for law enforcement agents, and aggregation of more objectively reliable information is, on the whole, a positive development. However, in the current context of ongoing terrorist threats, a person's life can be devastated if it becomes publicly known that he or she is suspected of, or linked to, terrorism. The consequences can be severe, and the damage may be irreparable. Once errors become cyber-embedded, it can be exceedingly difficult to correct them. Redundancy is generally practiced to protect against any number of file-corruption possibilities. Moreover, databases are routinely bought, traded, and merged, thus making it very difficult to purge all records of an incorrect entry. Personal credit histories are notoriously problematic for this reason, often requiring seemingly endless and extraordinary effort to set the record straight. In any event, this kind of reputational injury cannot be undone easily, if at all.

The harrowing experiences of Mr. Rene Ramon Sanchez, long-time resident of the Bronx, illustrate the severe consequences that can result from such errors. Somehow the local police and federal agents misidentified Sanchez and associated the fingerprints of another man with him in their electronic databases. Sanchez was arrested a number of times in the 1990s and spent several weeks in detention for drug-related crimes actually committed by Leo Rosario. Sanchez brought legal action against the authorities for his troubles and obtained a court order in 2002 to have the records corrected so that he would no longer need to live under a cloud of suspicion and ongoing threat of arrest. Nonetheless, in spring 2004 Sanchez found himself in court once again, facing deportation proceedings, based on fingerprint evidence of continued criminal activities. Rosario, it seems, was a busy man. Charges were finally dropped on the spirited effort of Sanchez's attorney, who again sought complete correction of the electronic files. Sanchez's ordeal may not yet be over, however. In May 2004, when the Sanchez lawyer went back to court seeking a copy of his client's records, "a clerk began searching in the computer . . . but seemed confused by what came up. 'Are you looking for Mr. Sanchez,' she asked, 'or Mr. Rosario?'" (Weiser 2004).

Sharing of data among public agencies also poses the risk that information will be used for purposes that are entirely unanticipated and that transgress norms regarding government decisions. Although a particular agency is entitled to information about individuals' lives relevant to its functions, personal privacy is jeopardized when the same information (stock trades, international travel, bankruptcy, driver's licenses, charitable donation histories, and so on) is made available to other agencies with completely different functions. Indeed, the possibility for outright abuse or leaking of private information by government employees has already been manifested.[7]

In addition, advanced technologies also raise broader concerns about the kind of society in which we live. Is something important lost when people feel as if they cannot move about anonymously, have a pervasive sense of "being watched," or experience loss of control over personal information? Here, the aggregation of data is especially relevant. Advanced technologies enable database cooperatives to construct a frighteningly detailed portrait of an individual's life out of electronic markers he or she scatters about through the course of everyday activities. Awareness that the government is engaged in comprehensive data collection and profiling may prompt individuals to avoid innocent actions out of concern that they may at some point be tagged as suspicious.

Privacy Law and the Challenge of Technology Development

In order to place technology advances into the broader context of democracy, we assess the development of privacy as a constitutional issue. Although the right to privacy is not explicitly mentioned in the U.S. Constitution, the Supreme Court has repeatedly recognized that a number of provisions in the Bill of Rights protect individuals from overly intrusive actions by public authority. The Court did not always acknowledge the implications of new technologies, but by the middle of the twentieth century it had become clear that the implications could not be ignored. Moreover, the contemporary era is not the first in which technologies have triggered debate over privacy rights. Political leaders have often confronted questions over how to apply long-standing safeguards to newly developed investigative techniques; prominent examples include wiretaps, air surveillance of private homes, and remote sensing devices for detecting sources of heat. After a brief introduction, we consider a number of actions by the U.S. Supreme Court as the justices have attempted to balance individual privacy interests and responsible government in the face of rapidly developing technologies, particularly in the field of communications.

This tension was visible in the early republic, with issues arising as the nation's first communications system was put into operation. Many years before cell phones and e-mail were to become ubiquitous, the founders understood the social, political, and economic values of information collection and exchange. Not only did they provide for a regular census of population to permit rational policy and planning, but they also laid the groundwork for a total-coverage postal system, connecting people from distant locations and allowing them to communicate even at great distances. The first Post Office Act of 1792 prohibited postal workers from opening letters, reflecting the high regard Americans attached to privacy. Indeed, the policy was widely considered a significant improvement over the British and French systems, in which personal letters seemed to be fair game (John 1995). In practice, however, and despite legal restrictions to the contrary, the temptation to tamper with the mail was too great. Virtually every public figure complained at one point or another about opened mail, sent or received. "Thomas Jefferson was so disgusted with the frequency with which the contents of his supposedly private letters found their way into the opposition press, that he vowed in 1801 'never to write another sentence of politics in a letter'" (John 1995, 43; this was written in a letter to Madison!).

In a *Harvard Law Review* article published in 1890, Louis Brandeis and Samuel Warren worried over the privacy implications of photography, writing: "Instantaneous photographs and newspaper enterprise have invaded the sacred precincts of private and domestic life; and numerous mechanical devices threaten to make good the prediction that 'what is whispered in the closet shall be proclaimed from the housetops'" (Brandeis and Warren 1890, 195). Constitutionally based privacy rights, however, were largely limited by the traditional view that the Fourth Amendment applied only to physical intrusions on the "persons, houses, papers, and effects" explicitly protected from unreasonable searches and seizures. In considering the implications of new technologies (especially in photography and newspaper production), Brandeis and Warren emphasized the importance of expanding upon that notion, stating:

> That the individual shall have full protection in person and in property is a principle as old as the common law; but it has been found necessary from time to time to define anew the exact nature and extent of such protection. . . . In very early times, the law gave a remedy only for physical interference with life and property. . . . Later, there came a recognition of man's spiritual nature, of his feelings and his intellect. Gradually the scope of these legal rights broadened; and now the right to life has come to mean the right to enjoy life—the right to be let alone." (Brandeis and Warren 1890, 193)[8]

The influential article attracted significant attention and created the intellectual foundations for a more expansive construction of privacy rights. But those roots were slow in sprouting; decades would pass before a majority of the Supreme Court significantly broadened the scope of Fourth Amendment principles.

Development of the "Expectation of Privacy" Standard

Nearly thirty years later, Brandeis, by then a U.S. Supreme Court justice, was unable to persuade the Court majority to adopt his view of the Fourth Amendment's application to wiretapping. The 1928 case of *Olmstead v. U.S.* (277 U.S. 438) involved wiretaps in support of a Prohibition Era conviction for illicit alcohol trade. Roy Olmstead and his partners ran a large bootlegging operation between Seattle and Vancouver. Prohibition officers obtained evidence against Olmstead by tapping his office and home phones. Olmstead challenged his conviction on the grounds that listening to his phone conversations without a warrant constituted an unreasonable search and seizure. In the Court's view, however, no seizure had been effected, since the wiretap did not require an actual trespass on Olmstead's property. Writing for a 5–4 majority, Chief Justice Taft explained why no search or seizure had taken place:

> The evidence was secured by the use of the sense of hearing and that only. There was no entry of the houses or offices of the defendants. . . . The language of the [Fourth] amendment cannot be extended and expanded to include telephone wires, reaching to the whole world from the defendant's house or office. The intervening wires are not part of his house or office, any more than are the highways along which they are stretched. . . .
>
> The reasonable view is that one who installs in his house a telephone instrument with connecting wires intends to project his voice to those quite outside, and that the wires beyond his house, and messages while passing over them, are not within the protection of the Fourth Amendment. (277 U.S. at 464–66)

In his famous dissent, Justice Brandeis echoed themes from his 1890 privacy article and presented a prescient argument that resonates well in our contemporary technology-rich environment:

> The progress of science in furnishing the government with means of espionage is not likely to stop with wire-tapping. Ways may some day be developed by which the government, without removing papers from secret drawers, can reproduce them in court, and by which it will be enabled to expose to a jury the most intimate occurrences of the home. . . .
>
> The makers of our Constitution . . . recognized the significance of man's spiritual nature, of his feelings and of his intellect. They knew that only a part of the pain, pleasure and satisfactions of life are to be found in material things. They sought to protect Americans in their beliefs, their thoughts, their emotions and their sensations. They conferred, as against the government, the

> right to be let alone—the most comprehensive of rights and the right most valued by civilized men. To protect that right, every unjustifiable intrusion by the government upon the privacy of the individual, whatever the means employed, must be deemed a violation of the Fourth Amendment. (277 U.S. at 464–66, 478)

Justice Brandeis was not the only member of the Court who eloquently pleaded for a more expansive approach to reconciling the Fourth Amendment with advancing technology. In *Goldman v. U.S.,* 316 U.S. 129 (1942), for example, Justice Murphy argued that a seizure had occurred under the Fourth Amendment when police officers used a detectaphone device, enabling them to record the defendant's conversations through an adjoining wall without physically penetrating it. The majority refused to distinguish *Olmstead,* even though the seized conversation took place entirely within the house. In dissent, Justice Murphy stated:

> Insistence on [Fourth Amendment rights] does not mean that a person has anything to conceal, but means rather that the choice should be his as to what he wishes to reveal, saving only to the Government the right to seek out crime under a procedure with suitable safeguards for the protection of individual rights. . . . The conditions of modern life have greatly expanded the range and character of those activities which require protection from intrusive action by Government officials if men and women are to enjoy the full benefit of that privacy which the Fourth Amendment was intended to provide. (316 U.S. 129, at 137–38)

The arguments of Brandeis, Murphy, and others notwithstanding, it would be nearly forty years after *Olmstead* before the Supreme Court significantly expanded its interpretation of the Fourth Amendment to accommodate technologically enhanced searches and seizures. Like *Olmstead, Katz v. U.S.,* 389 U.S. 347 (1967) concerned the privacy of telephone conversations. But this time the question involved the constitutional status of conversations in a public telephone booth. The defendant used the phone booth to place an illegal $300 wager, and the contents of the conversation were obtained by FBI agents with an electronic listening and recording device placed on an exterior wall of the booth. The Court could have applied the *Olmstead* rule to decide the case. The defendant was not at his home but in a public station, and the agents had not intruded into his physical space to record his conversation. Indeed, the parties in the case had focused their arguments on whether the phone booth was a constitutionally protected area. The Court, however, declined to frame the case around that question.

Justice Stewart, writing for the Court, concluded that the Fourth Amendment "protects people not places" (389 U.S. 347, at 351). The defendant did not forfeit his Fourth Amendment rights simply because he ventured outside his home; the protections apply as well to "an individual in a business office, in a friend's apartment, or in a taxicab" (389 U.S. 347, at 352). The justices found that it was essential to take into account the implications of evolving methods of communication. Thus, when a person "shuts the door behind him . . . [he] is surely entitled to assume that the words he utters into the mouthpiece will not be broadcast to the world. To read the Constitution more narrowly is to ignore the vital role that the public telephone has come to play in private communication" (389 U.S. 347, at 352). The Court also effectively overturned *Olmstead* in holding that the defendant was justified in relying on the privacy of his conversation. The justices concluded that the FBI agents had violated the defendant's privacy and had unconstitutionally conducted a "search and seizure" under the Fourth Amendment without a warrant (389 U.S. 347, at 353).

In a brief concurring opinion, which must rank as one of the most influential concurrences per word in the judicial annals, Justice Harlan elaborated upon the Court's view with a formulation still central to Fourth Amendment jurisprudence: "My understanding of the rule that has emerged from prior decisions is that there is a twofold requirement, first that a person have exhibited an actual (subjective) *expectation of privacy* and, second, that the expectation be one that society is prepared to recognize as reasonable" (389 U.S. 347, at 361; emphasis added).

Voluntary Disclosures and the Expectation of Privacy

Although *Katz* was crucial in freeing Fourth Amendment jurisprudence from the confining *Olmstead* rule, it did not begin to address all of the issues relating to privacy rights and technology advancements. Indeed, an observation by Justice Stewart foreshadows what has become a central difficulty in this area of law: "What a person *knowingly exposes to the public,* even in his own home or office, is not a subject of Fourth Amendment protection. . . . But what he seems to preserve as private, even in an area accessible to the public, may be constitutionally protected" (389 U.S. 347, at 351; emphasis added). Stewart's proviso regarding what a person *knowingly exposes to the public,* while never easy to interpret and apply, has taken on added significance in light of the technological developments discussed earlier.

Voluntary disclosure was central to *U.S. v. Miller,* 425 U.S. 435 (1976), in which the pivotal issue was whether a search or seizure had actually occurred. The defendant was found not to have any "Fourth Amendment interest" in the copies of checks and other bank records that federal agents had obtained from his bank. Mitchell Miller had come under suspicion of operating an illegal moonshine business in Georgia, and of writing checks from two bank accounts to purchase his supplies. Both banks complied with a Bureau of Alcohol, Tobacco, and Firearms subpoena upon the banks to obtain Miller's account records, but neither informed Miller about any of the proceedings. Upon conviction on several charges, Miller moved to suppress the account information, arguing that the subpoena amounted to an illegal search and seizure, and thus an improper violation of his privacy.

Miller specifically advanced the argument that he maintained a reasonable expectation of privacy in his financial records—even after he disclosed them to the bank—because he had made them available to the bank for only a limited purpose. The Court, however, rejected that argument. By conveying information to a third party, a person forfeits the Fourth Amendment interests in privacy attached to it, and assumes the risk that the third party will make the data available to others, including the government.

In dissent, Justice Brennan took issue with the majority's view concerning voluntary relinquishment of information. For Brennan, the fact that the defendant knowingly made records available to the banks should not be determinative: "For all practical purposes, the disclosure . . . of . . . financial affairs to a bank is not entirely volitional, since it is impossible to participate in the economic life of contemporary society without maintaining a bank account" (425 U.S. 435, at 451). Brennan also emphasized the troubling implications of the majority's view in light of the wide range of personally revealing records that bank depositors routinely turn over to third parties:

> In the course of such dealings, a depositor reveals many aspects of his personal affairs, opinions, habits and associations. Indeed, the totality of bank records provides a virtual current biography. While we are concerned in the present case only with bank statements, the logical extension of the contention that the bank's ownership of records permits free access to them by any police officer extends far beyond such statements to checks, savings, bonds, loan applications, loan guarantees, and all papers which the customer has supplied to the bank to facilitate the conduct of his financial affairs upon the reasonable assumption that the information would remain confidential. (Ibid.)

Justice Brennan's reasoning spotlights the implications of the *Miller* Court's approach. As we noted earlier, individuals willingly (but often unknowingly) provide a wide range of information to third parties in today's electronic society. How far does the notion reach that once disclosed to any third party, individuals lose all expectations of privacy in information? *Smith v. Maryland,* 442 U.S. 735 (1979), answered that question with respect to phone call data. In that case, Baltimore police authorities asked the telephone company to install a pen register to record the numbers called from Michael Lee Smith's residence. Although no warrant had been issued, the data were then used to indict and convict Smith of rape and robbery. Smith argued that the pen registry evidence should be suppressed, but a closely divided U.S. Supreme Court found that no "expectation of privacy" is associated with the electronic trail we leave as we make telephone calls.

Writing for the five-member majority, Justice Blackmun concluded that neither prong of the "expectation of the privacy" standard was satisfied. That is, individuals held neither subjective nor objectively reasonable expectations of privacy in regard to such data. Individuals have no expectations of privacy, Blackmun reasoned, because they are aware that they convey contact information to the telephone company, which has the ability to record and store the numbers permanently.[9]

The failure of the High Court's jurisprudence to keep pace with advancing communications technology is highlighted by a 2001 federal district court case involving online communications.[10] In *Hambrick,* the defendant had adopted a false screen name to keep his identity private. After observing his incriminating behavior in a chat room, an undercover police detective obtained a state subpoena, which he served on the defendant's Internet Service Provider (ISP), seeking identifying records. The district court confronted the question of whether the manner in which law enforcement had obtained information revealing Hambrick's identity had infringed upon his Fourth Amendment privacy rights.

Judge James H. Michael Jr.'s decision turned on the principle enunciated in *Katz, Miller,* and other cases—one forfeits Fourth Amendment protection relating to private information with voluntary disclosure to a third party. In this case, Judge Michael observed, the defendant had knowingly identified himself in communications with his ISP and thus had no reasonable expectation of privacy in the information (55 F. Supp. 2d 504, at 508–9). Although constrained by Supreme Court precedent, the judge in this case did not refrain from expressing his own view that the nature of online communications requires reconsideration of existing doctrine:[11]

> The court finds the defendant's implicit argument that certain information in cyberspace should be private requires careful consideration. Legal scholars and Congress have noted the ubiquity of cyberspace in the lives of all Ameri-

> cans. . . . The members of our society increasingly live important parts of their lives through the Internet. Cyberspace is a nonphysical 'place' and its very structure, a computer and telephone network that connects millions of users, defies traditional Fourth Amendment analysis. So long as the risk-analysis approach of Katz remains valid, however, this court is compelled to apply traditional legal principles to this new and continually evolving technology. In so doing, the court must deny Mr. Hambrick's motion to suppress. (55 F. Supp. 2d 504, at 508; citations omitted)

To be sure, the High Court has at times demonstrated its willingness to adapt Fourth Amendment doctrine to newly enhanced technology in the hands of law enforcement. In *U.S. v. Kyllo,* 533 U.S. 27 (2001), the Court held that the use of a thermal-imaging device to detect an indoor crop of marijuana plants amounted to an unlawful search. Writing for the Court, Justice Scalia stated: "It would be foolish to contend that the degree of privacy secured to citizens by the Fourth Amendment has been entirely unaffected by the advance of technology" (533 U.S. 27, at 33–34). The decision, however, turned on the fact that Mr. Kyllo's home was the focus of investigation and left untouched the principle under which Judge Michael felt so constrained in *Hambrick*—that voluntary disclosure of information to a third party relinquishes claims to Fourth Amendment privacy interests.

Voluntary Disclosure, Privacy, and the Technology Future

The information and communications revolution of the late twentieth and early twenty-first centuries is far-reaching, and it has clearly not run its full course. New breakthroughs continue to occur in computer power and speed, as well as technologies allowing the collection, transfer, retrieval, and analysis of vast quantities of disparate bits of information. At the same time, it is increasingly difficult to create an adequate legal standard to distinguish between information held entirely private and information made public through exposure to any third party, as individuals leave locational and transactional footprints virtually at every turn.

A sign of what may lie ahead came in fall 2004 when the FDA approved the marketing and use of a microchip for medical purposes (FDA 2004). The size of a grain of rice, the VeriChip, once implanted under the skin, stores a unique sixteen-digit verification number that can be detected with RFID technology. The number links to databases via encrypted Internet access. Used successfully for years to track the movement of livestock, zoo animals, and pets, the chip has been approved by the FDA for implantation in humans to facilitate quick and reliable access to medical histories. It does not take much imagination to understand what magnificent potential this technology promises, especially for emergency medicine. The chip can also be implanted into Alzheimer's patients and children so that, in combination with GPS satellite technology, their location at any given time can be pinpointed within a matter of feet. Similarly, it could be used to keep tabs on parolees and criminal suspects under house arrest.[12] The developer also suggests that the chip will someday replace identification cards and other "primitive" technology now used for security access to restricted buildings and facilities. The first known application of the technology was reported in the *Financial Times* in February 2006, noting that an Ohio company had recently implanted silicon microchips in two of its workers in a pilot project (Waters 2006). Individuals with implanted chips can be identified unobtrusively and quickly to allow entry to limited access areas and for other related purposes. Detractors argue that the chips represent an appalling potential threat to personal privacy (see e.g., Feder and Zeller 2004).

As these technologies are more deeply woven into the fabric of contemporary society, it is hard to imagine any personal information that will not be made accessible to another party. The pervasive and growing role of the Internet is also a major ingredient in the communications technology equation, as market forces largely push in the direction of greater disclosure of personal information in an online environment. Through a variety of means, including exchange of cookies,[13] for example, entities operating online can acquire information about anyone engaging in electronic transactions, services, and communications (Helms 2001, 293–300). Moreover, businesses have an obvious interest in establishing accounts with known individuals and in acquiring information relevant to credit worthiness and likely purchasing patterns. Consumers, meanwhile, are drawn to the conveniences associated with electronic services (ibid., 290). Those who advocate anonymous participation in online communities are immediately met with concerns about the implications for law enforcement and personal accountability (ibid.).

The reasoning in Justice Brennan's dissent in *Miller* is especially apropos on this point. As noted earlier, Brennan asserted that maintaining a bank account is not optional in contemporary society for anyone who wants to participate in economic life. Recent developments in online activity, as well as new devices like the VeriChip transponder, make the Court's current notion of voluntary disclosures and privacy expectations seem almost quaint, and at the very least, out of touch with contemporary reality.

Ongoing developments in communication and information technologies will require reconsideration of privacy rights. In his opinion in *Hambrick,* Judge Michael observed that: "The objective reasonableness prong of the privacy test is ultimately a value judgment and a determination of how much privacy we should have as a society" (55 F. Supp. 2d., at 506). It is precisely this question of "how much privacy we should have" that calls for reconciliation of long-standing rights with emerging technologies. In revisiting these questions, judges and other policy makers will need to take the measure of changing cultural realities. Given the expanding scope of electronic transactions and activities logged in digital databases, it is questionable whether the assumption of "voluntary disclosure" to third parties is truly valid. As Helen Nissenbaum argues, societal norms regarding what kinds of information we should reveal to whom are complex and often contradictory (Nissenbaum 2004, 119). The existing framework provides inadequate guidance to individual citizens, consumers, policy makers, and judges alike.

Statutory Responses to Privacy Concerns

This chapter has focused on privacy rights as articulated in the Supreme Court's Fourth Amendment jurisprudence. Naturally, statutes comprise another important element in the effort to reconcile privacy with advanced technology. Legislation, of course, can, and often does, provide greater privacy protection than that afforded by judicial interpretations of the Fourth Amendment.[14] Indeed, a number of privacy statutes operate precisely by extending protection to information even after it has been disclosed to at least one other party. These laws recognize that privacy involves not only the closely kept secret, but also extends to the notion of retaining some control over personal information even after it has been partially exposed (Dempsey and Rosenzweig 2004, 2–3).

Nevertheless, legislation can be repealed and is subject to swings in political contexts and public opinion. In addition to its impermanence, existing statutory law provides rather limited privacy protections. Congress has, thus far, approached privacy in a piecemeal fashion—each law enacted addresses only a narrow issue, leaving numerous loopholes (Keck 2002, 92) and many activities unprotected, including travel records, real estate information, magazine subscriptions, and club memberships, among others. Moreover, the gaps include cyberspace, where existing privacy laws have quite limited application (Dempsey and Rosenzweig 2004, 1), and data mining.[15] To compound matters, computer and other technologies are changing so rapidly (Helms 2001, 313), and the nature of the Internet itself is subject to such continuous alteration, that legislation is ill-suited for handling the myriad issues likely to arise (Keck 2002, 92).

Conclusion

The Information Age does not represent the first time new technologies have created direct challenges to personal privacy and triggered reassessment of how we conceive privacy rights. Indeed, the Supreme Court significantly updated its Fourth Amendment jurisprudence in light of new technologies relating to telephones and wiretapping when it considered *Olmstead* in 1928. Yet nearly four decades passed before the Supreme Court determined that a person might have a reasonable expectation of privacy in telephone conversations outside the home (*Katz* 1967). By any measure, this represents a serious lag time and, given the acceleration in development and marketing of new technologies, it is a pace that will repeatedly result in law and legal principles badly out of synch with relevant real-world activities.

Given the wide array of devices and tools that will define our life in the early twenty-first century, and the diversity of approaches to reconcile them with individual privacy concerns, it is important to analyze carefully the nature of the risks a proposed solution is designed to address. Clearly, technology provides significant benefits that define life in a modern and wealthy society, ranging from consumer convenience to individually appropriate health care. Measures designed to protect privacy must also take into consideration the possibility that restrictions could inhibit the beneficial potential of some important new devices.

Legislative attempts to enhance privacy are generally reactive and targeted at specific activities, such as financial transactions and medical records. Moreover, because the technology to warehouse and cross-reference information is increasingly available, electronic transfer knows no political or geographic boundaries. Indeed, access can occur easily from remote locations, leading some to argue that privacy issues must be addressed internationally (e.g., Bennet and Grant 1999; Bennett and Raab 2006; Wood 2006), perhaps as part of the international human rights regime. Demand for more extensive systems of surveillance, data collection, and relational analytical techniques have increased substantially since the events of 9/11. At the same time, demands from the private sector for faster and more efficient and comprehensive database technologies are ongoing, and consumer appetite for greater convenience is unquenchable. These all seem to be inevitable trends that are likely to define a series of new political and legal conflicts. As we have noted throughout this essay, privacy is a core concern of democratic liberty and these issues are likely to appear frequently on legislative and judicial agendas in the years ahead. In addition, the same technologies that enable government surveillance programs, allow greater reach and efficiency in the business sector, and drive consumer convenience provide advantages for some—but certainly not all. Such differential impacts have the potential to enhance current power structures and to create new fissures among and across populations (and nations), and they may well become the source for political conflict.

Notes

1. According to the Department of Commerce, retail e-commerce sales have increased from $5.3 billion in the fourth quarter of 1999 to $31.5 billion in the first quarter of 2007. Available online at http://www.census.gov/mrts/www/current.html (accessed July 5, 2007).

2. TIA was set up in 2002 under the direction of former national security advisor, John Poindexter, to collect data from all available public and private-sector sources and develop ways to analyze it. The objective was to create digital dossiers on individuals as a means of detecting and deterring terrorists. Congress became uneasy about the program and it was reorganized under a new name, Terrorism Information Awareness, and new direction.

3. ECHELON is a top-secret international project led by the National Security Agency in cooperation with parallel agencies in Canada, Australia, New Zealand, and the United Kingdom. The objective is reportedly to collect satellite, microwave, cellular, and fiber-optic communications around the world. Computers then sort through conversations, faxes, and e-mails, searching for keywords, which then trigger transcriptions by the intelligence agencies for further investigation.

4. Carnivore is a computer program designed by the FBI to sift and sort through vast quantities of electronic communications, including e-mail messages and chat room exchanges, identifying those of interest. For a full discussion of the project, see testimony of Donald M. Kerr, assistant director, Laboratory Division, FBI, before the United States Senate, Committee on the Judiciary, September 6, 2000, "Carnivore Diagnostic Tool." Available online at http://www.fbi.gov/congress/congress00/kerr090600.htm.

5. Months after the 9/11 attacks, President Bush, by presidential order, secretly expanded the surveillance authority of the National Security Agency, allowing it to monitor international e-mails and phone calls without a warrant, as would ordinarily be required for domestic spying. See Risen and Lichtblau (2005). U.S. District Judge Anna Diggs Taylor's ruling that the program violates the U.S. Constitution is on appeal to the Sixth Circuit Court of Appeals. *ACLU v. NSA*, 438 F. Supp. 2d 754 (ED MI, 2006). See Eggen and Linzer.

6. See U.S. General Accounting Office, "Data Mining."

7. See Dempsey and Rosenzweig (2004, 3–4). For example, Dempsey recounts a story of an LA Police Department officer who accessed official files to obtain information about celebrities that he then sold to tabloid magazines (at p. 3, n8).

8. Judge Thomas Cooley is credited with coining the phrase "right to be let alone" (Cooley 1888, 29).

9. Citing *Miller*, Blackmun further concluded that, even if individuals did have actual expectations of privacy in a registry of numbers called, they were not reasonable expectations, because the data are voluntarily revealed to third parties (442 U.S. 735, at 743–44).

10. *U.S. v. Hambrick*, 55 F. Supp. 2d 504 (W.D. Va. 1999), aff'd. 225 F.3d 656 (4th Cir. 2000), cert. denied, 531 U.S. 1099 (2001).

11. In a related development, the National Science Foundation, through its special Approaches to Combat Terrorism program initiative, has recently funded research by a computer scientist at Rensselaer Polytechnic Institute to develop tools that can effectively be deployed to conduct surveillance of online chat room activity, in which an estimated twenty-eight million people have participated (See Camtepe, Krishnamoorthy, and Yener 2004).

12. A number of states have programs that allow continuous satellite tracking of known sex offenders, and governments in Australia, Canada, and the United Kingdom, among others, are contemplating similar plans (e.g., Nellis 2005).

13. A cookie is a small data file that a Web site can place on a user's computer entirely unobtrusively and without the user's awareness when a site is visited, to allow the Web site to store and retrieve data about that particular user. Some cookies also contain programs, such as a "web bug," that perform a variety of tasks and functions, retrieving ongoing information in communication with the Web site operator. See e.g., *In Re Pharmatrak, Inc. Privacy Litigation*, 329 F.3d 9 (lst Cir., 2003), which presented the Court with this very issue as a violation of privacy. Here, the cookie author, a Web site marketing research company, was interested in determining which Web surfers visited pharmaceutical sites seeking information about drugs, so that they could sell the information for targeted electronic advertising. The Court found that the activities probably violate the Wiretapping Act, and remanded the case for further study. Also see *In re Doubleclick Inc. Privacy Litigation*, 154 F. Supp. 2d 497 (S.D.N.Y., 2001), in which the district court found no violation of privacy rights in a similar case. DoubleClick ultimately settled, however, and ended its online profiling service.

14. E.g., Right to Financial Privacy Act of 1978, 12 U.S.C. §§ 3401–21 (with an aim towards limiting the holding in *Miller*, provides that banks not turn over records without a warrant and must alert the customer that her/his records have been requested); Cable Communications Policy Act of 1984, 47 U.S.C. 551 (2000); Driver's Privacy Protection Act of 1994, 18 U.S.C. 2721–25 (2000); Videotape Privacy Protection Act of 1988, 18 U.S.C. 2170 (2000); Health Insurance Portability and Accountability Act, (HIPPA), Pub. L. No. 104–91, 110 Stat. 1936 (1996).

15. At least one corporation, Global Information, has formed and has located itself in the Bahamas to avoid restrictions to protect privacy in the United States, with the express purpose of aggregating disparate data sets on citizens of multiple countries, which the company then plans to sell to the U.S. government and other interested parties (see e.g., O'Harrow 2004).

References

Anderson, Dean M. 2000. "The Cyber Cow Whisperer and His Virtual Fence." *Agricultural Research,* Nov., p. 4.

Bennett, Colin J., and Rebecca Grant, eds. 1999. *Visions of Privacy: Policy Choices for the Digital Age.* Toronto: University of Toronto Press.

Bennett, Colin, and Charles Raab. 2006. *The Governance of Privacy: Policy Instruments in Global Perspective.* Cambridge: MIT Press.

Brandeis, Louis D., and Samuel D. Warren. 1890. "The Right to Privacy." *Harvard Law Review* 4:193.

Camtepe, Ahmet, Mukkai S. Krishnamoorthy, and Bulent Yener. 2004. "A Tool for Internet Chatroom Surveillance." Available online at http://www.cs.rpi.edu/~yener/PAPERS/35.pdf (accessed Oct. 12, 2004).

Codd, Edgar F. 1970. "A Relational Model of Data for Large Shared Data Banks." *Communications of the ACM* 13 (6): 377–87.

Cooley, Thomas M. 1888. *A Treatise on the Law of Torts* (2d ed.). Chicago: Callaghan & Co.

Dahl, Robert A. 1956. *A Preface to Democratic Theory.* Chicago: University of Chicago Press.

Delli Carpini, Michael X., and Scott Keeter. 1996. *What Americans Know about Politics and Why It Matters.* New Haven: Yale University Press.

Dempsey, James X., and Paul Rosenzweig. 2004. "Technologies That Can Protect Privacy as Information Is Shared to Combat Terrorism" (May 26, 2004), http://www.cdt.org/security/usapatriot/20040526technologies.pdf.

Eggen, Dan, and Dafna Linzer. 2006. "Judge Rules against Wiretaps—NSA Program Called Unconstitutional." *Washington Post,* Aug. 18, p. A1.

Farhi, Paul. 2004. "Parties Square Off in a Database Duel: Voter Information Shapes Strategies." *Washington Post,* July 20, p. A1.

Feder, Barnaby J., and Tom Zeller, Jr. 2004. "Identity Chip Planted under Skin Approved for Use in Health Care." *New York Times,* Oct. 14, p. A1.

Helms, Shawn C. 2001. "Translating Privacy Values with Technology." *Boston University Journal of Science & Technology Law* 7:288.

John, Richard R. 1995. *Spreading the News: The American Postal System from Franklin to Morse.* Cambridge: Harvard University Press.

Keck, Matthew C. 2002. "Cookies, the Constitution, and the Common Law: A Framework for the Right of Privacy on the Internet." *Albany Law Journal of Science and Technology* 13:83.

Lowi, Theodore. 1969. *The End of Liberalism: Ideology, Policy, and the Crisis of Public Authority.* New York: Norton.
Lupia, Arthur, and Mathew D. McCubbins. 1998. *The Democratic Dilemma: Can Citizens Learn What They Need to Know?* New York: Cambridge University Press.
Macedo, Stephen, ed. 1999. *Deliberative Politics: Essays on Democracy and Disagreement.* New York: Oxford University Press.
Mills, C. Wright. 1956. *The Power Elite.* New York: Oxford University Press.
Nellis, Mike. 2005. "Out of This World: The Advent of the Satellite Tracking of Offenders in England and Wales." *Howard Journal of Criminal Justice* 44:125–50.
Nissenbaum, Helen. 2004. "Symposium: Technology, Values, and the Justice System: Privacy as Contextual Integrity." *Washington Law Review* 79:119.
O'Harrow, Robert, Jr. 2002. "Fed Super Database to Track Personal Travel Info." *Washington Post,* Feb. 1, p. A1.
———. 2004. "Bahamas Firm Screens Personal Data to Assess Risk; Operation Avoids U.S. Privacy Rules." *Washington Post,* Oct. 16, p. A1.
Risen, James, and Erich Lichtblau. 2005. "Bush Secretly Lifted Some Limits on Spying in U.S. after 9–11, Officials Say." *New York Times,* Dec. 15.
Rosen, Jeffrey. 2004. *The Naked Crowd: Reclaiming Security and Freedom in an Anxious Age.* New York: Random House.
Schattschneider, E. E. 1960. *The Semisovereign People: A Realist's View of Democracy in America.* Chicago: Holt, Rinehart and Winston.
Solove, Daniel J. 2004. *The Digital Person: Technology and Privacy in the Information Age.* New York: New York University Press.
U.S. General Accounting Office. 2004. "Data Mining: Federal Efforts Cover a Wide Range of Uses." Report to the Ranking Minority Member, Subcommittee on Financial Management, the Budget, and International Security, Committee on Governmental Affairs, U.S. Senate (May 2004).
Waters, Richard. 2006. "U.S. Group Implants Electronic Tags in Workers." *Financial Times,* Feb. 12. Available online at: http://www.ft.com/cms/s/ec414700-9bf4-11da-8baa-0000779e2340.htm (accessed Sept. 10, 2006).
Weiser, Benjamin. 2004. "Can Prints Lie? Yes, Man Finds to His Dismay." *New York Times,* May 31, p. A1.
Whitaker, Reg. 2003. "After 9/11: A Surveillance State?" In Cynthia Brown, ed., *Lost Liberties: Ashcroft and the Assault on Personal Freedom.* New York: New Press.
Wood, David Murakami, ed. 2006. *A Report on the Surveillance Society.* Surveillance Studies Network, Office of UK Information Commissioner. Available online at: http://www.privacyconference2006.co.uk.

Case References

ACLU v. NSA, 438 F. Supp. 2d 754 (ED MI, 2006).
Goldman v. U.S., 316 U.S. 129 (1942).
In re Doubleclick Inc. Privacy Litigation, 154 F. Supp. 2d 497 (S.D.N.Y., 2001).

In re Pharmatrak, Inc. Privacy Litigation, 329 F.3d 9 (lst Cir., 2003).
Katz v. U.S., 389 U.S. 347 (1967).
Olmstead v. U.S., 277 U.S. 438 (1928).
Smith v. Maryland, 442 U.S. 735 (1979).
U.S. v. Councilman, 373 F.3d 197 (1st Cir. 2004); rehearing *en banc* granted, 385 F.3d 793 (1st Cir., Oct. 5, 2004).
U.S. v. Hambrick, 55 F. Supp. 2d 504 (W.D. Va. 1999), aff'd. 225 F.3d 656 (4th Cir. 2000), cert. denied, 531 U.S. 1099 (2001).
U.S. v. Kyllo, 533 U.S. 27 (2001).
U.S. v. Miller, 425 U.S. 435 (1976).
Vernonia School District 47J v. Acton, 515 U.S. 646 (1995).
Wyoming v. Houghton, 526 U.S. 295 (1999).

7

Engineering Consent

The Persistence of a Problematic Communication Regime

W. LANCE BENNETT

In the early decades of the twentieth century, the emerging consensus among many elites, including public intellectuals such as Walter Lippmann, was that publics were so explosive and potentially threatening to national interests that governance required the new art of public relations to engineer consent. By the dawn of the twenty-first century, the evolved technologies for engineering consent have come to mediate most relations between elites and publics. Indeed, the national political communication apparatus has become thoroughly institutionalized and professionalized, with cadres of pollsters, image consultants, marketing specialists, and spin doctors attached to parties, candidates, and causes. These trends are most pronounced in the United States but are evident in other democratic systems (Blumler and Kavanagh 1999; Napolitan 2004). This chapter examines the arc of public communication processes over the last century with an eye to two broad questions about the present and future of political communication: What has this century-long institutionalization of highly managed public communication processes wrought for democracy? and, What are the democratizing prospects for new digital information and communication technologies to enable publics to communicate more independently of efforts by elites to manage election and policy discourse?

Engineering Consent: A Doctrine and Its Mixed Effects

It is easy to assume that sophisticated practices of political communication actually result in the engineering of consent, or, at least, in routinely influencing public opinion. Yet, in many cases, publics appear to form strong dispositions based on external factors (e.g., experienced shifts in peace, prosperity, and social stability) that seem immune to the best efforts of elites to shape perceptions to the contrary (Nardulli 2005; Zaller 2001). Many political scientists see election and public policy processes as being largely in tune with independent public preferences (Bartels 1991; Stimson 2004). What, in this view, is the effect of managed communication? Stimson (2004) argues that elite efforts at manipulation simply "update" inattentive citizens, which explains why "information terms" in statistical models often predict election results without incorporating data on communication campaigns. Yet, in other situations, such as the highly managed Bush administration selling of the Iraq War, opinion was substantially shaped by oft-repeated but poorly substantiated claims about weapons of mass destruction and alleged links between Iraq and the terror attacks of 9/11 (Entman 2004; Bennett, Lawrence, and Livingston 2007). Many other situations fall somewhere in between these extremes, with often staggering expenses on advertising and news management working at the margins to shift public responses. For example, Johnston, Hagen, and Jamieson (2004) show that based on externalities, the election of 2000 should never have been so close. They attribute the margin of the Bush vote to strategic advertising and news management choices on both sides.

Given this range of empirical results, it is not surprising that a lively academic debate has continued for decades over just how malleable publics really are. While this debate will surely continue, it is interesting that no side contests the degree to which the elite management of public discourse has become a doctrine of modern politics. Whatever its effects, communication management sets the tone for contemporary politics, resulting in many implications for democracy beyond its measurable effectiveness in shaping opinion. For example, the daily glimpses of politics and government offered up in the media are seen by media savvy audiences as contrived and often cynical efforts to fool at least some of the people some of the time. Jacobs and Shapiro (2000, xv) propose that the goal of most policy leaders is to "simulate responsiveness," or to create the "appearance of responsiveness" to their agendas by using polling and communication technologies to find "the most effective means to move public opinion closer to their own desired policies." They cite professional operatives, ranging from Frank Luntz (Republican architect of the Contract with America) to Dick Morris (erstwhile Clinton communication advisor), as advocating the use of polls not to reshape programs but to move public perceptions in line with desired policy outcomes (Jacobs and Shapiro 2000, xv).

Targeted audiences who are bombarded with strategic messages may end up confused, discouraged, tuned out, and, not infrequently, misinformed. Indeed, the collateral damages from the daily stream of managed political communication may include high levels of cynicism and disaffection in relations among press, publics, and leaders. The predominant popular perception is that contemporary politics is a game involving collaboration, distortion, and posturing between politicians and the news media. The result is a veil of public cynicism that has descended around politics, press, and government (Cappella and Jamieson 1997; Patterson 2000; Bennett 2005a). The declining levels of public trust and legitimacy also seem important to understand as communication effects. Similarly, the spiraling cost of communicating in this environment needs to be considered as another important effect of this regime of managed public communication. Taken together, both cynicism and the high price of communication restrict public voice and participation, while giving disproportionate salience to the messages that money can buy (Jamieson 2001; McChesney 2004). All of these democratic outcomes transcend specific situational effects of managed communication on opinion.

The ranks of professional communication managers are seldom preoccupied with collateral damage to public trust and civic engagement. They generally proclaim their immunity on grounds that their sole obligation is to help their clients win, period. Others can worry about democracy (Johnson 2001). Even if politicians do worry about how their public performances affect democratic life, their overwhelming reliance on scripted, one-way, managed communication models verges on a near religious faith. Politicians, and even many activists and cause advocates, believe that they cannot operate politically without the help of communication professionals. Being scrutinized and attacked by opponents when public performances run off script proves this conventional wisdom right. Even when they are not being attacked by opponents, public officials risk being savaged by the press if they fail to spin their cases well. As damage control has become the byword of elite-mass relations, alternatives to a public life involving less managed communication remain largely unexplored on the elite side of the democratic divide.

From a democratic standpoint, the formulaic strategies of public communication seem poorly suited to bringing people and their representatives into subtle or satisfying interaction. At the same time, increasing numbers of citizens are trying to circumvent this great wall of communication by using interactive digital technologies to create large-scale public networks for producing and distributing more credible and less dispiriting forms of political information and organization.

Communication at a Crossroads: Stealth versus Transparency

Those committed to top-down management of public debate have developed technologies to target right-sized populations of individuals who may be united only by their demographic traits. The result is the emergence of an increasingly stealthy communication process that may go under the radar of public debate by getting messages directly to individual recipients yet still contribute to an aggregation of individual-level political decisions (Howard 2006). Ironically, the diminution of public opinion as a social, genuinely public expression may not be missed by citizens, who may well prefer stealth democracy in all senses of that term (Hibbing and Theiss-Morse 2002). If most citizens lean in the direction of avoiding politics, and new technologies for managing political communication take much of the opinion mobilization process out of public view, then an important general effect of the evolution of managed communication may be to diminish the common bonds of citizenship (see Rahn 2008).

Countering these trends in elite-to-mass communication is the rise of grassroots digital communication networks organized by activists who wish to restore more visible and transparent communication to public life. This sharply diverging path involves new communication technologies that offer far more transparent, public, and interactive capacities for online deliberation, as well as "many to many" and bottom-up channels of communication. These "net roots" communication possibilities challenge the current managerial communication paradigm, from the war-room mentality of campaigns, to the endless polling, message marketing, and media monitoring practices of conventional public relations. The capacity now exists for open source software applications to enable large numbers of individuals to form networks to exchange ideas, search information databases, produce and share information, set news agendas, meet online and offline, deliberate, and interact with more centralized campaign and issue organizations. Examples include the rapid, large-scale organization of transnational demonstrations against world trade regimes and the Iraq war (Bennett 2005b), as well as the role of technology in the campaign of Howard Dean in the 2004 U.S. presidential primaries (Iozzi and Bennett 2003).

The development of such divergent, stealth versus transparent, digital communication capacities suggests that we are at a crossroads from which clear new directions in public communication practices may emerge. Which path will be taken? The current path dominated by coteries of professional communication consultants is not likely to be abandoned easily. Inertia (path dependence) exerts considerable force on parties, politicians, communication professionals, journalists, and information consumers. But as the current path grows rockier with the various indicators of exclusion and citizen dissatisfaction noted above, increasing numbers of citizens with access to new information and communication technologies are likely to explore the alternatives. Bottom-up communication initiatives, from citizen journalism to networked issue activism, may challenge the long-standing regime of managed, top-down public communication. Yet if citizens who seek to "reclaim the media" (as one reform organization is called) are to create dominant, many-to-many communication spaces in the public sphere, they must contend with the resistance of elites and practitioners who cling to the faith that their political success requires tightly controlled public relations and media performances.

Challenges Posed by a Managed Public Communication Regime

How has the doctrine of managed public communication become so tenacious and so potentially at odds with levels of citizen satisfaction and engagement in public life? It makes sense to think of the currently evolved collection of beliefs and practices regarding the management of public communication as a regime—that is, a normative system that has been reinforced at key junctures along its historical path by conventions and agreements among players (notably, politicians, communication strategists, and the elite press) who generally punish those who defect. Regimes can become so binding that they govern the behavior of actors, even when their personal preferences may not always coincide with the rules of the game. Witness the numbers of politicians and journalists who privately wish they could communicate and report in more spontaneous and transparent ways but who cannot find ways to do so.

Thinking of managed public communication as a normative regime may help explain why it has become so binding on political actors despite various signs of dysfunction, such as its mixed success at shaping opinion, its spiraling costs, and the growing dissatisfaction of citizens. Engineering consent in democracy is like other dubious but entrenched regimes, such as the cold-war nuclear defense regime of Mutually Assured Destruction (appropriately named MAD), in that the faith-based activities of inside players seem less functional the farther one moves away from the center of power. As regime dysfunction strains the values of the larger human system, pressures for regime change may increase. And so we witnessed the rise of nuclear disarmament and nonproliferation regimes. In the managed communication regime, growing public dissatisfaction has given rise to continued experimentation with bottom-up technologies, from weblogs to automated political networks, along with continued pressure for campaign finance reforms and the restoration of various public service media regulations (McChesney 2004).

Despite a public outcry for reforms, the central tenets of the regime hold because they are reinforced by myriad secondary conditions. In campaign reform, meaningfully restricting the flow of money would change things a good deal, but money literally talks, as Supreme Court rulings equate it with free speech. On another front, campaign communication formats could be changed by regulatory legislation. For example, why not limit or ban spots of ad-length communication, and require television license holders to provide free air time for longer messages? This will not happen as long as broadcasters lobby (and contribute) vigorously to protect their commercial formats and the fat profits they make from election ad buys. Even if the vast sums of campaign money end up buying little beyond droning sound bites, the cult of communication experts is there to assure clients that sound bites work on an inattentive public. As the infamous Dick Morris once observed, "There is literally no such thing as an idea that cannot be expressed well and articulated to today's voters in thirty seconds" (Bennett 2005a, 113). And so, candidates grub for money and isolate themselves from much meaningful contact with their followers by relying on professional managers who maintain that isolation by employing a war-room campaign model.

The exception that proves the rule of heavily managed, top-down electoral communication is the candidacy of Howard Dean in 2004. Dean took an early lead in the Democratic primaries through unconventional transparent communication methods, from blogs to encouraging self-organizing meetings of supporters. But Dean was eventually brought down, at least in part, through opposition research that his primary opponents fed to the press. The media damage from opponent spin was compounded by Dean's failure to develop a conventional communication strategy to manage the press effectively. Thus, the run-up to the Iowa caucuses saw a steady rise in stories implying that Dean was emotionally unstable (i.e., unscripted) and, thus, unelectable (Iozzi and Bennett 2003). The uniform journalistic editing and sound mixing of the infamous "Dean Scream" after his loss in Iowa provided the perfect ending to a well-spun press narrative. Dean's campaign also offers other lessons about the pressures to conform to the managed communication regime. Although he was late in adopting a conventional communication operation, Dean was in the process of doing so at the time of the fatal Iowa meltdown, according to Joe Trippi, who helped deploy the early grassroots interactive communication strategies. Trippi suggests that as Dean became more successful he encountered more pressure to adopt a conventional, war-room campaign model (Trippi 2004).

The evolution of this managed communication regime does not imply that publics are manipulated or duped. However, reframing issues and positions to fit popular predispositions turns out to be a somewhat different game (Jacobs and Shapiro 2000). Edelman (1964) sagely described the secret of symbolic politics as inducing quiescence, or acceptance, in publics that might otherwise challenge elite policy initiatives. Despite their often desultory effects on the democratic experiences of citizens, the norms of this communication regime offer a competitive defensive advantage for adherents. Much as advertising may have dubious effects, failure to advertise leaves one's product at the mercy of those who do.

Engineering Consent: The Origins of the Managed Communication Regime

How did such a strange communication system emerge in America? The story dates back to a time, roughly a century ago, when a lively public debate existed about how to best organize the flow of ideas, information, and citizen involvement in the American democracy. From those debates about what kind of public communication system best suited an emerging world power facing challenges at home and abroad, a remarkable consensus emerged on the part of many elites, who adopted what might be termed the *doctrine of engineered consent*. This doctrine owes its importance to many key figures and events, but it is indelibly associated with Edward L. Bernays (1928) as the chief architect, and Walter Lippmann as its often-conflicted intellectual legitimator. From these origins, a regime of managed public communication has evolved through the last century, taking on various forms as society, politics, and communication technology have changed.

As noted earlier, a consensus formed among elites that unmanaged publics were explosive and threatening to the interests of business and global expansion. The shocking experiences of the Paris Commune of 1870 were revived and linked to the rise of a militant socialist labor movement in the United States. One of the most popular authors of the day among business, intellectual, and political circles was Gustav Le Bon, whose book *The Crowd* would surely have had a long run atop the bestseller lists if they had existed in the early 1900s. Among Le Bon's *bon mots* was the notion that "the divine right of masses is about to replace the divine right of kings" (Le Bon 1969, 10). He followed this admonition with a bit of advice to elites: "It is only by obtaining some insight into the psychology of crowds that it can be understood how slight is the action upon them of laws and institutions, how powerless they are to hold opinions other than those which are imposed upon them, and that it is not with rules based on theories of pure equity that they are to be led, but by seeking what produces an impression on them and what seduces them" (Le Bon 1969, 13).

This view was vigorously contested in the widely read "muckraking" press that had launched prominent investigations of business and governmental corruption, labor abuses, food quality, and child welfare. The idea that people at the grassroots could have an independent voice in defining and solving the problems facing society was the watchword of early investigative journals, such as *McClure's Magazine*. In June of 1898, *McClure's* hit a circulation level of four hundred thousand per issue (Tarbell Archive 2004). Controlling for national population, this would put *McClure's* somewhere between the *New Yorker* and *U.S. News and World Report* in national circulation today. A January 1903 sellout issue of *McClure's* contained an installment of Ida Tarbell's celebrated investigation of the Standard Oil Trust, another of Lincoln Steffens's investigations of machine corruption in the nation's cities (Minneapolis), and a Ray Stannard Baker report on the plight of mine workers and business efforts to break their unions.

Journals such as *McClure's* and dozens of others set high standards for evidence, and for linking information to citizen and decision-maker actions in policy areas from municipal reform to trust busting. To put it mildly, this journalism challenged the idea that people should leave the representative work of democracy up to their elected officials, many of whom seemed at the time to work for party machines with corrupting ties to big business. Countering the emerging elite consensus that publics needed to be managed, Steffens and others raised grand questions such as: How might the people rule? and, Is democracy possible? (Ewen 1996, 60–61). None other than a young college graduate named Walter Lippmann responded to these calls in 1910 and signed on as a writer for *Everybody's* magazine, with Steffens as his mentor (ibid., 61).

The tone of this pivotal public debate quickly began to change when Theodore Roosevelt, a popular president and great reformer, criticized the grassroots press and citizen reformers as setting a negative tone that undermined the trust and credibility so necessary for business and government to operate. In a 1906 speech, Roosevelt stuck the then pejorative label "muckrakers" on the activist press and called for reform and restraint (Tarbell Archive 2004). It turns out that Roosevelt had long been a fan of Le Bon. When the two finally met in 1914, he told Le Bon that he had always kept a copy of his book at hand during his presidency (Ewen 1996, 65).

Walter Lippmann would soon become persuaded by Roosevelt's concerns, and he came to regard the rising tide of social activism as a threat to private property and political stability. He, too, came to see *the crowd* as needing mastery. The muckrakers contributed to growing instability and drift. Lippmann's new direction was signaled with the publication of *Drift and Mastery* on the eve of World War I. For the next several decades, he continued advising leaders and publics alike. To leaders, he advocated the use of social science to formulate policies and prevent the corruption of propaganda. To publics, he often lamented that these ideals were not met in communication practice, and that publics knew little of the world they witnessed through received authoritative images of it (Lippmann 1922).

The person most responsible for showing the way to creating those authoritative images was Edward L. Bernays, who brought the idea of Le Bon's crowd together with the thinking of Gabriel Tarde that crowds would be replaced by organized publics with the right cultivation of ideas (Bernays 1928). The laboratory for forging these ideas was World War I, which saw Bernays and Lippmann joined together with prominent journalists such as George Creel to form the Committee on Public Information under the guidance of that practicing political scientist Woodrow Wilson. This propaganda operation forged a national communication network to sell the war to a divided public who had been promised peace just the year before when Wilson ran for president. The success of this national campaign set a precedent for the positive uses of propaganda to engineer popular consent. Bernays saw the future of democracy in these early initiatives. He also saw that the manufacture of images could produce cynicism, but he concluded that no amount of cynicism would outweigh the basic need for individuals in agitated crowds to seek the comfort of reassuring illusions: "No matter how sophisticated, how cynical the public may become about publicity methods, it must respond to the basic appeals, because it will always need food, crave amusement, long for beauty, respond to leadership. . . . Propaganda will never die out. Intelligent men must realize that propaganda is the modern instrument by which they can fight for productive ends and help to bring order out of chaos" (Bernays 1928, 168).

The activist press soon died out through a combination of factors, including commercial pressures from advertisers to tone down political attacks on business and the economic distress of subscribers during the depression of the early century. Ultimately, the range of national political discourse was narrowed through the withering fire of business and government propaganda, combined with the silencing and de-radicalizing of labor and leftist party movements through the passage of the Espionage and Sedition Acts of 1918. The rise of a reformed, professional press in the 1920s completed the foundation for the managed communication regime that evolved through the rest of the century. As Ewen describes this formative moment, "This revamped vision of a public—a pliant and 'spiritual collectivity' bound together by the agency of newspapers—provided a suggestive counterpoint to the horrifying phantasm of the crowd. While antibusiness muckraking had clearly demonstrated that even a 'spiritual collectivity' might prove menacing to the status quo, the notion of a media-made public proposed other possibilities as well" (Ewen 1996, 72–73).

Two world wars and the specter of communism helped spread this view of governance through the ranks of opinion leaders, from prominent journalists such as Walter Lippmann, to national networks of moderate labor, religious, and civic groups, which formed Putnam's vision of the golden age of civil society and citizenship (Putnam 2000). What is interesting about the historical force of the idea of managing consent is that it has endured and evolved over the course of a century marked by important changes in the key institutions of media and society that affect the regime, including changes in political institutions (e.g., the rise of popular primaries, growing numbers of independent voters, the growing influence of interest groups), changing social structures (declining group memberships, the rise of a more fluid social network society), and the growth of a far more complex media system (decline of concentrated mass media channels, the resulting fragmenting of audiences, and the rise of a 24/7 news system with an insatiable appetite for spin). In other words, the practices associated with managing consent have continued to evolve and change as political institutions, social structures, and media systems have changed dramatically.

Yet the current incarnation of the regime presents a set of problems that have not been associated with past eras. As noted earlier, the most important individual-level communication effects may not be the degree to which public communication works well to forge opinions and cue citizen action (although such effects continue to be documented), but, rather, the degree to which managed communication formulas alienate and discourage citizens from participating in government and public life. The core question is whether the grassroots agitation for more transparent, personally engaging political communication processes can find some place within the still centralized and increasingly stealthy communication management regime.

Three Eras of Managed Communication

It should not be surprising that the organization of politics and society affects the communication practices between publics and leaders. The relationship is not deterministic, yet the core idea of engineering consent persists due to risk-averse choices supported by adaptive communication technologies. For example, a grand arc of social change and communication in the past half century is framed nicely by the work of Katz and Lazarsfeld (1955) and Mutz (1998). Katz and Lazarsfeld describe the importance of *personal influence* from opinion leaders in helping individuals interpret mass media messages from elites. Mutz documents the contemporary isolation of individuals from groups and political discussion, resulting in the *impersonal influence* of messages that are directly targeted to audiences and interpreted in relative social isolation. This arc of social and communication change can be described as a movement from a two-step (socially intermediated) to a one-step (direct) flow of messages in society (Bennett and Manheim 2006). Yet through all this change, the doctrine of engineering consent has held firm.

Tracing the historical adaptation of managed communication helps to integrate and organize different theoretical understandings about changes in media, society, and citizen engagement. For example, in their overview of the evolution of political communication in the Western democracies, Blumler and Kavanagh (1999) outline three ages of communication since World War II. They are, briefly: a party-centered era in which messages were cued heavily by party ideologies and group memberships; a mass media era in which messages from more sources reached fairly homogeneous mass television audiences; and the current era of highly professionalized communication in which media channels have proliferated, and professional consultants design formulaic communication campaigns to assemble fragmented publics. Bimber (2003, and in this book) takes an even longer look at the American political order in information terms. He argues that the first half of the twentieth century was organized by a vast pluralistic interest-group system that used information both to mobilize supporters and convince policy makers. He, too, claims that this system crumbled with the rise of mass media and its capacity to reach large audiences more directly at relatively low cost. Bimber argues that with the rise of digital information technologies in the 1990s, we have entered an era of information abundance in which individuals are less dependent on groups or mass media in forming interest networks.

Other analyses of social (audience) change converge on similar turning points in history:

- Putnam's (2000) association of civic decline with the fragmentation of particular kinds of social group memberships and the rise of television;
- Bennett's (1998) linkage of political identity and communication shifts to a broader set of social and economic changes flowing from globalization;
- Schudson's (1998) analysis of changing styles of citizenship that affect the importance of political information and how it is received and used;
- Swanson's (1997) observation of the rise of a political media complex spanning the last half century; and
- Patterson's (1993) linkage of the weakening of political parties and the rise of journalists as national communication filters dating from the late 1960s.

These and other works inform my attempt to identify the punctuating eras of modern American public communication. However, more so than many of the above authors, I am inclined to see the overriding continuity of a normative order through all of these eras of change. This continuity will, I hope, help us grasp the historical importance of the present era of strain that may challenge this venerable communication regime. In the following sections I briefly outline three broad eras in which the gold standard of engineering consent has taken very different forms, based on different communication practices, with different effects and levels of citizen engagement.

THE STRONG CIVIL SOCIETY ERA—TWO-STEP COMMUNICATION FLOW (1920S–1950S)

In this era, interest organizations and parties transmitted messages through social membership groups that cued individuals. This was the so-called minimal effects era of media studies, reflecting a different social order with different channels of communication reaching audiences, including the proliferation of messages in theaters, parades, and simultaneously coordinated local publicity events featuring respected social figures. The scholarly preoccupation with opinion formation as the defining indicator of media effects distracted attention from possibly more important regime impacts. For example, Walter Lippmann (1922) reminded us that the biggest effect of all was the hardest to measure: the elite screening and framing of information that removes potentially important data from public consideration. It is even more ironic that communication scholars labored over the minimal effects controversy for years after this era ended. It is now clear, however, that measurable communication effects accompanied the rise of a mass media and a fragmenting social order (Iyengar and Kinder 1987; Iyengar 1991).

THE GROUP DECLINE—MASS MEDIA ERA (1960S–1980S)

In this era, managed communication was redefined by a combination of political party electoral reforms and declining social group memberships, resulting in weakened social cueing and increasing reliance on getting media messages to mass audiences. The rise of a mass media with relatively few channels, along with national news programs, made journalists the mediators of the political process. This era saw the rise of a symbiotic relationship between press and government, in which mainstream news organizations coproduced the messages that enabled elites to reach large media audiences.

The saturation of society with television, alone, does not help us understand how communication became adapted to this medium, or what kinds of communication resonated with audiences who were beginning to pull away from what Putnam (2000) has described as the golden age of civil society. One significant communication development in this era emerges in Patterson's (1993, 2000) analyses of the decline of parties as communication sources and the rise of journalists as political interpreters of politics. Both the weakening of party communication and the fragmentation of civil society memberships put journalists in the position of being prominent and often direct communication links to large but socially disconnected audiences. This made journalists and political actors increasingly mutually dependent for accomplishing their different communication missions. The dependency between journalists and political communication sources resulted in the establishment of symbiotic relationships that defined the interactions between reporters and officials (Cohen 1963; Sigal 1973).

Since messages could no longer be cued predictably through social networks oriented to parties and ideologies, they needed to be crafted for delivery through journalists (and, increasingly, through advertising) to mass audiences. This initiated the rise of serious polling, message development, testing, and marketing operations of the sort that characterized daily communication practices in the Reagan administration (Hertsgaard 1988). These practices helped Reagan become the Great Communicator—a title bestowed on him, of course, by a well-spun national press corps. Swanson (1997) refers to this governing partnership between the press and political elites as the *political-media complex.* Cook (1998) describes the institutionalization of the press as mediator of national politics as constituting the fourth branch of government. This political communication apparatus was forced to adapt again, due to the rise of new communication channels from cable TV to the Internet that made mass audiences more difficult to reach and hold.

THE ISOLATED CITIZEN ERA—ONE-STEP FLOW OF COMMUNICATION (1990S–PRESENT)

This era is defined by increasingly independent individuals who avoid politics and the press, while dispersing as audiences in the proliferation of cable and digital media channels. As audiences become harder to reach, new technologies for targeting them have evolved (Turow 1997). Messages targeted at strategic demographic audiences are introduced into various communication channels, making the media an *echo chamber* in which the repetition of messages from different trusted outlets substitutes for the social reference and validation process of groups in the old two-step model. The symbiotic interdependence of officials and journalists begun in the last era is now managed by professional consultants.

This managed communication regime in this era is defined by the proliferating ranks of communication professionals deploying demographic targeting technologies and marketing logics that had been developed in product advertising over the past two decades. Not surprisingly, this became the age in which journalists and publics came to perceive politics as a strategic game, often devoid of substantive ideals, and aimed at swaying audiences to create impressions of support for leaders and policy positions (Capella and Jamieson 1997; Patterson 2000; Jacobs and Shapiro 2000). One observer referred to the institutionalization of product marketing and professional communication formulas in both political and journalistic circles as a "crisis of communication for citizenship" (Blumler 1997). This era introduced stealth communication technologies with the capacity to send messages directly to individuals whose responses can be monitored and added to growing databases of individual-level consumer and political preferences.

This current era of managed communication finds the citizen in relatively isolated social and media environments, surrounded by a professionally managed public sphere. Patterson describes post-9/11 America as bereft of spontaneous and interconnected civic life, with little for motivated citizens to do but fly the flag on their own:

> The organizations they might have joined fifty years ago are now run by professional managers, who solicit dues but do not invite active participants. The war in Afghanistan was fought by professional soldiers, the bioterrorism threat was relegated to professional scientists, homeland security was entrusted to professional law enforcement and intelligence officers. Even the appeal to sacrifice was missing. Americans were urged to keep spending, lest the economy sink. . . . The modern campaign, too, is a thoroughly professional operation. Voters have no expectation that they will be asked to do anything more than send a check and vote on election day. (Patterson 2003, 186)

For public officials and policy organizations in this system, the press becomes a surrogate public for whose attention (i.e., news space) political actors often desperately compete (Herbst 1998). Hiring teams of professional communicators is perceived by regime insiders as the only means to succeed in political contests. This system depends on the implicit cooperation of news organizations in reporting the well-crafted pronouncements of officials and interest organizations, while savaging those who fail to spin them well. The core political communication logic behind managing the public in this third era of the regime entails

- Developing messages through market research on targeted publics,
- Embedding them in news events, advertising, and other publicity, and
- Creating an echo chamber (e.g., news coverage of ads) that gives manufactured ideas the ring of conventional wisdom in a society where social reference is weak

Since sending communication through the one-step flow works best if the echo-chamber effect can be created and maintained, other elements of the managerial regime have evolved to include

- Constant repetition of a few simple messages—staying on message is thought to enhance attention and impact;
- Continuous assessment of market response (polling, focus groups, relaying personal canvass information back to databases);
- Constant refinement of the message mix and reinforcement through individual-level stealth communication that appeals to known dispositions of targeted demographics.

Since the press function has shifted from national interpreter to many points of retransmission (or dissonance) in the echo chamber, the rules of press management become brutally simple:

- Spin the media to accept a dominant message as a valid news story frame (the Iraq War weapons of mass destruction story is a classic example);
- Failure to spin effectively may result in being savaged by opponents and the press.

Politicians who drift from this regime are punished in the press—if not always in public opinion. The Clinton administration offers something of a natural experiment on this point. Its favorable press coverage rose, and then fell, with the entry and exit of David Gergen—yet Clinton's continuing approval ratings were generally buoyed by externalities. By contrast, the sudden demise of Howard Dean in the 2004 presidential primaries offers an illustration of the costs of poor press management. At the same time, the Dean campaign illustrates the potential for substantially different forms of public communication. The clash between the effective use of transparent, grassroots communication technologies and the centralized professional campaign communication operation that emerged toward the end of the Dean campaign reflects the central strain in the current era of the regime (Trippi 2004).

Strains in the Third Era of Managed Public Communication

The current era of the managed public communication regime is facing serious strains that may stimulate even greater changes than in past transitions. Regime change may be a more serious possibility than at any time in the past century. Journalism reviews and books by concerned practitioners discuss the crisis in news organizations fed by commercial pressures, loss of audiences, and drift on the part of managers who have little sense of how to adjust the relations between news organizations, investors, consumers, and public responsibility (e.g., Kovach and Rosenstiel 1999). Social scientists talk about the drift of voters from parties, deteriorating news, and the generalized public antagonism toward politics (e.g., Patterson 2003).

From the standpoint of the public communication regime, all of these factors result in growing difficulties in reaching citizens with top-down messages, whether in elections or issue campaigns. Ironically, these developments further drive communication into the hands of professional consultants, whose formulaic stamp on public communication has become clear. Political news often focuses on communication itself, with reports on elite communication strategies, image battles, war-room conflicts, accounts of provocative ads, and public responses to communication campaigns. The media increasingly covers itself—perhaps out of a realistic sense that what passes through the echo chamber is the core stuff of politics in the present era. All the while, audiences continue to drift away.

In this communication system, advertising may become more important than news, and campaign ads are often amplified as they are reframed in news coverage. The so-called Swift Boat ads that questioned John Kerry's war record in the 2004 presidential campaign became echoed widely in the news, carrying their ad messages to far larger numbers than ever saw the original ads, and adding the legitimating context of news frames. Such communication patterns raise concerns about what the role of journalists should be.

The costs of communication in this system present another source of strain involving public access, political influence, and who is included in, and excluded from, national political discourse. Television advertising and related communication costs in the 2004 campaign for all offices were estimated at $1.6 billion, more than twice the amount spent in 2000 (McDermott and Drinkard 2004). The off-year election of 2006 topped $2 billion, as the parties struggled fiercely for control of Congress. All of this occurred after a serious round of campaign finance legislation, raising questions about the capacity for reform on the part of those who have learned to use this communication system to their political advantage (Rutenberg 2004).

What may be lost in the hand-wringing about the costs of communication in the third era of the regime are the strange effects of the marketing process on citizens. For those who are targeted to receive messages, the repetition of those messages in hotly contested campaigns may be nothing short of deadening. Meanwhile, the majorities who are not targeted are essentially left out of the democratic communication loop. The Wisconsin Advertising Project estimates that 4,644 campaign spots were run in the Albuquerque, New Mexico, television market in a two-week period (Sept. 24–Oct. 7, 2004), a market that ranked second only to Miami for both Bush and Kerry campaigns. This means that over three hundred ads a day appeared on local channels (Wisconsin Advertising Project 2004). Meanwhile, if 2004 marketing patterns resembled those of 2000, fully half the potential voting audience never saw a campaign ad—except incidentally on the news or in outlets such as *The Daily Show* with Jon Stewart (Johnston, Hagen, and Jamieson 2004).

In keeping with our linkage between communication eras and social change, it makes sense to look for emerging patterns of social organization that may push new technologies and communication practices forward in attempts to address these strains. One does not have to look far to see the importance of technology-assisted social networking as a means for individuals to construct new political relationships in what Bimber (2003, and in this volume) calls the post-bureaucratic era of American politics. Perhaps more important, new information and communication technologies enable citizens to communicate outside of the fragmenting mainstream news system that has been an integral part of the managed communication process.

A Fourth Era of Managed Communication, or Regime Change?

The image of isolated individuals bombarded with all manner of simplistic one-step communication input does not sit easily alongside the trend that finds many individuals resisting their daily media feedings by forming social networks and sharing information across them. Bottom-up, networked communication technologies offer much more transparency in identifying other members of the network, and in identifying the producers of communication and their goals. Moreover, participants are able to opt in or out of these communication networks and actively contribute their own content to the information flow. Digital media networks come in many forms and sizes, including weblogs, which enable people to create content about issues or candidates and share it across large networks of linked information nodes that can be traveled or surfed at hyper-speed. See, for example, Blog for America, the transformation of the Howard Dean campaign weblog into a grassroots action network for Democratic candidates and progressive issues (http://www.blogforamerica.com/).

Other transparent social networking technologies are driven by even more spontaneous, or emerging, network engines, such as the Meetups network (www.meetups.com). Meetups was designed by Scott Heiferman and a group of friends who read Robert Putnam on social capital and decided they could design digital technologies to build social capital in the network society (Heiferman 2003; Meskill 2004). Meetups, and social technology platforms like them, enable people with common interests to find each other, meet face to face, and share records of their encounters across networks of often distant others. Meetups are held weekly in neighborhood locations (which often provide an income stream for the Meetups business model). The most popular Meetups in early 2003 included Elvis fans, Chihuahua owners, and car buffs. These networks were soon overshadowed by a burgeoning network of Howard Dean followers who found a relatively unknown candidate who spoke for their concerns about a war in Iraq.

Even as the proliferation of citizen-to-citizen communication networks grows, the managers of the ever-resilient engineering consent doctrine develop new capacities to identify and assemble their own large demographic information networks from increasingly fine-grained databases on individuals (Howard 2006). The Republican and Democratic parties have currently assembled individual-level databases on upwards of 160 million potential voters. The Republican "Voter Vault" boasts over three hundred pieces of information on many of those individuals (address, e-mail, income, voting histories, political issue concerns, shopping and lifestyle characteristics, and more). The Democrats claim to be going one better, by adding a second-tier database dubbed "Demzilla." Demzilla assigns key respondents from the core database to a strategic, networking database. Selection into the latter pool is based on information—such as their receptivity to particular appeals, whether they plan to vote, if they will write checks or otherwise work for party goals—derived from door-to-door contacts or telephone canvassers. Reports vary on the reliability of the code that generates these databases. But the evolving goal is to parse large individual-level information profiles to find collections of individuals who behave similarly enough to identify them as likely target-networks for political appeals (Howard 2006). Perhaps even more stealthy technologies lie in store, as government security initiatives monitor large volumes of individual communications sent through e-mail. The Bush administration's domestic eavesdropping program during the ongoing war on terror suggests the worrisome potential for large-scale monitoring of private communications, with serious implications for civil liberties.

Perhaps the defining difference between these stealth networks and more transparent communication networks is that, in many cases, individuals targeted by new generation communication management programs generally do not know when (or how) their consumer and political traces have been harvested for a database. Nor do they generally realize when, why, how, or with whom they have been assembled into a particular network. Yet, the proliferation of these *stealth* communication technologies represents one possibility for resolving some of the strains in the current communication system (e.g., lowering communication costs, finer matching of appeals to audience predispositions). At the same time, these developments may create new problems, such as the further reduction of active citizen engagement in the communication process, compounded with privacy issues. Indeed, stealth digital communication channels offer monitoring and feedback possibilities heretofore unseen in managed communication that travels through conventional media. Communication consultants working on new digital transmission and feedback software can now send e-mails (perhaps with animations or campaign ads embedded or linked) and record who opens them, what they do with them, to whom they are forwarded, and how those people respond (e-Voter 2003). The viral transmission of these messages provides a real map of the personal communication networks of targeted individuals that can then be used to adjust the database links and send more refined messages in the future. With most of these stealth communication technologies, individuals seldom know that they are providing feedback, or that their communications are being monitored.

Conclusion: Which Path for the Future of Public Communication?

By the end of the twentieth century, the evolved technologies for managing political communication had come to mediate most relations between elites and publics. The question for democracy in the new century is: Will the growing disillusionment with politics and the media force a regime change toward more transparent, citizen-to-citizen communication networks as organizational foundations for issue and electoral politics? It is doubtful that the regime will change easily from within, even though there is evidence that strategic communication produces few salutary democratic outcomes. Even if opinion management works in the short term, as in the case of selling the Iraq War, it can backfire badly when dissonant realities catch up with manufactured illusions. The cost of such disillusionment may be high in terms of trust in government and the media, both of which have spiraled downward since the early 1990s.

Rather than engineering broad consent, the technologies of strategic communication today often contribute to short-term symbolic victories, while creating collateral damage in terms of the epidemic levels of cynicism and disaffection in relations between publics, leaders, and the press. In addition, most marketing strategies leave large segments of the public out of the public communication process altogether, making exclusion from communication another kind of democratic effect (Turow 1997). The greatest irony of this system is that the audiences seem generally unhappy with what they hear, feeling variously excluded, deceived, bored, or overloaded. Moreover, most Americans blame the messenger for these problems. Most regard members of the press as filtering the news, and talking mainly to each other, as though they somehow constituted the public—which, in the eyes of politicians and their communication consultants, they do (Herbst 1998). Despite the many strains in the system, the goal of engineering consent in top-down communication strategies persists.

The key question facing the future of public communication is whether the inevitable growth of large, lower-cost digital communication networks will utilize stealth or transparent technologies. There is, of course, no reason why both technologies cannot continue to develop and be put into play, even complementing each other. Indeed, transparent communication technologies have become instrumental in organizing large-scale information and action systems in transnational protest networks (Bennett 2005b). However, in the arena of communication between citizens and elites, the top-down bias of the managed communication regime becomes something of a barrier to transparent technologies. This paradigm bias requires advocates of digital networking technologies to figure out how to use them alongside more conventional command-and-control communication strategies.

Thus, the key question for determining how the public communication system in America will develop from this juncture is this: Given the norms embodied in the long-dominant communication regime dedicated to engineering consent, how can technologies that enable more interactive, less centrally scripted public communication be brought into more prominent play in elections and policy contests? The uses of transparent technologies to raise money and mobilize voters in the 2004 election indicate that we will see more of them in the future. Yet stealth technologies seem to offer a quicker technological fix for some of the problems of audience fragmentation and high communication costs plaguing the current regime. Continuing path dependence would seem to favor stealth solutions even at the price of greater democratic dysfunction.

Thus, it is not surprising that stealth technologies are being deployed disproportionately by political elites via the professional consultants who work for them (Howard 2006). The results may be emotionally resonant in the short term for unwary citizens who find ever more personalized political messages showing up on their screens. But the public life of democracy may wither as communication becomes an endless appeal to *The Daily Me,* as Negroponte (1995) called the self-defined information service of the future. The speed, reach, and ever-lowering costs of these stealth technologies represent attractive alternatives for political consultants and their clients, but they also threaten to limit the broad public exchange of ideas as individuals become "a democracy of one."

Note

The author would like to thank Scott Althaus, Lew Friedland, and Peter Nardulli for their helpful comments on this essay.

References

Bartels, Larry M. 1991. "Constituency Opinion and Congressional Policy Making: The Reagan Defense Buildup." *American Political Science Review* 92:545–58.

Bennett, W. Lance. 1998. "The UnCivic Culture: Communication, Identity, and the Rise of Lifestyle Politics." *PS: Political Science & Politics* 31:741–61.

———. 2005a. *News: The Politics of Illusion* (6th ed.). New York: Longman.

———. 2005b. "Social Movements beyond Borders: Organization, Communication, and Political Capacity in Two Eras of Transnational Activism." In Donatela della Porta and Sidney Tarrow, eds., *Transnational Protest and Global Activism*. Boulder, Colo.: Rowman & Littlefield. 203–26.

Bennett, W. Lance, Regina G. Lawrence, and Steven Livingston. 2007. *When the Press Fails: Political Power and the News Media from Iraq to Katrina*. Chicago: University of Chicago Press.

Bennett, W. Lance, and Jarol B. Manheim. 2006. "The One-Step Flow of Communication." *The Annals* 608 (Nov.): 213–32.

Bernays, Edward L. 1928. *Propaganda*. Brooklyn: Ig Publishing.

Bimber, Bruce. 2003. *Information and American Democracy: Technology in the Evolution of Political Power*. New York: Cambridge University Press.

Blumler, Jay G. 1997. "Origins of the Crisis of Communication for Citizenship." *Political Communication* 14:395–404.

Blumler, Jay G., and Dennis Kavanagh. 1999. "The Third Age of Political Communication: Influences and Features." *Political Communication* 16 (3): 209–31.

Cappella, Jospeh, and Kathleen Hall Jamieson. 1997. *The Spiral of Cynicism: The Press and the Public Good*. New York: Oxford University Press.

Cohen, Bernard. 1963. *The Press and Foreign Policy*. Princeton: Princeton University Press.

Cook, Timothy E. 1998. *Governing with the News: The News Media as a Political Institution*. Chicago: University of Chicago Press.

Edelman, Murray J. 1964. *The Symbolic Uses of Politics*. Urbana: University of Illinois Press.

Entman, Robert M. 2004. *Projections of Power: Framing News, Public Opinion, and U.S. Foreign Policy*. Chicago: University of Chicago Press.

e-Voter. 2003. Conference on "Political Campaigns and the Use of Online Communications." La Jolla, Calif., Dec. 3–4.

Ewen, Stuart. 1996. *PR! A Social History of Spin*. New York: Basic Books.

Heiferman, Scott. 2003. Presentation. E-Voter Institute Conference on "Political Campaigns and the Use of Online Communications." La Jolla, Calif., Dec. 3–4.

Herbst, Susan. 1998. *Reading Public Opinion: How Political Actors View the Democratic Process.* Chicago: University of Chicago Press.

Hertsgaard, Mark. 1988. *On Bended Knee: The Press and the Reagan Presidency.* New York: Farrar, Strauss, & Giroux.

Hibbing, John R., and Elizabeth Theiss-Morse. 2002. *Stealth Democracy: Americans' Beliefs about How Government Should Work.* New York: Cambridge University Press.

Howard, Philip N. 2006. *New Media Campaigns and the Managed Citizen.* New York: Cambridge University Press.

Iozzi, David, and W. Lance Bennett. 2003. "Crossing the Campaign Divide: Dean Changes the Election Game." In Karen Jagoda, ed., *e-Voter 2003.* La Jolla, Calif.: e-Voter Institute. http://depts.washington.edu/ccce/assets/documents/iozzi_bennet_crossing.pdf.

Iyengar, Shanto. 1991. *Is Anyone Responsible? How Television Frames Political Issues.* Chicago: University of Chicago Press.

Iyengar, Shanto, and Donald Kinder. 1987. *News That Matters: Television and American Opinion.* Chicago: University of Chicago Press.

Jacobs, Lawrence R., and Robert Y. Shapiro. 2000. *Politicians Don't Pander: Political Manipulation and the Loss of Democratic Responsiveness.* Chicago: University of Chicago Press.

Jamieson, Kathleen Hall. 2001. "Issue Advocacy in a Changing Discourse Environment." In W. Lance Bennett and Robert M. Entman, eds., *Mediated Politics: Communication in the Future of Democracy.* New York: Cambridge University Press. 323–41.

Johnson, Dennis W. 2001. *No Place for Amateurs: How Political Consultants Are Reshaping American Democracy.* New York: Routledge.

Johnston, Richard, Michael G. Hagen, and Kathleen Hall Jamieson. 2004. *The 2000 Presidential Election and the Foundations of Party Politics.* New York: Cambridge University Press.

Katz, Elihu, and Paul F. Lazarsfeld. 1955. *Personal Influence.* New York: Free Press.

Kovach, Bill, and Tom Rosenstiel. 1999. *Warp Speed: America in the Age of Mixed Media.* New York: Century Foundation Press.

Le Bon, Gustave. 1969. *The Crowd.* New York: Ballantine.

Lippmann, Walter. 1922. *Public Opinion.* New York: Free Press.

McChesney, Robert. 2004. *The Problem of the Media: U.S. Communication Politics in the 21st Century.* New York: Monthly Review Press.

McDermott, Mark, and Jim Drinkard. 2004. "Election Ad Battle Smashes Record in 2004." *USA Today,* Nov. 24. http://www.usatoday.com/news/washington/2004-11-25-election-ads_x.htm. Accessed Mar. 18, 2005.

Meskill, Judith. 2004. "On Innovation, Bowling, Scott Heiferman, and Meetup." Posted Oct. 1, on *thesocialsoftwareweblog,* http://socialsoftware.weblogsinc.com/entry/9547655009821755/. Accessed Oct. 21.

Mutz, Diana. 1998. *Impersonal Influence: How Perceptions of Mass Collectives Affect Political Attitudes.* Cambridge: Cambridge University Press.

Napolitan, Joseph. 2004. "Thoughts on IAPC Beginning Its Fourth Decade." http://www.iapc.org/secondletter.asp.

Nardulli, Peter. F. 2005. *Popular Efficacy in the Democratic Era: A Re-examination of Electoral Accountability in the U.S., 1828–2000.* Princeton: Princeton University Press.

Negroponte, Nicholas. 1995. *Being Digital.* New York: Knopf.

Patterson, Thomas. 1993. *Out of Order.* New York: Knopf.

———. 2000. "Doing Well and Doing Good: How Soft News and Critical Journalism Are Shrinking the News and Weakening Democracy—and What News Outlets Can Do About It." Cambridge, Mass.: Joan Shorenstein Center on Press, Politics, and Public Policy. Kennedy School of Government, Harvard University.

———. 2003. *The Vanishing Voter: Public Involvement in an Age of Uncertainty.* New York: Random House.

Putnam, Robert. 2000. *Bowling Alone: The Collapse and Revival of American Community.* New York: Simon and Schuster.

Rahn, Wendy. 2008. "Globalization, the Decline of Civic Commitments, and the Future of Democracy." In Peter F. Nardulli (ed.), *International Perspectives on Contemporary Democracy.* Urbana: University of Illinois Press.

Rutenberg, Jim. 2004. "Scary Ads Take Campaign to a Grim New Level." *New York Times,* Oct. 17, p. A20.

Schudson, Michael. 1998. *The Good Citizen: A History of American Civic Life.* New York: Free Press.

Sigal, Leon. 1973. *Reporters and Officials: The Organization and Politics of Newsgathering.* Lexington, Mass.: D.C. Heath.

Stimson, James A. 2004. *Tides of Consent: How Public Opinion Shapes American Politics.* New York: Cambridge University Press.

Swanson, David L. 1997. "The Political Media Complex at 50: Putting the 1996 Presidential Campaign in Context." *American Behavioral Scientist* 40:1264–82.

Tarbell Archive. 2004. Allegheny College. Pelletier Library. http://tarbell.alleg.edu/mc2.html. Accessed Oct. 14.

Trippi, Joe. 2004. *The Revolution Will Not Be Televised: Democracy, the Internet, and the Overthrow of Everything.* New York: Harper Collins.

Turow, Joseph. 1997. *Breaking Up America: Advertisers and the New Media World.* Chicago: University of Chicago Press.

Wisconsin Advertising Project. 2004. "Ranking of Media Markets by Overall Number of Presidential Spots Aired." http://polisci.wisc.edu/tvadvertising/Press_Releases/Press_Release_PDFs/092404%20to%20101204%20Rankings%20of%20markets%20by%20presidential%20airings.pdf. Accessed Oct. 18.

Zaller, John. 2001. "Monica Lewinsky and the Mainsprings of American Politics." In W. Lance Bennett and Robert M. Entman, eds., *Mediated Politics: Communication in the Future of Democracy.* New York: Cambridge University Press. 252–79.

8

The Internet and Political Fragmentation

BRUCE BIMBER

Democracy requires the successful management of divisions in society. Often, the divisions of greatest concern for the health of democracy involve large-scale, persistent cleavages along well-demarcated lines: divisions within a state between linguistic or ethnic groups, or between regions with divergent economic structures and interests. At the outset of the twenty-first century, such persistent divides are central to the future of nations as diverse as Iraq and Belgium. In addition, a number of observers have argued recently that another form of division threatens the quality of democracies. The putative cause is political fragmentation, which can be defined as the ramification of political collectivities into numerous, temporary, diffuse groups where attachments are thin and narrow, and whose presence has the potential to displace some of the functions of traditional mediating organizations, such as civic organizations, parties, interest groups, and labor unions.

In one form or another, political fragmentation has been thematic in a wide range of scholarship, including work on postmodernism, political community, social capital, collective action, and the study of political communication. The thesis that polities are growing more fragmented is indeed congruent with many theories and findings about the contemporary state, yet this congruence makes fragmentation difficult to test empirically at most levels of analysis. The causes of fragmentation are generally held to be different from the sources of persistent societal cleavages along ethnic or linguistic lines, but they are variously attributed to an array of factors, ranging from the rise of post-material values to the spatial arrangements of community in advanced societies. Whether fragmentation is a distinct phenomenon, let alone whether it is an important one, is far from clear.

In this chapter I review the thesis of fragmentation through a focus on technologies of political communication. By many accounts, rapidly changing media are a significant part of the fragmentation phenomenon, as well as a central player in broader phenomena at the outset of the twenty-first century, from globalization to the changing nature of international conflict. A number of mechanisms ostensibly implicate the Internet and related "new" media in political fragmentation: the division of the public's political attention across more "channels" and consequent reduction in exposure to common political messages (Bagdikian 2000), reduced capacity of political elites and central institutions to shape coherent agendas for societies (Bennett 1999), the capacity of people to segregate themselves communicatively into myriad, homogenous in-groups (Sunstein 2001), and other effects. I review several such claims, with the aim of organizing them with respect to one another, as well as with respect to some historical developments relevant to the issue of fragmentation. I offer a simple, two-dimensional typology of political communication intended to illuminate what it is about media that may, and may not, contribute toward fragmentation. This brief sketch suggests that technological innovation is leading toward possibilities both for fragmentation and for its opposite.

The United States provides the central case study in this discussion, for several reasons. Though the United States was not an early industrializer, it was early among democracies to adopt the mass newspaper as a political medium, early to incorporate broadcast television deeply into its campaign process, and early to employ the Internet for political advocacy and campaigning. Observers as far back as Tocqueville have noted the important connection between new media and political structure in the United States (Bimber 2003). This makes the United States an interesting case for examining media change as well as connections between innovation in media and innovation in political structures. Also, for better and often for worse, American media content and structure have exerted substantial influence well outside the nation. Despite its many distinctive features among democracies, the U.S. media experience, therefore, has some relevance to the dynamics of other states as well, both for similarities and for reasons of contrast.

The Fragmentation Thesis Reviewed

The thesis that media changes are leading to political fragmentation is described well by Bennett (1999, 741), who refers to "the challenge to coherent societies and effective governments presented by the breakdown of broadly shared social and political experience, and the rise of personalized realities." The foundations of shared experience and common realities in any society are obviously many. Institutional arrangements, the distribution of cultural and linguistic frames on political questions, the structure of economic activity, and geography are some of the most important drivers of persistent political cleavages on a large scale. Yet the possibility of "personalized realities"—a concept that has been controversially embraced by authors such as Negroponte (1995)—entails a different form of challenge to political coherence. Personalized realities would involve a high degree of variation at the individual level over political perceptions and experience. In the substantial literatures relevant to political fragmentation, two general classes of argument can be found: erosion of centralized mass-elite linkages through changes in the structure of elites and their messages; and increasing personalized control at the individual level over political communication.

Arguments in the literature about the changing nature of political elites and their messages focus on news and, less often, on campaigns for office and the structure of political advocacy. In the U.S. case, observations about news trends often invoke as a baseline the apex of the "mass audience" in the decades of the 1960s, 1970s, and early 1980s. By the 1980s and 1990s, the argument goes, the multiplication of media channels through cable television, periodical publishing, and other media was sub-dividing and fragmenting political attention, and consequently eroding broad citizen attachments and perceptions of reality. For instance, the Pew Research Center's figures show about 60 percent of the public reporting that they regularly watched a national nightly network news program in 1993; this fell to about 30 percent at the end of the 1990s (PRCP&P 2002). The concern is not simply that fewer people are watching news, but that fewer people share common news experiences, frames, and agendas (Delli Carpini and Williams 2001), which then sets the stage for more personalized political realities. Nye (2002, 10) illustrates this view, arguing that the transformation from broadcasting to "narrowcasting" threatens to "fragment the sense of community and legitimacy" upon which democratic government depends.

Work on news content does suggest an evaporating common awareness of issues and political agendas (Bennett and Entman 2001; Hamilton 2004; Baker 2002). This would appear to threaten productive democratic deliberation, which requires several ingredients: common perceptions of what issues are to be decided, a rationale for one's own positions on those issues, and awareness of the positions and rationales of others. The necessity or possibility of a single national public sphere in which issues of state are deliberated can easily be challenged. But, the argument goes, if twenty neighbors receive their news from twenty personalized and idiosyncratic sources rather than just three, they are less likely to perceive a common set of democratic problems, to engage with one another about issues of the day, and to view as legitimate outcomes with which they disagree.

As in the case for diversification of news experiences, evidence can be found for specialization and narrowing in strategic communication in political campaigns of various kinds. Appeals by candidates and groups to broad coalitional interests of the kind associated with earlier eras of politics appear to many observers to be succumbing to specialized appeals aimed at the mobilization of core constituencies committed to positions on a small number of issues. The adoption of technologies and techniques from commercial marketing, such as data-mining, highly detailed profiling of neighborhoods, and micro-tailored communication are indeed on the rise in the United States (Gandy 2001; Turow 1997). As Bennett observes in the preceding chapter, at worst these threaten segmentation and individuation of the citizenry, as political communication is strategically customized to appeal to smaller subgroups, and as emphasis of communication shifts from persuading people of common positions to activating (or de-activating) people on the basis of their fixed positions. The result could be increasing alienation and the thinning of the public's commitment to democratic processes.

Increased citizen choice and control over exposure to political communication is the second broad mechanism to which some observers attribute a trend toward political fragmentation. These individual-level effects complement the diversification and specialization of elite messages, but are independent. As Galston (2003, 39) frames the problem, media abundance expands choice, and "as individual choice becomes more central, social bonds tend to weaken." He argues that choice and individual-level control afforded citizens by technology contribute to the trend toward a civic life dominated by "voluntary community" (Galston 2003; 1999). In such community, entry is by choice, barriers to exit are low, and intra-community relations are shaped by mutual adjustment rather than authority or coercion. The result of the voluntary character of community is that it tends to be homogenous and to be organized around a relatively narrow set of interests. Many variants on this argument exist. Sunstein (2001), for example, argues that the prevailing effect of greater control by citizens over their media experiences is selective exposure to like-minded messages, which produces polarization effects and fragmentation of political community. Shade (2004) sees sociopolitical interaction built online as particularly susceptible to commoditization and the transformation of communities of citizens into unconnected consumers of political products. Dreyfus (2004) views the Internet as the ultimate domain of postmodern, anonymous "spectatorship," where the meaningful and the trivial are accorded equal status, and where possibilities for substantive connections among the citizenry based on real community interests are diminished.

Historical Antecedents

Concerns such as these about fragmentation can be stated in more precise form as follows: Developments in the media at the outset of the twenty-first century are weakening political bonds that tie citizens together around broad civic interests, and are diminishing opportunities for elites to build crosscutting political agreement among groups. Though evidence can be marshaled that is consistent with this position, as suggested above, a good deal of evidence also contradicts it. For example, it is now fairly clear that, under the right conditions, highly mediated communication among citizens—in chat rooms for instance, or virtual environments—can produce interaction that meets a reasonable standard of "community" or that builds social trust (Castronova 2005; Shah, Kwak, and Holbert 2001; Katz and Rice 2002; Feenberg and Barney 2004). Some online news audiences are large and diverse, some interest groups and campaigns use new media to address broad rather than narrow interests, and in some circumstances citizens use new media to reinforce traditional, broad forms of political identification rather than segregating into ever smaller groups (Hamilton 2004; Hindman, Tsioutsiouliklisz, and Johnson 2003; Bimber and Davis 2003). While the Internet offers a diversity of specialized political messages and identities unprecedented in history, it also is a realm where traditionally influential interests and long-standing political cleavages appear and are reinforced. The question of *whether* the Internet and related new media are leading to political fragmentation, therefore, is badly framed. It is better to inquire about which features of new media might exert forces for fragmentation, which might facilitate integration, and which might work in other ways.

Answering this question reliably will require the passage of a good deal of time because the present remains a period of rapid change, when social innovation and technological innovation are tightly coupled and are developing quickly. Yet some clues can be obtained by looking backward in time, considering some of the high and low points of fragmentation and political cleavage, and asking what role prior developments in media may have played. The United States from the 1790s through the 1810s provides a good historical baseline for thinking about the structure of political elites and about individuals' political experience, and about shifts between forces for fragmentation and those tending toward integration. This period has been well described, and in a number of ways it exhibited problems akin to those in current discussions of fragmentation. Especially striking in most accounts of this period is the lack of a "broadly shared social and political experience," to employ Bennett's (1999) phrase. This forms in some ways a hallmark of the first two to three decades of U.S. democracy. Patterns of elite structure that would later be consolidated and organized by political parties had emerged at this time, especially in congressional voting and Electoral College outcomes. But the mass public did not yet exist. In place of "a public" were myriad local publics, a vast collection of isolated communities and cities defined by geographic boundaries (Young 1966; Aldrich 1995). Before the rise of the newspaper system via the Penny Press, no system of national political communication existed, and few means existed for organized collectivities to act beyond localities or to perceive the interests and actions of others. Goodman (1967, 86) describes the polity in this time as suffering from "a crisis of integration."

These original problems of integration or proto-fragmentation were centrally a function of the state of communication. In that time, it was the absence of adequate communication technology that circumscribed political communication, limiting people's political realities to the local and familiar (Schudson 1998; Bimber 2003). Now, at the outset of the twenty-first century, observers such as Sunstein argue that an abundance of technologies permits citizens to isolate themselves from the national public sphere—that is, in a way to re-create conditions reminiscent of the pre-nationalized period in American politics. Citizens who might be walled off behind media filters and specialized news feeds, who are plugged into social network software that reinforces narrow group interests, and who are targeted by political campaigns as if they were consumers with specialized tastes, are not so unlike the inhabitants of isolated towns and villages of Jefferson's day, knowing much of their neighbors and little of their nation. What is common to the two situations is a narrow horizon of communication, rather than the extent to which communication is mediated. In 1807, citizens had little choice but to communicate narrowly, remaining largely cut-off from national issues; in 2007, some worry that citizens have too much opportunity to do something similar.

The century and a half or so between the rise of the mass newspaper and the ascendance of television as the dominant political medium gives more clues about the relationship of media to political fragmentation, and especially the connection of centralized political elites to this relationship. In the United States, the mass party system that emerged by the 1840s began to organize broader political communication that could tie together a mass public, though the parties of mid-century are easily over-estimated as a contributor to political coherence and integration. The largely rural population, spread across half a continent, had yet to develop mechanisms for reliable national-scale public deliberation or the formation of deep ties transcending the local. The fact that the party system that emerged by the 1840s had splintered by the early 1850s says a great deal about the lack of political coherence and stable alliances. Before the realignment of the late 1850s and 1860s could take place, the emergent party system simply fell apart. The Whigs splintered; the Democratic Party divided over slavery; and Free-Soilers, Know Nothings, the Union and Liberty parties, and others competed to organize the system.

As a number of observers have noted, even the stable electoral system of the late nineteenth century in the United States did not rest on grand coalitions that integrated diverse interests throughout the polity (Hays 1994; Sundquist 1983; Skocpol 1999; Wiebe 1967). The issues dividing U.S. political communities were numerous and substantial: agrarianism, the populist movement, monetary policy, labor and industrialism in the cities, the racial divide, and surge of immigrants—much of this still overlaid on sectionalism dividing West, South, and Northeast. As Sundquist (1983, 158) writes, "For twenty years the two-party system had been based on dead issues of the past. It had offered voters no means of expressing a choice on the crucial issues of domestic economic policy around which the country had been polarizing—slowly at first, but beginning in the late 1880s at a headlong pace."

Alongside the major divisions of the late nineteenth century was a good deal of individual and community-level isolation. In his classic history of the period, Wiebe (1967, 1) writes that the country was "a society of island communities" with weak inter-group communication, little economic integration, and dispersed political power. Again evoking both contemporary criticisms of new media and the problems of much earlier times, Wiebe describes citizens as leading lives "narrowly circumscribed by a community or a neighborhood" (1967, 27), despite the existence by then of viable national political machinery. To be sure, the problems of the late nineteenth century were different from those of the present, but they suggest that political coherence, integration, and opportunities for shared political experience require more than effective political organizations competing on the national scale. This period presents a reminder that strong systems of party elites competing aggressively with one another on the national scale do not necessarily draw citizens together or create a meaningful body of shared political experiences.

In the twentieth century, two periods are typically identified for high levels of political integration and shared reality: the New Deal era, and the era of the mass audience for television. To the extent that concerns about contemporary political developments are victims of nostalgia, it is these periods that are likely the source. So it is important that these neither coincided with one another nor involved the same sets of institutions and elites; indeed the forces of the latter era worked against those of the first. Nationalized politics and policy making in the New Deal overcame the smaller-scale, localized way of life of the previous eras through partisan realignment and the building of national institutions of government. Electoral integration rested on the solidification of major lines of cleavage around a large portfolio of policy issues. The eventual decay of this high-water mark for party-based politics and policy making during the 1960s and 1970s is attributed to a number of factors, such as the rise of interest-group politics. It is conspicuous that one of these factors was the ascendance of television. The same broadcast media commonly credited with creating in the 1960s and 1970s the shared news experience, responsible gate-keeping, and effective contributions to national agenda-setting also permitted the growth of the individualized political campaign, the diminished role of parties in national politics, and political dealignment. By the 1970s, scholars examining the electoral and policy-making systems found it hyper-pluralized and fragmented, rife with alienation and conflict. It would not be long before scholars of communication would draw similar conclusions about the effects of media on politics.

Communication and Fragmentation

If nothing else, the history of American political development provides no shortage of illustrations that cable television and the Internet did not invent challenges to integration and coherence in the public sphere. Periods of political division and fragmentation, and episodes of response to such developments, have often involved changes in the structure of political communication. These changes are part of what I have elsewhere labeled the evolution of information regimes (Bimber 2003). Some changes, such as the rise of broadcast television and the Internet, as well as the building of New Deal institutions, altered the *degree of centralization* of political communication.

Other episodes, such as the development of interest-group based recruitment and mobilization, affected the specialization, or *reach across groups* of political messages. The distinction between centralization and reach in political communication structures is one lesson to be drawn from American political development.

The centralization of political communication might be defined as the extent to which the content and flow of messages is controlled by a small number of political elites or power centers, rather than by citizens themselves. Contemporary communication by electoral campaign organizations in the United States provides a good illustration of centralized political communication. Campaigns' traditionally military-style decision-making and communication structures emphasize top-down, tightly controlled, strategic messages directed at the public. Communication from mass media also reflects a high degree of centralization for similar reasons. Decentralized communication patterns, on the other hand, have traditionally been found in more informal contexts: at the local level and among groups of people known to one another. These entail control over the flow and content of message chiefly at the level of citizens themselves. Personal communication about politics among friends, neighbors, and co-workers is decentralized. So too is much communication among members of various community groups and civic associations, where people interact personally over time on a variety of agendas that are largely shaped without central control points or decision makers (Flanagin, Stohl, and Bimber 2006).

It should be clear that an organization exerting centralized control over communication may craft messages aimed at either broad or narrow audiences. Political interest groups illustrate a form of centralized communication structure that targets audiences narrower in scope than do parties or national news businesses. While a relatively large number of interest groups exist, compared with the number of parties and mass media organizations, individual groups have traditionally tended to construct political communication in a hierarchical way. Citizens who belong to groups communicate little information back toward the center or outward among themselves as a function of their membership.

The reach of political communication can therefore be usefully thought of as independent of centralization. Messages with a broad reach are those that span meaningful, persistent lines of political difference, while narrow communication is directed at well-bounded, homogenous audiences that might be defined by specific interests, regions, or ideologies. An archetypal example of political communication that spans diverse groups is the centralized broadcast news system. This was especially true in the United States' three-network configuration, which is perhaps overly praised for having distributed similar messages to broad audiences. Traditionally, political parties of the New Deal system also embodied broad communication reach, unlike that of interest groups. One reason interest groups were such a successful innovation in the U.S. policy-making process in the twentieth century is that they tailored political information and communication to specific interests within groups rather than across them.

Like centralized communication, messages that are decentralized in flow can also vary considerably in reach. At the local level, citizen associations can be broadly oriented and engage people with a variety of interests and backgrounds, such as in sports leagues or civic groups. They can also engage people with strong common identities, interests, or political orientations, such as in church groups. Because decentralized communication has traditionally been bounded by geography, the reach of its communication patterns may not be as varied as more highly centralized, national-scale communication structures.

Combinations of broad and narrow reach, and centralized and decentralized flows of communication, offer four cells if represented in two-by-two form, as shown in table 8.1. The cells in this matrix can be used to classify some of the key changes in American political communication. For instance, the historical shift in the United States from a partisan newspaper system to a professionalized, non-partisan system during the Progressive Era is widely described as beneficial to democracy. In the matrix, this represents movement from the lower right cell to the upper right: a change in the reach of news but without an accompanying change in the centralization of news organizations themselves. The claim that traditional, limited-channel mass media created a common, shared foundation for public opinion-formation

Table 8.1. A two-dimensional classification of political communication

	Decentralized Flow of Information	Centralized Flow of Information
Broad Reach	• Bridging social capital associations	• Party system • Broadcast news media • Professionalized newspaper system
Narrow Reach	• Bonding social capital associations • Personal political discussion networks	• Partisan newspaper system • Contemporary campaign communication • Specialized cable media • Interest group communication

in the mid-twentieth century represents an argument about the benefits of communication in the centralized-broad cell (Katz 1996). The functions of programmatic political parties as integrators of interests is also a centralized-broad phenomenon.

Literature on social capital can also be located on these two dimensions. The forms of community engagement that Putnam (2000, 2002) and others argue build norms of trust and networks of reciprocity are decentralized in nature, falling in the left-hand cells of the table. Putnam's distinction between "bonding" and "bridging" social capital, which are connected to the types of interaction that tend to build in-group versus out-group trust and reciprocity, respectively, differentiates decentralized-narrow from decentralized-broad communication.

Viewed this way, it becomes clear that many disparate concerns about political fragmentation and new media fall into the lower-right and lower-left cells of the table, where communication has limited reach. Concerns with the deleterious effects of targeted campaign communication (Gandy 2001; Turow 1997) and channel multiplication (Neuman 1991), as well as some critiques of the interest group system more generally (Lowi 1979), are in part problems of centralized-narrow communication. Concerns that citizens will use new media to selectively isolate themselves from those who are politically different is a problem of narrow-decentralized communication networks, while the capacity of citizens to create news filters and selectively navigate the world of political information is a phenomenon of narrow-centralized communication (Sunstein 2001).

Without denying the potential relevance of centralization and decentralization to aspects of political fragmentation, it would appear that a wide range of arguments in the literature about fragmentation and shared political experience have in common a set of concerns with the reach of communication, rather than the structure or identity of centralized elites. A simplified working proposition suggested by the work reviewed above is therefore that *all else being equal, the narrower the reach of systems of political communication, the greater the tendency toward political fragmentation.*

Effects of the Internet

This formulation helps focus consideration of the Internet and new media. Which forms of communication does technology facilitate? The answer is that technological innovation in media is facilitating all four combinations of reach and centralization in the structure of political communication. Consider first the Internet and the upper-right cell. The fact that the Internet facilitates centralized communication from elites and political organizers to large groups is often lost in observations about "narrowcasting," peer-to-peer communication online, and the other departures from traditional communication. It is now well known that the Web involves both very large audiences for a small number of web sites and very small audiences for a very large number of sites. Many traditional political organizations, especially campaigns and interest groups, use new media to reach narrow audiences *and* to communicate broadly with traditional segments of the public (Bimber and Davis 2003; Trippi 2004). Johnson (2001) measures audience concentration across all web sites and estimates the collective audience of the top ten sites to be about an order of magnitude larger than the audience of the next hundred web sites together. Hindman, Tsioutsiouliklisz, and Johnson (2003) examine a variety of political sites and find that audience concentration at the top political websites rivals audience concentration in traditional media. Studies of online news audiences have reported roughly the same thing (Hamilton 2004; Tewksbury 2003). Earlier views of the Internet as the exclusive domain of tiny, fragmented audiences have given way to the more contemporary "long tail" model, in which many specialized audiences coexist with mass audiences for a comparatively small number of news and information sites.

Centralized communication online also targets narrower audiences, as Sunstein and other argue. Traditional interest groups seeking to identify and interact with more specialized audiences have found the Internet to be a congenial medium. Environmental groups are an example. After a period of stagnating and declining membership, the capacity of a number of American groups to attract and mobilize citizens was reinvigorated in the late 1990s and early 2000s by new technologies interacting with political developments (Bimber 2003). As a result, environmental groups across the board reported increases in the number of citizens whom they contact and are able to mobilize. New media have permitted these organizations to take an already specialized group interest and subdivide it at ever finer-grained detail. The networks of specialized news and information sites, electronic newsletters, and issue-specific blogs conducting centralized communication to small audiences are another example. Yet at the same time, political elites are also using new communication techniques to assemble large-scale coalitions composed of diverse groups, such as the protests against the war in Iraq, the immigration rights protests of 2006, the anti-globalization protests as far back as the late 1990s, and the "Indymedia" movement (McCaughey and Ayers 2003; Bennett 2004; Bennett, Givens, and Breunig 2007).

The lower-left cell of the matrix is the locus of much concern about political fragmentation online. Decentralized, narrow-reach communication may have received more attention from journalists and scholars than is warranted, but clearly many examples exist that appear attributable to the Internet. These include narrowly focused groups assembled in chat rooms, bulletin boards, and other interactive domains online that are too numerous to count. As of this writing, a Google Group discussing education in Alabama had over five thousand "threads" or discussion topics; a group on atheism had over sixteen thousand, and a euthanasia group thirteen thousand. The boundaries of these groups do not follow traditional political fault-lines in politics, nor do most such specialized groups apparently have the potential to support broad coalitional politics.

As an empirical problem, it is impossible to assess meaningfully the fraction of politically relevant communication that falls in any of the cells of the matrix, or between them. Though it is tempting to speculate that the most frequent forms of communication are in one cell or another, or, more important, that the most consequential forms of online political communication are concentrated in one place, available evidence cannot sustain those kinds of conclusions. The most responsible claim that can be advanced at this stage in the research literature is that the Internet is structured in ways that advance both fragmentation and integration, and it appears to do so more as a function of the reach of communication across lines of difference than as a function of centralization or decentralization.

A defining feature of the Internet as a communication medium is in fact its heterogeneity compared to previous media, such as broadcasting. Many historical technologies led to political communication structures heavily biased toward one form or structure. Mass media for instance, simply made centralized, across-group communication vastly easier than other types. Interest groups advanced the state of centralized within-group communication. Because of the properties of the media themselves, along with the economic and institutional apparatus upon which they were based, patterns of communication have often exhibited a good bit of stability over time. One of the important features of the structurally heterogeneous political communication system made possible by new media may be more diversity and less predictability in communication patterns. In a more labile environment for political communication, outcomes could be less centrally a function of institutional imperatives and the momentum of long-standing cleavages and the organizations that embody them, and more commonly a function of the idiosyncratic strategies and identities of the political collectivities appearing on the stage at any particular moment. These, it appears, can involve broadly shared or narrowly circumscribed political realities and experiences.

Note

I wish to thank colleagues Cynthia Stohl and Andrew Flanagin at UC Santa Barbara, with whom I collaborated on many of the ideas that form the background to this work. This chapter extends analysis conducted jointly with them under NSF grant number 0352517 and reported elsewhere.

References

Aldrich, John H. 1995. *Why Parties? The Origin and Transformation of Political Parties in America.* Chicago: University of Chicago Press.

Bagdikian, Ben. 2000. *The Media Monopoly* (6th ed.). Boston: Beacon.

Baker, C. Edwin. 2002. *Media, Markets, and Democracy.* Cambridge: Cambridge University Press.

Bennett, W. Lance. 1998. "The UnCivic Culture: Communication, Identity, and the Rise of Lifestyle Politics" Ithiel de Sola Pool Lecture, American Political Science Association, published in *PS: Political Science* 31:741–61.

———. 2004. "Communicating Global Activism." In Win van de Donk, Brian Loader, Paul Nixon, and Dieter Rucht, eds., *Cyberprotest: New Media, Citizens, and Social Movements.* New York: Routledge. 123–46.

Bennett, W. Lance, and Robert M. Entman, eds. 2001. *Mediated Politics: Communication in the Future of Democracy.* Cambridge: Cambridge University Press.

Bennett. W. Lance, Terri Givens, and Christian Breunig. 2007. "Crossing Political Divides: Communication, Political Identification, and Protest Organization." In Stefan Walgrave and Dieter Rucht, eds., *Protest Politics: Anti-War Mobilization in Western Democracies.* Minneapolis: University of Minnesota Press.

Bimber, Bruce. 2003. *Information and American Democracy: Technology in the Evolution of Political Power.* New York: Cambridge University Press.

Bimber, Bruce, Andrew J. Flanagin, and Cynthia Stohl. 2005. "Reconceptualizing Collective Action in the Contemporary Media Environment." *Communication Theory* 15 (4): 365–88.

Castronova, Edward. 2005. *Synthetic Worlds: The Business and Culture of Online Games.* Chicago: University of Chicago Press

Delli Carpini, Michael X., and Bruce A. Williams. 2001. "Let Us Infotain You: Politics in the New Media." In Bennett and Entman, *Mediated Politics.* 160–81.

Dreyfus, Hubert. 2004. "Nihilism on the Information Highway: Anonymity versus Commitment in the Present Age." In Feenberg and Barney, *Community in the Digital Age.* 69–81.

Feenberg, Andrew, and Darin Barney, eds. 2004. *Community in the Digital Age: Philosophy and Practice.* Lanham, Md.: Rowman & Littlefield.

Flanagin, Andrew, Cynthia Stohl, and Bruce Bimber. 2006. "Modeling the Structure of Collective Action." *Communication Monographs* 73 (1): 29–54.

Galston, William. 2003. "If Political Fragmentation Is the Problem, Is the Internet the Solution?" In *The Civic Web: Online Politics and Democratic Values,* ed. David M. Anderson and Michael Cornfield. Lanham, MD: Rowman & Littlefield. Pp. 35–44.

———. 1999. "(How) Does the Internet Affect Community? Some Speculations in Search of Evidence." In Elaine Ciulla Kamarck and Joseph S. Nye Jr., eds., *Democracy.com? Governance in a Networked World.* Hollis, N.H.: Hollis Publishing. 45–62.

Gandy, Oscar H., Jr. 2001. "Dividing Practices: Segmentation and Targeting in the Emerging Public Sphere." In Bennett and Entman, eds., *Mediated Politics.* 141–59.

Goodman, Paul. 1967. "The First American Party System." In William Nisbet Chambers and Walter Dean Burnham, eds., *The American Party Systems: Stages of Political Development.* New York: Oxford University Press. 56–89.

Hamilton, James T. 2004. *All the News That's Fit to Sell: How the Market Transforms Information into News.* Princeton: Princeton University Press.

Hays, Samuel. 1994. *The Response to Industrialism: 1885–1914* (2d ed.). Chicago: University of Chicago Press.

Hindman, Matthew, Kostas Tsioutsiouliklisz, and Judy A. Johnson. 2003. "'Googlearchy': How a Few Heavily-Linked Sites Dominate Politics on the Web." White paper accessed at: http://www.princeton.edu/~mhindman/googlearchy—hindman.pdf.

Johnson, Steven. 2001. *Emergence: The Connected Lives of Ants, Brains, Cities, and Software.* New York: Touchstone

Katz, Elihu. 1996. "And Deliver Us from Segmentation." *Annals of the American Academy of Political and Social Science* 546:22–33.

Katz, James E., and Ronald E. Rice. 2002. *Social Consequences of Internet Use: Access, Involvement, and Interaction.* Cambridge: MIT Press.

Lowi, Theodore. 1979. *The End of Liberalism: The Second Republic of the United States* (2d ed.). New York: W. W. Norton.

McCaughey, Martha, and Michael D. Ayers, eds. 2003. *Cyberactivism: Online Activism in Theory and Practice.* New York: Routledge.

Negroponte, Nicholas. 1995. *Being Digital.* New York: Vintage Press.

Neuman, W. Russell. 1991. *The Future of the Mass Audience.* New York: Cambridge University Press.

Nye, Joseph S., Jr. 2002. "Information Technology and Democratic Governance." In Joseph S. Nye Jr. and Elaine Ciulla Kamarck, eds., *Governance.com: Democracy in the Information Age.* Washington, D.C.: Brookings. 1–16.

PRCP&P [Pew Research Center for the People and the Press]. 2002. Biennial Media Consumption Survey. Washington, D.C.: Pew Research Center for the People and the Press.

Putnam Robert D. 2000. *Bowling Alone: The Collapse and Revival of American Community.* New York: Simon & Schuster.

———, ed. 2002. *Democracies in Flux: The Evolution of Social Capital in Contemporary Society.* New York: Oxford University Press.

Schudson, Michael. 1998. *The Good Citizen: A History of American Civic Life.* New York: Martin Kessler.

Shade, Leslie Regan. 2004. "Gender and the Commodification of Community: Women.com and gURL.com." In Feenberg and Barney, *Community in the Digital Age.* 144–60.

Shah, Dhavan V., Nojin Kwak, and R. Lance Holbert. 2001. "Connecting and Disconnecting with Civic Life: Patterns of Internet Use and the Production of Social Capital." *Political Communication* 18:141–62.

Skocpol, Theda. 1999. "How Americans Became Civic." In *Civic Engagement in American Democracy,* ed., Theda Skocpol and Morris P. Fiorina. Washington, D.C.: Brookings Institution. 27–80.

Sundquist, James L. 1983. *Dynamics of the Party System: Alignment and Realignment of Political Parties in the United States* (rev. ed.). Washington, D.C.: Brookings Institution.

Sunstein, Cass. 2001. *Republic.com.* Princeton: Princeton University Press.

Tewksbury, David. 2003. "What Do Americans Really Want to Know? Tracking the Behavior of News Readers on the Internet." *Journal of Communication* 53:697–710.

Trippi, Joe. 2004. *The Revolution Will Not Be Televised: Democracy, the Internet, and the Overthrow of Everything.* New York: Regan Books.

Turow, Joseph. 1997. *Breaking Up America: Advertisers and the New Media World.* Chicago: University of Chicago Press.

Wiebe, Robert H. 1967. *The Search for Order: 1877–1920.* New York: Hill and Wang.

Young, James Sterling. 1966. *The Washington Community: 1800–1828.* New York: Columbia University Press.

Contributors

W. LANCE BENNETT is a professor of political science and the Ruddick C. Lawrence Professor of Communication at the University of Washington, where he also directs the Center for Communication and Civic Engagement (www.engagedcitizen.org). The general focus of his work concerns how communication processes affect citizen engagement with politics. His publications include *Mediated Politics: Communication in the Future of Democracy; News: The Politics of Illusion*, 7th ed.; and *When the Press Fails: Political Power and the News Media from Iraq to Katrina* (coauthored with Regina Lawrence and Steven Livingston). He has received the Ithiel de Sola Pool Award and Lectureship, and the Murray Edelman Career Achievement Award in Political Communication, both from the American Political Science Association.

BRUCE BIMBER is a professor in the Departments of Political Science and Communication at the University of California, Santa Barbara, and the director emeritus of the Center for Information Technology and Society. His research examines the relationship between evolving information technology and changes in human behavior, especially in the domains of political organization, collective action, social capital, and political deliberation. He is the author of *Information and American Democracy: Technology in the Evolution of Political Power,* which won the Don K. Price Award for Best Book on Science, Technology, and Politics, and *Campaigning Online: The Internet in U.S. Elections,* which won the McGannon Communication Policy Award for social and ethical relevance in communication policy research. He is also the author of numerous articles dealing with technology, democracy, and public life.

BRIAN J. GAINES is an associate professor of political science at the University of Illinois, Urbana-Champaign, and holds an appointment in the Institute of Government and Public Affairs. His research focuses on elections and public opinion, and his work has appeared in more than a dozen journals. Between February 2005 and January 2007, he ran marathons on all seven continents.

BERNARD N. GROFMAN is a professor of political science at the University of California, Irvine. Much of his work has dealt with issues of elections and voting rules, voting rights, and redistricting. He is the author of over two hundred articles and research notes and is the coauthor of *Minority Representation and the Quest for Voting Equality; A Unified Theory of Voting; A Unified Field of Party Competition;* and *Behavioral Social Choice.* He has edited or coedited sixteen other books, including *Quite Revolution in the South* and *Political Gerrymandering and the Courts.* His work on voting rights, and in volumes he has edited, has been cited repeatedly by federal courts, including the U.S. Supreme Court in a dozen different cases—perhaps most notably in *Thornburg v. Gingles*, 478 U.S. 30 (1986). He has testified as an expert witness in redistricting and voting rights cases in more than a dozen states. He is a fellow of the American Academy of Arts and Sciences and past president of the Public Choice Society.

WAYNE V. McINTOSH is an associate professor of government and politics at the University of Maryland. He is PI on two projects funded by the National Science Foundation: *Inter-Court Relations in the American Legal System: Using New Technologies to Examine Communication of Precedent* (Law and Social Sciences, SES-0416455 and SES-0519157); and *Digital Docket: Applying Computational Linguistics to the Study of Law and Courts* (HSD-DHB, BSC-0624067).

PETER F. NARDULLI is a professor of political science and law at the University of Illinois, Urbana-Champaign, and served as department head in the Department of Political Science from 1992 until July 2006. He is the founding director of the Cline Center for Democracy. He is the author of six books on various aspects of the American legal process and empirical democratic theory. His most recent book is *Popular Efficacy in the Democratic Era: A Reexamination of Electoral Accountability in the U.S., 1828–2000*. He has edited another five books and has authored a number of articles in journals such as the *American Political Science Review, Public Choice, Political Communica-*

tion, Political Behavior, and various law reviews. He is currently directing a global study, the Social Infrastructures and Development Project, which uses a number of innovative methodologies to examine the impact of democracy, free enterprise, and the rule of law on a wide range of societal developmental indicators (economic growth, environmental quality, human rights, social stability, and so on).

MARK Q. SAWYER is an associate professor of African American studies and political science at UCLA. He is also the director of the Center for the Study of Race, Ethnicity, and Politics. In the fall of 2005 he was a visiting associate professor at the Department of African and African American Studies at Harvard University. His book *Racial Politics in Post-Revolutionary Cuba* received the DuBois Award from the National Conference of Black Political Scientists and the Ralph Bunche Award from the American Political Science Association.

STEPHEN A. SIMON is an assistant professor of political science at the University of Richmond. He received his Ph.D. in government and politics from the University of Maryland, and a J.D. from the New York University School of Law.

PAUL M. SNIDERMAN is the Fairleigh S. Dickinson Jr. Professor of Political Science at Stanford University. He has been awarded the Woodrow Wilson Prize, the Gladys M. Kammer Prize, and the Ralph Bunche Award for best book of the year in political science, American politics, and ethnic and cultural pluralism, respectively. He is the author of a large number of scholarly articles that have appeared in a wide range of journals. He is a fellow of the American Academy of Arts and Sciences, the American Association for the Advancement of Science, and the Royal Society of the Arts. He is the grandfather of Sophie and Alexandra Lurie.

JACK SNYDER is the Robert and Renée Belfer Professor of International Relations in the Department of Political Science and the Saltzman Institute for War and Peace Studies at Columbia University. His books include *Electing to Fight: Why Emerging Democracies Go to War; From Voting to Violence: Democratization and Nationalist Conflict* (coauthored with Edward D. Mansfield); *Myths of Empire: Domestic Politics and International Ambition;* and *The Ideology of the Offensive: Military Decision Making and the Disasters of 1914.*

Index

Note: Numbers in *italics* indicate illustrative material, with *t* representing a table.

DEMOCRACY, FREE ENTERPRISE, AND THE RULE OF LAW

Domestic Perspectives on Contemporary Democracy
Edited by Peter F. Nardulli
International Perspectives on Contemporary Democracy
Edited by Peter F. Nardulli

The University of Illinois Press
is a founding member of the
Association of American University Presses.

Composed in 10.5/13 Adobe Minion Pro
with Meta display
by Jim Proefrock
at the University of Illinois Press
Manufactured by Cushing-Malloy, Inc.

University of Illinois Press
1325 South Oak Street
Champaign, IL 61820-6903
www.press.uillinois.edu